CW00568366

Jack the Ripper
SUSPECT
Dr. Francis Tumblety

Michael L. Hawley

SUNBURY PRESS
Mechanicsburg, PA USA

Published by Sunbury Press, Inc.
Mechanicsburg, Pennsylvania

SUNBURY
P R E S S

www.sunburypress.com

Copyright © 2018 by Michael L. Hawley.
Cover Copyright © 2018 by Sunbury Press, Inc.

Sunbury Press supports copyright. Copyright fuels creativity, encourages diverse
voices, promotes free speech, and creates a vibrant culture. Thank you for buying
an authorized edition of this book and for complying with copyright laws. Except
for the quotation of short passages for the purpose of criticism and review, no
part of this publication may be reproduced, scanned, or distributed in any form
without permission. You are supporting writers and allowing Sunbury Press to
continue to publish books for every reader. For information contact Sunbury
Press, Inc., Subsidiary Rights Dept., PO Box 548, Boiling Springs, PA 17007 USA
or legal@sunburypress.com.

For information about special discounts for bulk purchases, please contact
Sunbury Press Orders Dept. at (855) 338-8359 or orders@sunburypress.com.

To request one of our authors for speaking engagements or book signings, please
contact Sunbury Press Publicity Dept. at publicity@sunburypress.com.

ISBN: 978-1-62006-819-9 (Trade paperback)

Library of Congress Control Number: 2018942968

SECOND SUNBURY PRESS EDITION: April 2018

Product of the United States of America
0 1 1 2 3 5 8 13 21 34 55

Set in Bookman Old Style
Designed by Crystal Devine
Cover by Amber Rendon
Edited by Jennifer Cappello

Continue the Enlightenment!

Contents

Foreword

Is Francis Tumblety a legitimate candidate for committing the 1888 Whitechapel Murders? To answer that, people first need to avoid the reasoning that acquits a suspect of such terrible crimes due to sexual preference. It is wrong to simply employ the generalized perception that a homosexual male cannot kill a handful of female prostitutes. Whenever criminal profiling techniques are applied to the East End of London in 1888, a Ripperologist may get fooled and quickly decide that the spotlight of suspicion should no longer shine on Tumblety. After all, the man was a homosexual, so therefore, based on 21st century reasoning methods, he could not have been Jack the Ripper. This line of thinking is an ineffective approach to the dismissal of a Ripper suspect, yet the attempts to excuse Tumblety by this thought process have gone on for many years.

A respected researcher in our field, Roger Palmer, once said, "All crimes of this sort have one thing in common: they are profoundly social acts. And because society changes in profound ways, it is very misleading to take case histories from one society and superimpose them on another."

One example of a profound societal change from modern times to the days of 1888 is the medical treatment of the venereal disease syphilis. Criminal profilers should not take case histories involving homosexual murderers living in an age where the access to proper medication for syphilis is readily available and then proceed to utilize that data for the sake of imprinting those modern-day results upon a homosexual man of the 19th century. A century where no such medical aid existed to combat the awful brain maladies that syphilis caused. The suspicion that Tumblety had suffered from a progressed stage of syphilis in 1888 is real. He admitted to being in constant fear of death during that year due to illness. His facial markings were said to have been repulsive and required a cosmetic covering. That is a key point because it has been reported that 30% of individuals with untreated syphilis may develop facial lesions as the disease advances to its late stage.

Whitechapel mysteries author and historian Simon Wood once wrote about how the word "rheumatism" had been a euphemism for the symptoms of syphilis during the 1800s. This was a medical condition that was said to have bitten Tumblety. Newspapers reported of Tumblety's attempts to alleviate his "rheumatism" by attending a spa site in Arkansas containing sulphur spring water. Simon also reminded us that the *Journal of Cutaneous Diseases including Syphilis* stated that "Sulphur water (taken) internally and as baths acts brilliantly in syphilitic patients . . ." Men who suffered from this particular venereal disease sought out sulphur spring sites in those olden days.

Witnesses spoke of Tumblety's scary odd behavior during the autumn of 1888. His abrupt restless movements and impulsive travel gave notice that there was something medically wrong. His lifelong practice of promiscuous one-night stands with other men placed him in danger of syphilis at a time when the invention of penicillin was still over fifty years away. Due to the risky health environment of the 19th century, no exoneration from the title of Jack the Ripper should be granted to Tumblety solely because a modern criminal profiling method does not lead us to him. It is a method that cannot be trusted when applied to the year 1888 because society has changed in profound ways since then, especially in the field of medical care.

Another reason that has been recited in the hopes of dismissing Tumblety as a suspect has been the claim that he was too publicly flamboyant of character. The belief being that the Ripper must have been stealth-like and introverted. The truth, however, is that nobody really knows any of the personal qualities of the Ripper, so it is fruitless to reject the candidacy of a suspect due to his personality, height, age, sexual preference, or race. According to the official copy of Assistant Commissioner Sir Melville Macnaghten's memoranda, and as stated by Inspector Walter Andrews, nobody has ever seen the Ripper. So there really is very little basis for the rejection of a Ripper suspect on the grounds of personal mannerism or appearance. As for Tumblety's flamboyant behavior, in the summer of 1888 it looks like he was still using self-promotional tactics under the pseudonym The Great American Doctor. He printed some ads in a couple of Irish newspapers that sold his odd products. He was sexually active during that summer, so he probably circulated some of his autobiographical writing to impress young males. Tumblety wrote those extravagant pieces of literature for the sake of projecting a phony image of himself and to con potential mates into buying into his importance. The compositions presented him as a gentleman of high social and political standing, but still, that type of arrogance should not dissuade researchers when it comes to deciding if a man is a bona fide Ripper suspect. Actually, if you look at a 19th century mass murderer by the name of Dr. Edward Pritchard you will see some obvious similarities to Tumblety. As Roger Palmer has written:

> *Now let's look at Dr. Pritchard. We don't know much about his youth, but he was a social climber. He bragged endlessly. He lied his way into the Royal Navy and later padded his meager medical qualifications with bogus credentials. One of his greatest peculiarities was that he printed up dozens of daguerreotypes of his own image, in an age when that stuff wasn't cheap, and he liked handing them out to strangers. He owned a gold-cane walking staff engraved "From your great friend Garibaldi" - but, of course, he wasn't really Garibaldi's friend. Does this guy sound the least bit familiar to Ripper researchers? Because of their inadequate backgrounds, these blokes have enormous social pretensions. Enormous. And when it starts unraveling for them, they snap.*

Scotland Yard officials John Littlechild and Robert Anderson knew of Tumblety's boastfulness and sexual preference, yet both men still took this Ripper suspect seriously. Anderson went as far as to make investigative communications to America in the autumn of 1888 to obtain further information about the man. Tumblety is a legitimate Ripper suspect and should be treated as such. The author of this book, Mike Hawley, is an experienced researcher who lectured on Tumblety at the previous Ripper Conference in Baltimore in 2016 and in Liverpool, England, in 2017. Mike brings to the table a tremendous amount of scholastic achievements along with a proud military background. I think it is a fine tribute to Ripperology that a man of his credentials has chosen our field as a course of study and it is great to see him openly share his work and hold nothing back.

Mike's previous book, *The Ripper's Haunts,* touched upon a number of matters into the Whitechapel mysteries that were pioneer in its nature. One of the topics that stuck in my mind was Mike's chapter about the wax museum located on the Whitechapel Road in 1888 and how it displayed effigies of the Ripper victims. It was a chapter that was born of original thinking and it created a fresh approach into looking at how the Ripper may have been influenced by his East End surroundings. Another memorable topic was Mike's chapter that clearly defined the terms "woman-hater" and "misogynist" and how the words were expressed in 19th century literature. Mike's talent as an educator came forth in that writing, and it was interesting to learn the true meanings of those terms and how to correctly apply them when studying the Ripper murders. Let us now take our seats in Mike's classroom and read the pages of *Jack the Ripper Suspect Dr. Francis Tumblety.* I expect to be taught new facts about this eccentric "doctor" as well as being shown new angles on how to view the Whitechapel Murders.

by Joe Chetcuti

Author's Note

Because this book relies heavily on original source material, every effort has been made to preserve the integrity of the original language—including spelling and grammar. While the author and publisher are aware that some of these dated and unusual conventions may appear to be errors on the part of the author, they have been checked against original source material and have been left untouched and unmarked to retain the historical accuracy and flavor of the primary source. Since marking every single "error" would have been tedious and distracting to the reader, this note serves as the disclaimer that those "mistakes" knowingly exist in the manuscript. In addition to this note, there are still several prominent instances of mistakes in quoted source material, which have been marked (using "[*sic*]") throughout the following pages, as determined by editorial discretion.

To clarify, the use of brackets in quoted material throughout this book refers to interjections by the author; the use of parentheses in quoted material refers to either notes and asides found in the original source or this author's citation of said material.

Additionally, since much of the scholarship and primary and secondary source material in this genre comes from British authors, the UK spellings (and some punctuation) have been left unedited. While these conventions may seem unusual to an American reading audience, they are indicative of traditional British spelling and grammar practices and are not errors.

All efforts in these areas have been made to ensure quality scholarship practices and to help clarify the origins of source material for readers and other researchers in the field.

Preface

The volume of new evidence discovered on Francis Tumblety in the last few years is incredible, possibly exceeded only by the number of misconceptions dispelled about him. Case in point: It was concluded by many experts just a few years ago that Tumblety did not hate women, and that when he was referred to as a "woman hater" in the newspapers, this was either a product of sensationalism or merely a euphemism for his homosexuality. The recent evidence makes clear that Tumblety was indeed an extreme misogynist and harbored an unusual and bitter hatred of a certain type of women. This particular misconception is significant, since it goes to the heart of the reason why Scotland Yard took seriously the possibility that he was Jack the Ripper.

In 1993, retired Suffolk Constabulary police officer and crime historian Stewart P. Evans rediscovered Tumblety as a Whitechapel murder suspect when he acquired a private letter written by Chief Inspector John G. Littlechild, who headed Scotland Yard's Special Branch at the time of the murders. In it, Littlechild stated that Tumblety was "a very likely suspect." With the assistance of Paul Gainey, Evans researched extensively for the next two years, finding evidence that confirmed Scotland Yard's suspicions about Tumblety. Evans was asked by his publisher to publish his findings in 1995. He then made the decision to stop researching Tumblety but knew full well much more research was needed in order to gain a clearer picture. While Evans' and Gainey's conclusions were sound and fact-based, the evidence was limited enough that opposing explanations were argued to also fit the evidence. A number of experts favoring the opposing explanations published their own findings, reinforcing the belief that Tumblety was, at best, an insignificant Ripper suspect. These published works were so convincing that they won the day. By 2009, most experts believed the Tumblety story was complete, thus, few continued any research, save for three: Joe Chetcuti, Roger Palmer, and me. Discovery of new evidence began almost immediately, which was followed by research articles. It was not until 2015 that interest returned, and others began to research specific aspects of Tumblety's involvement in the Whitechapel case. I published these new findings in April 2016 in my book, *The Ripper's Haunts*, which allowed the experts to see the Tumblety story based upon a larger pool of evidence. Evans' and Gainey's conclusions were regaining favor.

A wealth of further evidence was discovered after the publication of *The Rippers Haunts*, and then, in January 2017, St. Louis filmmaker Michael Sandknop reached out to me requesting my assistance in his short film on Francis Tumblety. He knew Tumblety had died in St. Louis and thought there might be undiscovered evidence that he could find. I told him that Tumblety ignored the majority of his living relatives in his 1903 will and testament, which prompted them to file a lawsuit. They claimed Tumblety was not of sound mind and body, therefore, the will should be deemed null and void. In so doing, all of the living family members would then get equal share of his wealthy estate. I told Michael that these relatives would have information on Tumblety that no one else knew, which might very well be damning in the Whitechapel murders case. Michael began digging, and his relentless tenacity came through, discovering over 900 pages of documents not seen since the turn of the twentieth century. It was a goldmine for Tumblety research, adding 47 sworn testimonies of what Tumblety was like in the later years of his life.

This book is a compilation of the evidence on Francis Tumblety, both old and new. Although research continues, the volume of reliable evidence has painted a clear and startling picture of the Tumblety story, markedly different than previously known. Specific to the Whitechapel murders, Scotland Yard's suspicions may have been correct all along.

Acknowledgments

I owe a great debt of gratitude to Stewart Evans not only for laying the scholarly groundwork to further credible Tumblety research but also for allowing me to take up his time and tap into his vast knowledge and understanding of the entire Whitechapel murders case. I would like to thank two other pioneers in the field for giving me their expert advice in critical areas of my research, Paul Begg and Martin Fido.

Special thanks to Joe Chetcuti for providing me much-needed, almost daily guidance, advice, and research. Thank you, Roger Palmer, for the same. Joe and I are constantly amazed at your level of knowledge of the good doctor. I also took advantage of some outstanding researchers: Jonathan Hainsworth; Robert Linford; Neil Storey; Brian Young; A.j. Griffiths-Jones; Lauren Davies; David Barrett; Bernard Beaulé; Lindsay Siviter; Colleen Nugent, MD; Pete Grinnell; and Siobhán Pat Mulcahy. Your research/assistance was important and very much appreciated. I was honored by Michael Sandknop when he asked for my assistance, which resulted in a wealth of discoveries thanks to his tenacious investigative skills.

Further thanks goes out to my fellow Buffalonian, Brian Young, for partnering with me in order to ensure our research is as unbiased as it can be. Thank you, Robert Anderson, for your expert advice on many occasions and helping me understand the "secret disease." Thanks goes out to Howard Brown for maintaining an outstanding storehouse of evidence and information on the Whitechapel murders mystery at JTRForums, and further thanks to you and Nina Brown for finding important evidence and understanding its relevance. Thank you, Jonathan Menges, for allowing me to participate in the podcasts at Casebook.org's Rippercast, one of the most important peer review tools in the field. I certainly appreciate the help of Tom Wescott for understanding what I was looking for in front-cover description, his input capturing the essence of the story in one sentence.

Further appreciation goes out to Barbara DeWitt for editing my initial manuscript, and to Sunbury Press editor Jennifer Cappello and book designer Crystal Devine, for making such an excellent read. Amber Rendon, the book cover is outstanding.

I

Jack the Ripper and the Whitechapel Mystery

Not even during the riots and fog of February, 1886, have
I seen London so thoroughly excited as it is to-night. The
Whitechapel fiend murdered his fourth victim this morning and
still continues undetected, unseen, and unknown.
　　　　　　　—*New York Times*, September 8, 1888

The unusually dark night had a hint of red glow in the
overcast sky above the slums of the East End, Whitechapel
District, London, England, in the early hours of Friday,
August 31, 1888. At approximately 3:40 a.m., Charles Cross,
a carman, was walking in the rain through Buck's Row, a
side street from Whitechapel Road. The only light on the dark
street was a lone streetlamp at the far end. As Cross was
nearing the gateway entrance to Brown's stable yard between
a boarding school and some terrace houses, he noticed in
the dim light what he thought was a tarpaulin bundled on
the footpath opposite the Essex Wharf. As he approached,
he realized it was a woman lying on her back. Her skirt was
pulled up to her waist, and he thought the woman had just
been raped and was lying unconscious. He looked around
quickly, considering that he might have just scared the
attacker away, when he noticed another man casually walking
toward him—Robert Paul, a market porter, also on his way
to work. When Paul was about to pass him, Cross put his
hands on the newcomer's shoulder and said, "Come and look
at this woman." As they stared at her, Cross suggested they

help her up. Paul reached down, touched her face and hands, and noticed they were cold to the touch. He believed her to be dead, then after straightening her clothes to look a little more decent, he felt her heart and thought he detected a slight heartbeat. Because it was so dark, neither man saw the severe neck wound or the blood. Both men were concerned about getting to their respective jobs, so they left. They encountered Police Constable (PC) Jonas Mizen at a street corner and told him about the woman. Mizen rushed to Buck's Row but saw PC John Neil already hovering over the body, illuminating her with his bullseye lantern. Buck's Row was part of PC Neil's beat, though he had not walked through this section for nearly thirty minutes.

The woman was Mary Ann "Polly" Nichols, a casual prostitute, aged 43, graying dark brown hair, and missing front teeth. She was wearing a well-worn, reddish-brown ulster coat, a brown linsey frock, white chest flannel (the brassiere), two petticoats, side-spring boots, and a black straw bonnet. Like many casual prostitutes in Victorian London's East End slums, she left her family for the "demon" drink. She lodged in the various workhouses and supported her drinking habit and destructive lifestyle through prostitution, which is the reason these women were called "unfortunates." She was last seen alive, alone, and very drunk at two-thirty a.m. on the corner of Osborn Street and Whitechapel Road, walking toward Buck's Row, which was a half mile away.

Local surgeon Dr. Rees Llewellyn was called to the scene; he inspected the body and pronounced her dead based upon the deep throat cut. He found no marks indicating a struggle and no bloody trails as if she had been dragged to the location. Inspector Spratling gave the mortuary examination and noticed her throat had been cut deeply from left to right, with the windpipe, gullet, and spinal cord cut through, likely from a long-bladed knife. There was a bruise running along the lower part of the jaw on the right side of the face. A circular bruise was on the left side of the face, possibly indicating pressure from the fingers. The abdomen was cut open from the center-bottom of ribs on the right side and under the pelvis to the left of the stomach. The wound was jagged-shaped and there were two small stab wounds to the genital area.

Violent crime in a rough neighborhood such as the East End slums was not unusual, but this murder was different. Evidence of the usual motive behind a crime-related death on the streets, such as a mugging by a local gang, was absent at this crime scene. Nothing was stolen off her body. The murderer seemed to be killing for the sake of mutilating and taking life. The Nichols murder immediately made international news, not just because of its unusual brutality but because many—including in the press—believed that the East End had a ruthless killer on the loose. Polly Nichols was the third unfortunate to die so violently in the Whitechapel District in 1888; the first two murders were also unsolved.

The first brutal murder of an unfortunate occurred six months earlier, on April 16, 1888. Her name was Emma Elizabeth Smith. Smith was generally drunk, and her face was bruised and scratched thanks to her belligerent nature. Between four and five a.m., she walked into her lodging house on George Street, beaten up. She told the deputy-keeper of the lodging house that she had been brutalized by a number of men, and then robbed. Smith was taken to the London Hospital but died at nine a.m. due to the injuries caused by a blunt object, like a stick, being thrust into her genital area. Smith was likely the victim of local gang violence. The second murder of an unfortunate occurred around two-thirty a.m., August 7, 1888, just three weeks before the Nichols murder. This victim's name was Martha Tabram (or Turner), and she died on the first-floor landing of the George Yard Buildings. A John Saunders Reeves, aged 23, found Tabram's body positioned on her back, hands to her side, with her legs apart. Her body had thirty-nine stab wounds and was lying in a pool of blood. The left lung and heart were penetrated, but it was estimated that the knife was no more than three inches long. An eyewitness, another prostitute called Pearly Poll, stated she saw Tabram with two soldiers—a corporal and private in the Guards from the London Tower—from ten p.m. to about 11:45 p.m. A subsequent investigation did not identify any of the soldiers.

Many in Scotland Yard and the press believed the three unfortunates were killed by the same hand, and the Whitechapel murders investigation went into full swing. Chief

Inspector Donald Swanson was placed in full charge of the investigation, and three first-class detective inspectors from headquarters, Frederick Abberline, Henry Moore, and Walter Andrews, were assigned to assist the detectives assigned to the Whitechapel District, called H Division. Abberline was senior and in charge. He was the perfect fit, since before being assigned to headquarters the year before, he was head detective at H Division.

Chief Constable of Scotland Yard's Criminal Investigation Division Sir Melville Macnaghten joined the Metropolitan Police Department near the end of the Ripper murders investigation in June 1889, and had full access to the extensive files on the case. His hindsight on the case is arguably one of the most important perspectives. He became convinced that Nichols was actually the first victim of the Whitechapel fiend. Years later, in 1914, he stated, "The first real 'Whitechapel murder' . . . took place on the 31st of August, when Many Ann Nichols was found in Bucks Row with her throat cut and her body slightly mutilated."

The next victim would soon meet her horrific end. On Saturday morning, September 8, 1888, at 4:45 a.m., John Richardson of 2 John Street, Spitalfields District (next to Whitechapel), went outside and sat on the steps of the backyard to cut a piece of leather off his boot. Although the sun was yet to rise, Richardson could see the adjoining backyard of 29 Hanbury Street clearly in the predawn light, and it was empty. At 5:25 a.m., Albert Cadosh of 27 Hanbury Street, went into his backyard neighboring 29 Hanbury Street and heard people talking but could not see anyone because a five-foot wooden fence separated the two backyards. He did recognize the word "no" being said. He then went into the house, but three minutes later he went back outside and heard a noise from the backyard of 29 Hanbury Street, as if something were falling against the fence. He thought nothing of the noise and went back inside. At six a.m., John Davis, a resident of 29 Hanbury Street, saw the body of a woman just in front of the back door next to the wooden fence. It was the body of unfortunate Annie Chapman. Chapman had left a common lodging house at 35 Dorset Street drunk and penniless at 1:45 a.m. and planned on earning enough for a bed to sleep in that night.

The divisional surgeon, Dr. Bagster Phillips, examined the body. As in the case of the Nichols murder, Chapman's throat was cut deeply and with a jagged incision. Her abdomen was also mutilated with a long knife, but in this case, the body was eviscerated; the small intestines and other tissues were removed—yet still attached—and placed above her right shoulder. The womb and surrounding tissue were taken. Abrasions on her ring finger indicated that the two rings she owned were taken as well. Phillips gave his professional opinion that the murderer possessed "anatomical knowledge from the manner of the removal of the viscera" and used a sharp knife with a six- to eight-inch blade, such as a small amputating knife or a slaughterman's knife. The right temple and upper chest had bruises, but it was discovered that these came about because of an earlier fight with a woman named Eliza Cooper.

An eyewitness, Mrs. Elizabeth Long, claimed to see a man and a woman, who seemed to fit Chapman's description, talking near 29 Hanbury Street at five-thirty. She stated that the man was "apparently over 40 years of age," appeared to be a little taller than the woman, and looked like a foreigner, although, she admitted, she did not get a good look at his face and would not be able to recognize him. Coroner Wynne E. Baxter took Long's testimony seriously at the inquiry, but there is a contradiction. She saw the couple *after* Cadosh likely heard the murder taking place. In his October 19, 1888 report, Chief Inspector Swanson, the man Commissioner Warren directed to take charge of all inquiries in the Whitechapel murders investigation, seemed to be of the opinion that the time discrepancy put Long's testimony in doubt. Long claimed to hear the five-thirty a.m. strike of the clock, but Swanson surmised she may very well have heard the five-fifteen strike.

While many police officials, including Detective Abberline, did not believe Smith and Tabram were killed by the same offender who murdered Nichols, all were convinced Chapman was; thus, all now had a single-minded focus to capture a single killer. Two days later, Detective Sergeant William Thick arrested John Pizer, aged 38, on suspicion of the Chapman murder. His nickname was "Leather Apron." Once he gave a valid alibi, he was cleared. Numerous other suspects were arrested, but all seemed to be dead ends.

On the fifth day of the Chapman inquest, September 26, 1888, Coroner Baxter stated that a sub-curator of a pathological museum was asked months earlier by an American to acquire a number of uterus specimens—the same organ that was missing from Chapman's body. This detail was generally dismissed, because any medical professional could acquire these specimens at a relatively low price. Baxter, however, never suggested an American physician was the suspect of the crimes, but proposed a theory that the killer—likely "some abandoned wretch"—having knowledge of a demand for uterus specimens, was attempting to possess these organs by murdering unfortunates. He was convinced that there was indeed a market for organs. Baxter stated at the inquest:

> It has been suggested that the criminal is a lunatic with morbid feelings. This may or may not be the case; but the object of the murderer appears palpably shown by the facts, and it is not necessary to assume lunacy, for it is clear that there is a market for the object of the murder.

Many modern researchers believe once it was made known that a Philadelphia gynecologist was likely the person requesting the uterus specimens in 1887, Scotland Yard discounted the theory. But notice the following statement made in 1907 by famous journalist George R. Sims in the *Sunday Referee*, regarding a particular theory he received from Scotland Yard officials. Sims was in direct communication with the top officials in Scotland Yard and "highly respectable people":

> The other theory in support of which I have some curious information, puts the crime down to a young American medical student who was in London during the whole time of the murders, and who, according to statements of certain highly-respectable people who knew him, made on two occasions an endeavour to obtain a certain internal organ, which for his purpose had to be removed from, as he put it, "the almost living body."
> Dr. Wynne Baxter, the coroner, in his summing up to the jury in the case of Annie Chapman, pointed out the

significance of the fact that this internal organ had been removed.

But against this theory put forward by those who uphold it with remarkable details and some startling evidence in support of their contention, there is this one great fact. The American was alive and well and leading the life of an ordinary citizen long after the Ripper murders came to an end.

This article, written years later, suggests many in Scotland Yard rejected the Philadelphia gynecologist explanation, apparently because of "startling evidence." What is not a surprise is Scotland Yard allowing the public to believe the harvesting theory as being rejected. Note a report in the *Chicago Tribune* on October 7, 1888, written by the *New York World* London correspondent:

. . . An American who used to live in New York keeps an herb shop now in the Whitechapel district. A detective called at his place this week and asked him if he had sold any unusual compound of herbs to a customer since August. Similar inquiries were made at other shops in the neighborhood. The basis of this investigation has a startling Shakespearean flavor. An eminent engineer in London suggested to the police the theory that the murderer was a medical maniac trying to find the elixir of life and was looking for the essential ingredient in the parts taken from the murdered bodies; that, like the witches in "Macbeth," he spent the time over a bubbling caldron of the hellbroth made from the gory ingredients looking for the charm.

One day after the Philadelphia gynecologist story went out, Scotland Yard was investigating additional harvesting theories. How coincidental that this Dr. Jekyll and Mr. Hyde harvesting theory was of interest to Scotland Yard while the play *Dr. Jekyll and Mr. Hyde* was being performed in two separate London theaters. Surprisingly, Bram Stoker, author of *Dracula*, was the business manager at one of these theaters, the Lyceum Theatre. Many of the employees at the Lyceum Theatre were members of a Masonic-like group called the

Order of the Golden Dawn, and one of the main goals of this group was to discover the Philosopher's Stone—specifically, the elixir of life.

One day after Baxter's statement, on September 27, 1888, the Central News Agency received a letter possibly from the Whitechapel fiend, now known as the 'Dear Boss' letter:

> *Dear Boss,*
>
> *I keep on hearing the police have caught me but they wont fix me just yet. I have laughed when they look so clever and talk about being on the <u>right</u> track. That joke about Leather Apron gave me real fits. I am down on whores and I shant quit ripping them till I do get buckled. Grand work the last job was. I gave the lady no time to squeal. How can they catch me now. I love my work and want to start again. You will soon hear of me with my funny little games. I saved some of the proper <u>red</u> stuff in a ginger beer bottle over the last job to write with but it went thick like glue and I cant use it. Red ink is fit enough I hope <u>ha. ha.</u> The next job I do I shall clip the ladys ears off and send to the police officers just for jolly wouldn't you. Keep this letter back till I do a bit more work, then give it out straight. My knife's so nice and sharp I want to get to work right away if I get a chance. Good Luck.*
>
> *Yours truly*
>
> *Jack the Ripper*
> *Dont mind me giving the trade name*
>
> *PS Wasnt good enough to post this before I got all the red ink off my hands curse it No luck yet. They say I'm a doctor now. <u>ha ha</u>*

This is the first time the Whitechapel fiend was referred to as Jack the Ripper. Scotland Yard initially considered this letter a hoax, but this changed once the next murders occurred just days later. At around one o'clock in the morning, on September 30, 1888, a jewelry salesman named Louis Deismschutz drove his cart and pony into Dutfield's Yard, which was adjacent to the International Working Men's Educational Club. Upon entering the pitch-black yard, the pony abruptly stopped and refused to continue. Deismschutz noticed what he thought was a bundle in front of the pony, approached, and touched it with his whip. He struck a match, and in the low light he realized the bundle was a woman's body. Evidence suggested to the coroner that Deismschutz and his cart and pony interrupted the offender before he could complete his mutilation. First, the pony exhibited unusual behavior, more in line with surprising a living, threatening figure as opposed to just a lifeless body. The coroner also noted that the body was warm to the touch for a significant amount of time after the discovery, suggesting the attack must have been at the time of the surprise encounter.

The unfortunate's name was Elizabeth Stride, or "Long Liz," aged forty-two years, wearing an old black skirt and a black jacket trimmed with fur. Her bonnet was on the ground near her head. Her right hand was open, and her left hand was partially closed, holding onto a packet of cachous wrapped in tissue paper. Around her neck was a silk scarf that was pulled tight. Her throat was cut very similarly to the Nichols and Chapman bodies, but there was no abdominal mutilation. Stride was lying on her left side with her face looking toward the adjacent building, the International Working Men's Educational Club.

A second, even more horrific murder occurred within the same hour. Although less than a mile away from the Stride murder, the second murder actually took place outside the jurisdiction of Scotland Yard, or the Metropolitan Police, and fell within the jurisdiction of the City of London Police, at Mitre Square, Aldgate. While some argue that Stride was not a victim of Jack the Ripper because there was no evidence of abdominal mutilation, this second murder has few doubters. PC Edward Watkins was walking his beat and entered the square on Mitre Street. He shined his bullseye lantern in the gloomy south corner and spotted a woman lying on her back with her feet facing him. She was a casual prostitute named Catherine Eddowes. Her throat was cut deeply, and her clothes were ripped away, revealing her abdomen, which was gutted open from the pubic area all the way up to the sternum. She was lying in a pool of blood with her arms out and hands facing down, and her head was turned to the left. The attacker had cut her face, and the lobe and auricle of the right ear were cut through. Watkins was shocked and immediately ran to the east side of the square, spotted a nightwatchman in an adjoining building—an ex-Metropolitan police officer—and yelled, "For god's sake, Mate, come to my assistance! There is another woman cut to pieces! She has been ripped like a pig in a market!" The body was later found to be missing the left kidney; the police surgeon, Dr. Frederick Brown, stated that it was carefully removed with the uterus. The vagina was not attacked, and there was no indication of sexual intercourse. Dr. Brown believed the murderer must have had "considerable knowledge of the position of the organs in the abdominal cavity and the way of removing them." The conclusion at the inquiry was that Eddowes was murdered sometime between 1:35 a.m.—the time a witness walked by and saw nothing—and 1:45 a.m.—when the body was discovered.

This is a very short amount of time to murder, eviscerate the body, then leave.

The night was later dubbed the "Double Event." Just forty or so minutes between the two murders also suggests to some researchers that there were two killers responsible for the events of September 30, but if Jack the Ripper was hell-bent on accomplishing his murderous agenda that night, it was physically possible. Once the Ripper left the first murder site, all he had to do was rush off in a westerly direction to the intersection of the two busy thoroughfares, spot an unfortunate—in this case Eddowes—and either solicit her or more likely just follow her. The next murder site was just off the beaten path of this intersection, at a place called Mitre Square. Since Mitre Square was just outside of the Whitechapel District and within the city limits of London, the London City police were now involved in the case.

These attacks also had a number of Jewish connections, almost as if Jack the Ripper were taunting the police with the recent popularity of the Jewish Leather Apron. Elizabeth Stride was killed in a Jewish-populated area. While Catherine Eddowes was murdered in an area less populated by Jews, part of her apron was torn off and discovered a few blocks away in a highly populated Jewish area. Above the apron, written in chalk, was a note that stated (in one version), "The Juwes are the men that will not be blamed for nothing." It may only have been a coincidence that the apron was discovered below this message, since a note referencing 'Juwes' within a Jewish population makes sense.

Eddowes' ear being attacked could be interpreted as what the author of the Dear Boss letter meant, so the police took the letter very seriously—and then it was followed by a second letter. On October 1, 1888, a postcard was received by the Central News Agency; it was clearly penned by the same author as the Dear Boss letter written four days earlier:

> *I was not codding dear old Boss when I gave you the tip, you'll hear about Saucy Jacky's work tomorrow double event this time number one squealed a bit couldn't finish straight off. ha not the time to get ears for police. thanks for keeping last letter back till I got to work again.*
> *Jack the Ripper*

Scotland Yard decided to publish the letter in the London dailies on October 5, 1888, in hopes that someone might recognize the handwriting. An unintentional consequence was that the shocking name of Jack the Ripper stuck. Another result of the Dear Boss letter was Scotland Yard's suspicions that the Whitechapel fiend may be American; the letter possessed numerous Americanisms. Note the following editorial in London's *Evening News* on the very same day it was published:

> *THE EDITOR'S DRAWER.*
> *THE WHITECHAPL MURDERS.*
> *TO THE EDITOR OF "THE EVENING NEWS."*
> *Sir—Having resided for nearly ten years in America, and having carefully examined the facsimile letters you published this afternoon from "Jack the Ripper," I have not the slightest hesitation in saying they are written by an American, or by a person who had resided many years in the States. They are full of Americanisms from beginning to the end, such as boss, fix me, right track, real fits, shan't quit, squeal, fit enough, give it out straight, right away. Many of these expressions are in constant use by all classes of Americans, but never by Englishmen. This fact might become important in tracing the assassin.*
> *—Evening News, October 5, 1888*

The London correspondent for the *New York World* also reported on the American connection and noted how Scotland Yard was identifying Americans on the street by their American hat:

> *Horror-Stricken.*
> *[Special Cable to the Evening World]*
> *London, Oct. 2 – The London police are still working at random in the Whitechapel cases. No arrests have yet been made this morning, though it is not at all unlikely that a half a dozen suspicious characters maybe taken into custody before night, as was done yesterday. . . . With this indefinite and aimless policy on the part of the police, it is hard to tell whether any real detective work is being done. The detention of Fitzgerald, the hauling up of the poor German who quarreled with a woman he had met by chance and the late seizure of the mysterious gentleman with the "American hat" are proceedings which have only gone to strengthen the discredit with which the populace regards the police efficiency in this emergency.*
> *The curious disposition to connect the crimes with an American has been carried to an absurd extreme. "An American hat," "an American medical student," an American what not! An English friend, who has travelled enough across seas to become imbued with a just idea of things, whispers half reluctantly in my ear that if, instead of giving such a direction to their suspicions, the London detectives would give an American directness and sim-plicity to their researches and investigations, they might hope sooner to strike a trail which would lead them to the desired accomplishment . . .*
> *—The Evening World*, October 2, 1888

Note that the Dear Boss letter was not yet published when this October 2 special report was written, so the London correspondent had no idea about the Americanisms in the letter and was convinced Scotland Yard's American suspicion was evidence of their incompetence. On October 6, 1888, the *Saturday Budget* reported an arrest of a tall American wearing an American slouch hat, which is a soft felt hat having a wide brim and turned down the middle:

MORE WHITECHAPEL MURDERS.
A man was arrested at midnight last night on suspicion
of having committed the horrible murder in Whitechapel.
He is a tall man with dark beard and wore an American
slouch hat, by which he was traced from the locality of
the latest murder, where it is reported he was seen on
Saturday night, to Albert Chambers on Union street, in the
Borrough of South London, where he was found. The Bor-
rough is across the river and far away from Whitechapel
quarters. When arrested he was unable to give any ac-
count of himself during the previous night. The police are
investigating his antecedents and movements; of which it
is said he refuses to give any information.
—The Saturday Budget, October 6, 1888

Yet another connection to an American doctor occurred
near the Stride murder site on Batty Street. The following
newspaper report records a temporary non-English lodger in
the *Daily News*, October 16, 1888:

According to a Correspondent, the police are watch-
ing with great anxiety a house at the East-end which is
strongly suspected to have been the actual lodging, or a
house made use of by someone connected with the East-
end murders.
Statements made by the neighbours in the district
point to the fact that the landlady had a lodger, who since
the Sunday morning of the last Whitechapel murders has
been missing. The lodger, it is stated, returned home early
on the Sunday morning, and the landlady was disturbed
by his moving about. She got up very early, and noticed
that her lodger had changed some of his clothes. He told
her he was going away for a little time, and he asked her
to wash the shirt which he had taken off, and get it ready
for him by the time he came back. As he had been in the
habit of going away now and then, she did not think much
at the time, and soon afterwards he went out. On looking
at his shirt she was astonished to find the wristbands
and part of the sleeves saturated with wet blood. The ap-
pearance struck her as very strange, and when she heard

of the murders her suspicions were aroused. Acting on the advice of some of her neighbours, she gave information to the police and showed them the blood-stained shirt. They took possession of it and obtained from her a full description of her missing lodger. During the last fortnight she has been under the impression that he would return, and was sanguine that he would probably come back on Saturday or Sunday night, or perhaps Monday evening.

The general opinion, however, among the neighbours is that he will never return. On finding the house and visiting it, a reporter found it tenanted by a stout, middle-aged, German woman, who speaks very bad English, and who was not inclined to give much information further than the fact that her lodger had not returned yet, and she could not say where he had gone or when he would be back. The neighbours state that ever since the information has been given two detectives and two policemen have been in the house day and night. The house is approached by a court, and as there are alleys running through it into different streets, there are different ways of approach and exit.

It is believed from the information obtained concerning the lodger's former movements and his general appearance, together with the fact that numbers of people have seen the same man about the neighbourhood, that the police have in their possession a series of most important clues, and that his ultimate capture is only a question of time.

The reporter's information clearly came from neighbors who gave the landlady advice, meaning they had knowledge of the incident with the landlady as their source. The police seem to have told the lady not to speak with the press, as evidenced by her reticent response.

Note an additional report in the *Manchester Evening News* on October 17, 1888:

. . . The German lodging-house keeper could clear up the point as to the existence of any other lodger absent from her house under the suspicious circumstances referred to, but she is not accessible, and it is easy to understand that the police should endeavour to prevent her making any

statement. From our own inquiries in various directions yesterday afternoon a further development is very likely to take place.

With regard to the statements current as to finding a bloodstained shirt at a lodging house in Whitechapel, the Central News says: 'The story is founded on some matters which occurred more than a fortnight ago. It appears that a man, apparently a foreigner, visited the house of a German laundress at 22, Batty-street, and left four shirts tied in a bundle to be washed. The bundle was not opened at the time, but when the shirts were afterwards taken out, one was found to be considerably bloodstained. The woman communicated with the police, who placed the house under observation, the detectives at the same time being lodged there to arrest the man should he return. This he did last Saturday, and was taken to Leman-street Police Station where he was questioned, and within an hour or two released, his statements being proved correct.'

In the *Yarmouth Independent* of February 25, 1911, was an article from famous British journalist George R. Sims, titled "Adventures of a Journalist, Part VIII 'On the Track,'" in which he seems to have recalled the Batty Street incident:

JACK THE RIPPER.

The crimes of Jack the Ripper are still debated and from time to time the discussion as to his identity is revived in the Press.

... Three years ago, when the discussion as to Jack's identity cropped up again in the Press, I wrote on the subject. Soon afterwards a lady called upon me late one night. She came to tell me that the Whitechapel fiend had lodged in her house. On the night of the double murder he came in at two in the morning. The next day her husband, going into the lodger's room after he had left it, saw a black bag, and on opening it discovered a long knife, and two bloodstained cuffs. The lodger was a medical man, an American. The next day he paid his rent, took his luggage and left. Then the police were communicated with but nothing more was heard of the American doctor with the suspicious black bag.

'But,' said my lady visitor, 'I have seen him again this week. He is now in practice in the North West of London.'

She gave his name and address and the names of two people who were prepared to come forward and identify him as the lodger with the black bag, the knife, and the incriminating cuffs. The next day I took the information, for what it might be worth, to the proper quarters. But the doctor was not disturbed in his practice. There was ample proof that the real author of the horrors had committed suicide in the last stage of his maniacal frenzy.

The similarities between the two accounts are uncanny. Both involve a female landlady and a male renter; the renter is identified as a lodger; the incident occurred on the night of the double event murder; the lodger was out during the night and only returned in short time intervals; and lastly, the landlady noticed bloodstained "wristbands"—sleeves or cuffs. Interestingly, the slight differences in the accounts might not be differences at all. First, they are different sources. The 1888 *Daily News* account came from the neighbors, while the 1911 Sims account came directly from the landlady. Second, both are reporting on slightly different events involving the incident. The *Daily News* account describes when the lodger came in on the evening of the murders then asked the landlady to wash his clothes. The Sims account reports on the man's return on the night of the murders at two in the morning. The neighbors' account suggested she received the bloodstained clothes directly from the suspect that night, differing from the Sims account, but the *Manchester Evening News* story of the Batty Street lodger clarifies that it was later: "The bundle was not opened at the time, but when the shirts were afterwards taken out . . ."

Scotland Yard continued to take seriously American suspects, as evidenced by the following October 29, 1888, article in the *Echo*:

> EAST-END ATTROCITIES
> POLICE ACTIVE—STILL NO CLUE
> *The various districts are being patrolled by extra constables, and their zeal has lead them into several excesses, notably, an arrest of three young men made on Thursday night in Berner-street. The police, according to a morning*

contemporary, have so much in mind the vague stories of an American perpetrator of the dastardly crimes that any person in a wide-a-wake or soft felt becomes an object of suspicion. A comic singer was unfortunate enough during a professional visit on Thursday to Whitechapel to wear one of these hats; and when during the interval he and two friends strolled round the neighbourhood, to view the scene of the Berner-street tragedy, they were promptly denounced by some too quick-sighted citizen and marched off by the police. It is only due to the latter to say they were detained but a very short time, sufficient to test the truth of their statement. It is stated that the words, "I shall do another murder, and will receive her heart," have been found written in chalk on the on the footway in Camplin-street, Deptford.

 —*Echo*, October 29, 1888

No murders attributed to Jack the Ripper occurred on the East End in the month of October 1888, likely because the police departments increased the number of constables and detectives on the street, plus the public was on high alert. Reinforcing this explanation is the fact that the last murder occurred when the police force was busy with the annual ceremonial event known as the Lord Mayor's Show, suggesting the murderer saw this as an opportunity. Also, the last victim was murdered indoors, away from any police constable walking his beat.

The last of the canonical five Ripper murders occurred on November 9, 1888, and this time it was indoors in the victim's room, allowing the killer hours of uninterrupted time with the body. Mary Ann Cox, an unfortunate who lived at 5 Miller's Court, was on the streets that night and saw fellow unfortunate Mary Jane Kelly walking with a man around eleven forty-five p.m. She followed them as they turned into Miller's Court, and Kelly went into her room with the man. He was around five feet and five inches tall, in his mid-thirties, had a blotchy face, and a carroty moustache on a clean-shaven face. He was dressed in shabby clothes, a "longish" dark overcoat, and a billycock hat. Ms. Cox told Ms. Kelly, "Good night," and noticed that her neighbor was very drunk. Kelly replied, "Good night; I am going to have a song." Cox noticed the man was carrying a quart can of beer. Cox left then returned at one o'clock a.m. and heard Kelly singing. Cox left yet again and returned at three a.m. This time Kelly's room was dark and silent. Another witness claimed to see Kelly back on the street at two a.m., and yet another even claimed to have seen her at eight thirty that morning.

Another unfortunate living in the Court, a Ms. Elizabeth Prater, claimed she heard a woman screaming a few times at three thirty or four a.m. and then heard a woman say, "Oh, murder," in a faint voice. She actually thought nothing of it and went back to bed. Prater woke up and left at five thirty a.m. to the Ten Bells club and had some rum. Thomas Bowyer, employed by John McCarthy, was tasked to go to Kelly's room to collect rent. He arrived at ten forty-five a.m., knocked on the door, walked around the rear of the room, and opened up the curtains through a crack. He was shocked by what he saw.

Police Surgeon Dr. George Bagster Phillips arrived at Miller's Court at eleven fifteen a.m., but was not allowed to enter the room until one-thirty p.m. A Dr. Thomas Bond, the police surgeon from A Division, was called in to assist. Sections of his report state:

> The body was lying naked in the middle of the bed, the shoulders flat but the axis of the body inclined to the left side of the bed. The head was turned on the left cheek. The left arm was close to the body with the forearm flexed at a right angle and lying across the abdomen. The right arm was slightly abducted from the body and rested on the mattress. The elbow was bent, the forearm supine with the fingers clenched. The legs were wide apart, the left thigh at right angles to the trunk and the right forming an obtuse angle with the pubes.

Bond then went into great detail on the extensive abdominal and facial mutilation and extraction of organs. The neck was cut to the vertebrae, as in the case with the four earlier victims, and Dr. Bond stated that, "the heart was absent." The mutilation was the most extreme of all the victims, which makes sense since the murderer had hours to conduct his sinister work, uninterrupted.

Even after the Kelly murder, Scotland Yard considered the possibility of an American Jack the Ripper as they investigated all suspect theories. Note the article published in the *Brooklyn Daily Eagle* on November 10, 1888:

London's Reign of Terror

The assassin of Whitechapel has claimed his ninth victim, having planned and executed his latest crime with all the deliberation and cunning that characterized his former exploits . . . It has been said among other things that the assassin is an American, because he wears a slouch hat . . .

George Hutchinson watched Mary Jane Kelly with a suspicious man in Commercial St late Friday night, November 9, 1888. His description:

dress long, dark coat, collar and cuffs trimmed astracan [sic] and a dark jacket under, light waistcoat, dark trousers, dark felt hat turned down in the middle, button boots and gaiters with white buttons, wore a very thick gold chain, white linen collar, black tie with horse shoe pin, respectable appearance walked very sharp . . . [Author's note: This conforms to a slouch hat.]

Matthew Packer keeps a shop in Berner St. has a few grapes in window, black & white.

On Sat night about 11pm a young man from 25-30—about 5.7 with long black coat buttoned up -soft felt hat, kind of yankee hat rather broad shoulders—rather quick in speaking, rough voice. I sold him 1/2 pound black grapes 3d. A woman came up with him from Back Church end (the lower end of street) She was dressed in black frock & jacket, fur round bottom of jacket with black crape bonnet, she was playing with a flower like a geranium white outside and red inside. I identify the woman at the St. George's mortuary as the one I saw that night . . .
—*Brooklyn Daily Eagle*, November 10, 1888

Note the following excerpt in an article published in the *San Francisco Chronicle* on November 18, 1888, written by the London correspondent from the *New York World*, E. Tracy Greaves:

> GOSSIP OF LONDON.
> *A Heavy Swell Arrested in Whitechapel. A Score of Prisoners, but No Clew.*
> *LONDON, November 17.*
> *. . . That was the case with Sir George Arthur of the Prince of Wales set. He put on an old shooting coat and a slouch hat and went to Whitechapel for a little fun. He got it. It occurred to two policemen that Sir George answered very much to the popular description of Jack the Ripper.*
> —*San Francisco Chronicle*, November 18, 1888

Not only was Scotland Yard still interested in a possible American killer, but the report suggests the police constables were directed to look for anyone suspicious wearing an American slouch hat.

The monthly murders stopped after the Kelly murder, and a few months later, in early 1889, Scotland Yard even reassigned Inspector Frederick Abberline, the detective they had directed to head the investigation in the East End. Following the Kelly murder, there were two more murders of unfortunates, which at the time convinced many in Scotland Yard that Jack the Ripper was still on the loose. Alice Mackenzie was murdered on July 17, 1889. The coroner, Dr. Thomas Bond, believed that "the murder was performed by the same person who committed the former series of Whitechapel murder." Metropolitan Police Commissioner James Monro was also convinced, and he even deployed an extra two sergeants and thirty-nine constables to the Whitechapel District. Because of the knife wounds being dissimilar to the wounds found on the earlier victims, few now consider Mackenzie a Ripper victim. On February 13, 1891, casual prostitute Francis Coles was murdered. Her throat was cut, but she did not have any abdominal wounds. A number of officials at the time believed that Coles was a Ripper victim, while most modern-day researchers now reject this and believe Kelly was the last victim.

Officially, the case remains unsolved to this day. Scotland Yard and the City of London Police investigated countless angles and suspects during and just after the murders. As years passed, many officials directly involved in the case gave their opinions—publicly and privately—as to whom they believed was the murderer known as Jack the Ripper. These opinions have been taken very seriously by modern researchers and enthusiasts, especially since those sources lived through the investigation. Curiously, there was no consensus. For example, Assistant Commissioner Anderson and his faithful subordinate, Chief Inspector Swanson, seemed to have been convinced of a Polish Jew. Assistant Chief Constable Melville Macnaghten was convinced it was Montague John Druitt. The first-class inspector running the investigation in the East End, Frederick Abberline, highly suspected George Chapman. The subject of this book, Scotland Yard suspect Dr. Francis Tumblety, was named by the head of Special Branch, Chief Inspector John G. Littlechild.

Police officials at the time had no alternative but to place heavy emphasis upon eyewitness testimony, but there are a number of inherent problems with using a person's memory as the determining factor in selecting one suspect over another. First, in this case, no one saw the murders, thus, it is only an assumption that a particular eyewitness described the offender. Second, even if they did, their recollections may have been in error.

Recently, a compelling study by the Innocence Project out of the School of Law at Yeshiva University demonstrated the weakness of eyewitness testimony. They studied 239 cases where the determining factor for conviction was eyewitness testimony. Shockingly, 73% of these convictions were overturned by DNA testing. Additionally, surveys reveal that most jurors give priority to eyewitness testimony over other types of evidence, believing human memory is accurate and unalterable. Psychologists explain that false memory is a reality, produced by a process called memory reconstruction. Not believing a particular memory has been unknowingly altered is also a reality.

Contemporary Scotland Yard officials had no idea of the weakness in eyewitness testimony. When nearly three-quarters of convictions by eyewitness testimony can be overturned by DNA evidence, it seems prudent to be less emboldened about a favored suspect.

In February 1993, retired Suffolk constabulary police officer and crime historian Stewart Evans discovered that Scotland Yard had suspected an American in the Whitechapel murders case: a Dr. Francis Tumblety. Evans acquired a private letter from a book dealer, written by the chief inspector of Scotland Yard's Special Branch division at the time of the murders—John G. Littlechild. The letter, dated September 23, 1913, was addressed to well-known British journalist George R. Sims, who had previously written a letter to the retired chief inspector asking about the twenty-five-year-old Whitechapel murders case. The following are excerpts from the letter dealing with Tumblety:

> *Dear Sir,*
>
> *I was pleased to receive your letter which I shall put away in 'good company' to read again, perhaps some day when old age overtakes me and when to revive memories of the past may be a solace.*
>
> *Knowing the great interest you take in all matters criminal, and abnormal, I am just going to inflict one more letter on you on the 'Ripper' subject. Letters as a rule are only a nuisance when they call for a reply but this does not need one. I will try and be brief.*
>
> *I never heard of a Dr D. in connection with the Whitechapel murders but amongst the suspects, and to my mind a very likely one, was a Dr. T. (which sounds much like D.) He was an American quack named Tumblety and was at one time a frequent visitor to London and on these occasions constantly brought under the notice of police, there being a large dossier concerning him at Scotland Yard. Although a 'Sycopathia Sexualis' subject he was not known as a 'Sadist' (which the murderer unquestionably was) but his feelings toward women were remarkable and bitter in the extreme, a fact on record. Tumblety was arrested at the time of the murders in connection with unnatural offences and charged at Marlborough Street, remanded on bail, jumped his bail, and got away to Boulogne. He shortly left Boulogne and was never heard of afterwards. It was believed he committed suicide but certain it is that from this time the 'Ripper' murders came to an end.*

With regard to the term 'Jack the Ripper' it was generally believed at the Yard that Tom Bullen of the Central News was the originator, but it is probable Moore, who was his chief, was the inventor. It was a smart piece of journalistic work. No journalist of my time got such privileges from Scotland Yard as Bullen. Mr James Munro when Assistant Commissioner, and afterwards Commissioner, relied on his integrity. Poor Bullen occasionally took too much to drink, and I fail to see how he could help it knocking about so many hours and seeking favours from so many people to procure copy. One night when Bullen had taken a 'few too many' he got early information of the death of Prince Bismarck and instead of going to the office to report it sent a laconic telegram 'Bloody Bismarck is dead'. On this I believe Mr Charles Moore fired him out.

It is very strange how those given to 'Contrary sexual instinct' and 'degenerates' are given to cruelty, even Wilde used to like to be punched about. It may interest you if I give you an example of this cruelty in the case of the man Harry Thaw and this is authentic as I have the boy's statement. Thaw was staying at the Carlton Hotel and one day laid out a lot of sovereigns on his dressing table, then rang for a call boy on pretence of sending out a telegram. He made some excuse and went out of the room and left the boy there and watched through the chink of the door. The unfortunate boy was tempted and took a sovereign from the pile and Thaw returning to the room charged him with stealing. The boy confessed when Thaw asked whether he should send for the police or whether he should punish him himself. The boy scared to death consented to take his punishment from Thaw who then made him undress, strapped him to the foot of the bedstead, and thrashed him with a cane, drawing blood. He then made the boy get into a bath in which he placed a quantity of salt. It seems incredible that such a thing could take place in any hotel but it is a fact. This was in 1906.

Now pardon me—it is finished. Except that I knew Major Griffiths for many years. He probably got his information from Anderson who only 'thought he knew'.

Faithfully yours, J. G. Littlechild

Chief Inspector John G. Littlechild stated that Francis Tumblety was "amongst the suspects, and to my mind a very likely one." Here was a man privy to the private discussions of those directly involved with the Whitechapel murders investigation in the detective division called the Criminal Investigation Department (CID), including Assistant Commissioner Anderson, and he not only challenged Anderson's opinion, but he also claimed Tumblety was very likely Jack the Ripper. This was a big surprise, since Francis Tumblety was not part of the discussions on the possible identity of Jack the Ripper throughout the twentieth century. Yet, here is a key Scotland Yard player at the time of the murders stating Tumblety was a very likely suspect. This fact alone has caused many researchers to take Tumblety seriously as a viable Whitechapel murderer candidate. Littlechild even explained to Sims why CID considered Tumblety "amongst the suspects." He stated, ". . . but his feelings toward women were remarkable and bitter in the extreme, a fact on record."

Was Jack the Ripper a serial killer and can we identify his motive?

Scotland Yard was convinced they had a single killer who murdered two or more victims in separate events in the Whitechapel and Spitalfields Districts in late 1888, thus, Jack the Ripper fits the modern definition of a serial killer. What was not a consensus in Scotland Yard was which victims were killed by one offender. All told, there were well over a dozen victims of violent crimes on the East End in the period in question. As in any research discipline, there are groupers and splitters. Some see the slightest similarities as justification to group together, while others focus upon the differences and split the groups apart. There are even modern researchers who are convinced there was no Jack the Ripper, and all of the casual prostitutes were murdered by separate offenders. Most experts, though, agree that the number of Jack the Ripper victims is in the middle, between four and six.

To add to the confusion, three useful tools that modern law enforcement use on a daily basis were not available to the Metropolitan Police and the City of London Police in 1888. First is the use of modern forensics and the utilization of latent physical evidence at the crime scene, such as fingerprints, fibers, DNA, and massive suspect databases.

Second, they did not understand the common behavior patterns of serial offenders, such as the identification of modus operandi (MO) and offender signature. The MO is what the offender must do in order to commit a crime, such as leading the prostitute away from public places, the method of control, and the type of knife used. The offender signature serves to satisfy the emotional and psychological needs of the offender through fantasy, such as torture, location of mutilation, or staging and posing the body. The MO between successive murders may be similar, but may change and evolve with a changing environment, or the offender discovers a better method of accomplishing his agenda. The offender signature tends not to change, since it involves the same fantasy from one murder to the next.

In 2005, the FBI's Behavioral Analysis Unit Two from the National Center for the Analysis of Violent Crime Division facilitated a symposium of experts in the fields of law enforcement, mental health, and academics in order to assist in investigations on violent offenders. They came up with a broad definition for serial murder, "the unlawful killing of two or more victims by the same offender(s), in separated events." The experts also concluded, after reviewing case studies, that serial killers differ in many ways, but all possess certain traits: lack of remorse or guilt, impulsivity, need for control, and predatory behavior. The experts also came up with the following list, albeit not intended to be a complete measure of identified categories of serial offender motives: Anger, Criminal Enterprise, Financial Gain, Ideology, Power/Thrill, Psychosis, and Sexually-based.

Understanding MO and offender signature can lead to identifying serial motive. Identifying these attributes to assist law enforcement—and in our case to evaluate the Whitechapel murders—has produced a boost in a methodology called forensic victimology. Forensic victimology is defined as the scientific study of violent crime victims for the purpose of addressing investigative and forensic issues. It is studying evidence that establishes the relationship between the victim, the suspect, and the crime scene, in the backdrop of social-political, legal, and natural environments. Forensic victimology is an applied discipline, as opposed to merely a theoretical one, and has assisted in the successful apprehension and prosecution of countless offenders. This approach in criminology is perfect for studying Jack the Ripper and the Whitechapel murders of 1888, since direct, physical evidence in the case is long gone yet the details of the crime scenes are well-documented. Elements of this modern forensic methodology were used in the Whitechapel murders investigation. The divisional police surgeon in Victorian England was the equivalent to today's forensic pathologist and was responsible for the body of the deceased and the forensic evidence, such as wound-pattern analysis in the case of the Whitechapel victims and how it may relate to them in the act of casual prostitution. The coroner was responsible for discovering the means by which the death occurred and took into account the behavior of the offender.

The difference between the Kelly murder and the previous four is that it was done indoors, which has caused many to believe it was a different offender. If we assume Kelly was murdered by Jack the Ripper, there has been a change in MO and offender signature frequency. The first four were outdoors, and the offender only had minutes to complete his agenda, thus, MO dominates the crime scene over offender signature. The offender had hours with the Kelly body, thus, he could actualize his entire fantasy, producing a well-developed offender signature.

Forensic scientist and criminal profiler Dr. Brent Turvey, PhD, explains how behavioral patterns of violent offenders identified at the crime scene are relatively consistent and classified as Behavioral-Motivational Typology. The patterns found at crime scenes resulting from violent offenders are Power Reassurance, Power Assertive, Anger Retaliatory, Sadistic, and Administrative Behaviors. In 1989, forensic pathologist Dr. William Eckert, MD, headed an investigation, which studied the victims of Jack the Ripper and concluded the offender exhibited what Turvey terms as non-sadistic, anger-retaliatory behaviors. More recently, Dr. Turvey studied the Whitechapel murders, specifically the crime scenes and victims from Polly Nichols to Mary Kelly, and also interpreted the offender's behavior as non-sadistic, observing a lack of sexual assault to the victims, lack of torture while alive, post-mortem humiliation through mutilation, and display. Turvey observed experimental behavior, as opposed to ritualistic, and a need to instill fear or terror in the public. Turvey states, "they [offender behaviors] describe an offender who evidences both anger-retaliatory and reassurance-oriented behaviors." Specific to anger-retaliatory, the offender attacks the very identity of a woman, indicative of misogyny. Reassurance-oriented behaviors come from a feeling of personal inadequacy and are intended to restore self-confidence and self-worth. Collecting souvenirs, such as the organs or Chapman's rings, is a "token of remembrance." Turvey states this is commonly associated with reassurance-oriented needs.

Another obstacle was that Victorian officials did not understand the mind of a serial killer; what causes their behavior. During the Whitechapel murders, most law enforcement officials, physicians, and psychologists, known at the time as alienists, were convinced the killer was an insane, sadistic, bloodthirsty maniac. Case in point is the following news cable dispatch picked up by the *Bismarck Daily Tribune*:

> *The London Horror.*
>
> *Alienists are unanimous in the opinion that the murderer is a monomaniac with a homicidal turn; and many add that he is what medical science calls a "sexual pervert"—that is, a man in whom the natural instincts have been changed by disease or excess into a blind hatred and desire to kill and mangle . . . His cunning is wonderful—not an uncommon thing in monomaniacs. Dr. William Hammond, the eminent alienist, very sensibly says that the police have gone wrong from the start, because they have looked only for a self evident villain, a man "whose face would go far to hang him," while the probabilities are many to one that the perpetrator is a decorous and soft spoken gentleman, living an apparently virtuous life, a man whose closest acquaintances do not suspect of crime . . .*
>
> —*Bismarck Daily Tribune*, October 11, 1888

Even today we—the public as well as experts, such as therapists—have a difficult time understanding how different a psychopathic serial killer is to us and even to other violent offenders. Case in point, in the 1980s, serial killer David Michael Krueger, birth name Peter Woodcock, was one of numerous offenders in a psychopathy treatment program at Oak Ridge Psychiatric Facility in Ontario, Canada. In 1991, he seemed to be responding positively to the treatment, so he was released to a minimum-security hospital in Brockville, Ontario. During a weekend pass, Krueger murdered a fellow inmate within hours of being released. After reviewing the program, the therapists realized their treatment was actually having a negative effect upon psychopaths. Krueger admitted that the therapy did not work, and he merely gained an understanding on how to manipulate the therapists.

Cognitive neuroscientists have made great inroads into understanding the minds, or the neurologic pathways, of psychopaths, including serial killers. A series of recent discoveries has identified abnormal brain processing patterns in the various types of violent offenders. It is a brain processing pattern involving both the emotional center (the limbic system) and the cognitive center (the cerebral cortex). The specific emotion-producing organ involved in violent and aggressive behavior is the amygdala, in which is part of the limbic system. Among other attributes, the amygdala is the source of emotion for fear and rage. The cognitive part of the brain that controls our emotional reactions is a section in the cerebral cortex called the prefrontal cortex. The prefrontal cortex connects emotions to thoughts and decisions, allowing humans to self-moderate social behavior, such as controlling sexual or anger impulses. An overactive amygdala can result in impulsive violent behavior. This can be caused by the body releasing too much testosterone, which has been identified in numerous violent offenders. At the other end of the brain processing pattern, damage to the prefrontal cortex can make people less able to control their emotional reactions. Certain violent offenders have been identified as having damage to the prefrontal cortex. Serotonin is a chemical in the prefrontal cortex that acts as a break for emotional impulses. The body releasing low serotonin levels can cause a lack of control of aggressive impulses. So, too much testosterone in the limbic system and/or too little serotonin in the cerebral cortex can cause a normal person to exhibit unusual aggressive behavior.

Studies have demonstrated that the origins of these abnormal brain processing patterns are a product of both genetics and severe child abuse and neglect. Some are genetically predisposed to producing low levels of serotonin, while severe child abuse and neglect can impair the neural connectivity needed for controlling aggressive impulses. Professor Peter Smith at the University of London, an expert on child psychology, studied the development of early aggressive behavior. Professor Smith's research suggests that until the age of three, impulses for aggressive behavior run wild due to urges in the emotional center of the brain. At this time, the part of the brain that controls these urges, the prefrontal cortex, begins to develop. The gray matter in the prefrontal cortex builds up. Smith discovered that being taught to share and control aggressive behavior actually changes the physical structure of the brain, strengthening the connections between the emotional center and the prefrontal cortex. Childhood abuse and neglect retard these structures, thus creating less gray matter.

Psychopathic serial killers exhibit a different abnormal brain pattern than other violent offenders. Their brains show a lack of reactivity in the amygdala, while the prefrontal cortex exhibits relatively normal activity. Because of this, these serial killers have the ability to control impulsive abnormal emotional behavior.

The hallmark behavioral pattern in psychopaths, sociopaths, and especially with serial killers, is an extreme lack of empathy. This leads to a third section of the brain that connects the prefrontal cortex with the amygdala: the insula. The insula, which is housed within the prefrontal cortex, is associated with pain, anger, fear, disgust, joy, and sadness. A groundbreaking study conducted by Decety, Chenyi, Harenski, and Kiehl, published in *Frontiers in Human Neuroscience*, September 24, 2013, demonstrated that when psychopaths were introduced to information about themselves undergoing pain, such as cutting themselves with a knife, sections of the prefrontal cortex (the anterior midcingulate gyrus and somatic cortex), the anterior portion of the insula, and the right amygdala became active. When the same psychopaths were introduced to information about others undergoing the same pain, the prefrontal cortex-insula-amygdala pathway showed no activity, and in fact, brain activity increased in the areas known for pleasure called the ventral striatum. They seemed to enjoy watching others suffer. When specifically asked about the pain of others, the prefrontal cortex–insula–amygdala pathway activated, albeit slightly, suggesting that psychopaths have the ability to feel empathy. It was clear, though, that the normal pathway for experiencing empathy was weakly connected and was overshadowed by the pleasure pathway. Note how this resonates with the comments made by psychopathic serial killer David Kruger. He stated in an interview that when he was in the act of mutilating a child, he felt like God, felt pleasure, and felt a feeling of accomplishment. He then stated, "Now, if I for one instance thought, well, this is a human being, this is someone who is being badly hurt by me, I think I would have stopped. The fact that I didn't shows that those feelings are really secondary."

Another common pattern in serial killers is a history of child abuse and neglect, and its physical effects in the prefrontal cortex now explain why psychopathy is not the only ingredient in the formation of a serial killer. Psychopathic serial killers are indeed born, possessing low-functioning amygdalas, but then child abuse reduces the neural connections among the prefrontal cortex, the insula, and the amygdala. Thus, the transformation of a psychopath to a psychopathic serial killer is a combination of both nature and nurture. Sociopathic serial killers may have begun with a normal amygdala and brain functions, but extreme child abuse caused excessive neurological pathway damage, resulting in a violent offender who possesses an extreme lack of remorse.

According to modern psychology experts studying abnormal violent behavior, serial offenders as a whole are not insane, meaning they know right from wrong but just do not care. Based upon decades of study, modern psychologists now understand that serial killers have personality developmental disorders. One such developmental disorder is Antisocial Personality Disorder (APD), fully expressed by violence and a lack of remorse. It is labeled as a cluster B personality in the *Diagnostic and Standard Manual of Mental Disorders*, fourth edition (*DSM-IV*; published in the American Psychiatric Association (APA), 1994), and is connected to psychopathy. Not all individuals with APD are considered psychopathic, but those who have minimal empathy and feelings of grandiosity are likely psychopathic. According to the *DSM-IV*, a characteristic of APD is a "pervasive pattern of disregard for, and violation of, the rights of others that begins in childhood or early adolescence and continues into adulthood." Individuals with APD fail to conform to social norms and instead engage in deviant behavior, such as sexual assault, and many have criminal records and repeated arrests. Included with the lack of remorse are consistent irresponsibility, impulsivity, irritability, and aggressiveness. One study in 2002, headed by Dr. Janet I. Warren, DSW, involving violent offenders in prison, identified six diagnostic patterns: "antisocial-narcissistic, paranoid-antisocial, borderline-antisocial-passive-aggressive, borderline, compulsive-borderline and schizoid." Jeffrey Dahmer was diagnosed as having schizoid traits.

Another personality disorder diagnosed in violent offenders is Borderline Personality Disorder (BPD). BPD is characterized by emotional instability, anxiety, and psychotic-like symptoms. Individuals with BPD also have a lack of empathy and can suddenly become very paranoid or suspicious of others. BPD has also been connected with impulsive aggression. This impulsive aggression can be brought about by environmental triggers.

Narcissistic Personality Disorder (NPD) is a personality disorder characterized by "a pervasive pattern of grandiosity, need for admiration, and lack of empathy that begins by early adulthood and is present in a variety of contexts." Those diagnosed with NPD show signs of selfishness and a lack of interest in and empathy for others. Dr. Anthony Benis, ScD, MD, states in his book, *Toward Self & Sanity*, that aggressive narcissists "love to travel." The criteria in the *Diagnostic and Statistical Manual of Mental Disorders* gives the following features for NPD:

- Having an exaggerated sense of self-importance
- Expecting to be recognized as superior even without achievements that warrant it
- Exaggerating your achievements and talents
- Being preoccupied with fantasies about success, power, brilliance, beauty or the perfect mate
- Believing that you are superior and can only be understood by or associate with equally special people

- Requiring constant admiration
- Having a sense of entitlement
- Expecting special favors and unquestioning compliance with your expectations
- Taking advantage of others to get what you want
- Having an inability or unwillingness to recognize the needs and feelings of others
- Being envious of others and believing others envy you
- Behaving in an arrogant or haughty manner

It is often difficult to differentiate between Antisocial Personality Disorder and Narcissistic Personality Disorder, since they share many characteristics. For example, seventy-three psychologists from the APA Division participated in a study on the personality structure of serial killer Ted Bundy. Psychologists Samuel and Widiger reported in the *Journal of Abnormal Psychology* in 2006 that 96% of the psychologists gave Bundy a diagnosis of Antisocial Personality Disorder; however, 95% also saw Bundy meeting the criteria for Narcissistic Personality Disorder.

While the first obstacle faced by Victorian officials is still an obstacle for modern researchers studying the Whitechapel murders, since the physical evidence in the case is no longer available, the second and third obstacles are less so. Because the details of the crime scenes and suspects are still available, we can review them with twentieth-century eyes and compare our modern understanding of serial offenders with the Whitechapel murders investigation. Victorian officials, though, did not understand serial offenders as we do now, as evidenced by the comments made by Chief Inspector Littlechild when he stated the murderer was unquestionably a sadist. Today, it is not considered an unquestionable conclusion, since experts Dr. Eckert and Dr. Turvey concluded that Jack the Ripper was non-sadistic. How curious that the only reason Littlechild had any sort of reservation about Tumblety—that the herb doctor was not sadistic—actually conforms better to the modern experts' conclusions on the motive behind the Whitechapel fiend.

This particular issue has also caused confusion amongst researchers. Note his statement, "he [Tumblety] was not known as a 'Sadist' (which the murderer unquestionably was) but his feelings toward women were remarkable and bitter in the extreme, a fact on record." Some have concluded that Littlechild did not consider Tumblety a suspect because he was convinced Jack the Ripper was a sadist and stated that Tumblety was not. A problem exists with this line of reasoning, though. Why did Littlechild state Tumblety was "a very likely" suspect if he did not mean it? Modifying the term suspect with "very likely," logically means Littlechild believed the suspect was very likely the killer. This creates a contradiction, especially considering the fact that Littlechild brought up Tumblety as a suspect as a better alternative to "Dr. D" and Assistant Commissioner Anderson's favorite suspect.

Littlechild's Special Branch division was not responsible for investigating the Whitechapel murders case, yet they were involved on certain occasions. His boss, Assistant Commissioner Anderson, and CID were directly responsible, though. These points, plus the fact that Sims asked Littlechild about it years later, means Littlechild was privy to the direction of investigation at the highest level.

A logical answer to the seeming conflict is a logical explanation that creates no conflict. Littlechild never stated Tumblety was not a sadist; he stated Tumblety was not *known* as a sadist. Littlechild was explaining that Tumblety's sadistic behavior was not on record in the large dossier. It is the reason he commented upon others like Tumblety "given to 'contrary sexual instincts' and 'degenerates' are given to cruelty." The very definition of 'sadistic' is "willing to cause pain and suffering, i.e., cruelty." In other words, Littlechild was explaining why he believed Tumblety was sadistic even though there was no record of his sadism. It is also the reason why Littlechild stated Tumblety's hatred of women *was* a fact on record, stating this in the very same sentence. Reinforcing this interpretation is the very last statement Littlechild made about Tumblety and the Whitechapel murder: ". . . but it is certain from this time the 'Ripper' murders came to an end." Littlechild was explaining to Sims why he should take Dr. T. more seriously than Dr. D.

Another claim dismissing Littlechild's comments about Tumblety being a very likely suspect is the chief inspector's Victorian England-belief that all gays, or those with 'contrary sexual instincts,' are given to cruelty. This is a misreading of Littlechild's statement. He did not state, "those given to 'Contrary sexual instinct' are given to cruelty," he stated, "those given to 'Contrary sexual instinct' and 'degenerates' are given to cruelty." Littlechild was stating that gays who are also degenerates are given to sadistic behavior, and he believed Tumblety was a degenerate with a bitter hatred of women—the very gender mutilated by Jack the Ripper.

What is undeniable about Littlechild's comments is, he stated Tumblety was "amongst the suspects," a suspect list generated by CID, the department in charge of the investigation. Upon investigation, Stewart Evans discovered a volume of evidence corroborating Littlechild's statement that Francis Tumblety was amongst the suspects, much coming from contemporary US newspaper articles. The November and December 1888 London Central Criminal Court calendars recorded exactly what Littlechild stated, that Tumblety was "arrested at the time of the murders in connection with unnatural offences and charged at Marlborough Street." Littlechild did make one mistake when he stated, "It was believed he committed suicide. . ." Because his earlier comments were amazingly accurate and detailed, this mistake was likely not the result of forgetfulness, but rather not being directly involved in Tumblety's case after he was spotted in France. Littlechild did not state, "He committed suicide"—he stated, "It was believed . . ." This means Littlechild only heard of Tumblety's death through later rumor, as opposed to a timely official report.

While it is true that the Littlechild letter brought back to light one of Scotland Yard's suspects in the Whitechapel murders investigation, it is only corroborating evidence, not the key piece of evidence connecting Tumblety to the Jack the Ripper murders case. Recently uncovered evidence, such as the sworn testimony of Richard S. Norris, a young man Tumblety met each year in New Orleans from 1881 to 1901, only reinforces Scotland Yard's suspicions. The following chapters are the result of a detailed synthesis of previously known evidence with the newly discovered evidence.

2

The Whitechapel Investigation
and Dr. Francis Tumblety

He [Francis Tumblety] *told me they were awarded to him by the English Government. Then there was a sort of tray in the trunk, and there were all sorts of large knives in there, surgical instruments . . .*

—Richard S. Norris, sworn testimony to
Judge Gabriel Fernandez, May 12, 1905

Thirty-year-old E. (Edwin) Tracy Greaves was the chief European correspondent for the *New York World* stationed in London, England, at the time of the Whitechapel murders in the fall of 1888. He was born in England in 1858, educated in Hartford, Connecticut, then eventually moved to New York City. In 1885, Greaves worked for the *New York Times*, having already worked for the *New York Herald*. In 1886, he came to the *New York World* as a night editor of its *Evening World* paper, and in 1887, he was promoted to managing editor until January 1888. He was then assigned to the London office as a subordinate reporter to the then highly esteemed chief correspondent, T. C. Crawford. Crawford had been in the position for three years, but within a few months of Greaves' arrival, the *New York World* thought it necessary to bring Crawford back to the United States to cover the Hatfield & McCoy feud, which was making headlines across the United States. This left Greaves alone to perform his duties.

Foreign correspondents were also known as special correspondents, and the *New York World* was not the only newsgathering organization with special correspondents stationed in London. The list included the *Boston Herald* with Arthur Warren, the *New York Times* with Harold Frederick, the *New York Tribune* with George W. Smalley, the *New York Sun* with Arthur Brisbane then Frank White, the Associated Press with James Maclean, and the *Freeman's Journal* with James Tuohy. Professionally, the reporters were competitors, fighting for breaking stories, but personally, they socialized with each other; all were members of London's Savage Club. Because of this, Greaves was able to receive much-needed advice even without Crawford's assistance, especially from the experienced and well-connected James Tuohy. By 1889, Touhy was on the *New York World's* payroll.

Amongst all the US foreign correspondents, Greaves was considered the hard-charger of the group. Note the comments made in *The Day* (New London, Connecticut), in their September 22, 1891, issue:

> *GETTING LONDON NEWS, Yankee Correspondents at, the World's Capital.*
> *LONDON, Sept. 7. – There is probably no post in jour-nalism which American newspaper men desire so much as that of London correspondent . . . By common consent the hardest working American newspaper man in London is Mr. E. Tracy Greaves, correspondent for the New York World. He has offices in Trafalgar Square, where you may have a reasonable chance of finding him at any hour of the day or night.*

In the same month the very first Whitechapel murder occurred, August 1888, Greaves was permanently appointed as the chief correspondent, yet he was still on his own. The chief European correspondent position was sometimes called chief London correspondent, since the office was in the West End of London near Trafalgar Square, but Greaves was responsible for collecting news out of both England and the entire European mainland. With such a large area of responsibility, a small budget to work within, and a constant fight against the clock to publish and transmit articles to Home Office in New York City, Greaves took advantage of the well-equipped London newspapers for daily European news—a common practice with all of the foreign correspondents.

The well-established and well-financed London newspaper organizations had a massive newsgathering infrastructure throughout Europe. Since New York and the East Coast of the United States are five hours earlier in time than England, the correspondents would pick up the morning London newspapers "fresh off the press," cut and paste newsworthy stories, then transmit them via telegraph across the Atlantic, allowing the New York office enough time to publish the stories in the United States on the very same day. Newsworthy stories out of London were a slightly different story. While Greaves and his competitor foreign correspondents continued to gather stories from the London papers, they also investigated themselves in hopes of breaking a significant story, especially with the very popular Whitechapel murders. It was common practice to solicit the police for news on the case, and Greaves' office was only 700 yards away from Metropolitan Police Headquarters, better known as Scotland Yard. The following article, written by Greaves, shows not only his practice of using both the London dailies and the police, but the practice being used by all of the special correspondents:

> *[SPECIAL CABLE TO THE EVENING WORLD.]*
> *LONDON. Nov. 2.—The excitement over the alleged tenth attempt . . . The sensational London evening papers and the police themselves are responsible for the reports sent out from London to all parts of the world yesterday by special correspondents and the Associated Press . . .*
> *—Evening World, November 2, 1888*

Greaves actually reported having a Scotland Yard informant, and published this fact, as evidenced by the following two articles authored by him:

> *THE WHITECHAPEL HORRORS.*
> *SPECIAL CABLE DISPATCH TO THE TRIBUNE.*
> *[Copyright, 1888, by the Press Pub. Co., N. Y. World.]*
> *LONDON, Oct. 6.—The horrors of Whitechapel are no blacker than they were a week ago, but the terror in the district and the public excitement are not one whit decreased. The maniac murderer is still in the district and no one knows when he will select another victim for merciless*

mutilation. I learned today from a Scotland Yard man working on the case that the mysterious American who was here a few months ago offering money for specimens of the parts taken from the bodies of the victims has been discovered . . .

He [Sir Charles Warren] made a rule this week that every newspaper man calling at Scotland Yard must register his name and business in a book.

—*Chicago Tribune*, Sunday, October 7, 1888

A STARTLING THEORY.
Is It "Dr. Jekyll and Mr. Hyde" in Real Life?
[SPECIAL CABLE TO THE EVENING WORLD.]
LONDON. Oct. 9.—I am informed by a gentleman, who stands in close relations at Scotland Yard, that several of the leading detectives have thrown over the clues and ideas heretofore taken up a dare working on an entirely new and most remarkable theory. My informant tells me that a well-known . . .

—*The World (Evening Edition)*, October 9, 1888

Sir Charles Warren, Commissioner of the Metropolitan Police Department, demanded his subordinates not speak with the press, but after the Mary Kelly murder on November 9, 1888, Warren resigned, which allowed special correspondents easier access into Scotland Yard. On November 14, 1888, Arthur Brisbane, special correspondent for the *New York Sun*, struck it big and received an interview with Assistant Commissioner Robert Anderson:

Notes from Whitechapel.
LONDON, Nov. 14—Though extremely busy, Dr. Anderson, the head for the hour of the Metropolitan Police, has been kind enough, on knowing that I was a representative of THE SUN, to give me a few minutes of his just now priceless time. . . . I asked Mr. Anderson why the bloodhounds were not employed. His answer was: "At 11 o'clock the last murder was discovered, and we knew of it here in Scotland Yard a few minutes later. The officer who had wired us . . ."

—*The Sun*, November 14, 1888

Not to be outdone, Greaves received an end-of-the-week update on the Whitechapel investigation on Saturday, November 17, 1888, just one week after the Kelly murder, and collected breaking news. He reported on multiple stories involving the Whitechapel investigation and then wired the news cable article off to the *New York World*'s Home Office in New York City. Repeater stations automatically transmitted the story to North American newspapers, paying the *New York World* for their massive newsgathering services, as in the case with the *Boston Globe, San Francisco Chronicle, Chicago Daily Tribune*, and *Ottawa Free Press*. The headliner, which took up half the article, was the arrest on suspicion of the Whitechapel crimes of captain of the Royal Horse Guard, Sir George Arthur:

DOING WHITECHAPEL.

London, Nov. 17—Just think of it! One of the Prince of Wales' own exclusives, a member of his household and cavalry and one of the best known swells about town who glory in the glamor of the Guelphs, getting into custody on suspicion of being the Whitechapel murderer. It is the talk of all clubdom tonight.

Just now it is a fashionable fad to slum it in Whitechapel and every night scores of young men who have never been in the East End before in their lives, prowl around the neighborhood of the murders talking with frightened women. So long as two men keep together and do not make nuisances of themselves, the police do not interfere with them. But if a man goes off alone and tries to lure a woman off the street into a secluded corner, he is pretty sure to get into trouble.

This was the case of Sir George Arthur of Prince Wales set. He put on an old coat and slouch hat and went to Whitechapel for a little fun. He got it. It occurred to two policemen that Sir George answered very much to the description of Jack the Ripper and they watched him and when they saw him talking with a woman they collared him. He protested and threatened them with the vengeance of the royal wrath, but in vain. Finally, a chance was given him to send to a fashionable West End Club and prove his identity and he was released with profuse apologies for the mistake. The affair was kept out of the newspaper, but the jolly young baronets at the Brooks Club considered the joke too good to keep quiet.

Another arrest was a man who gave the name of Dr. Kumbelty of New York. The police could not hold him on suspicion of the Whitechapel crimes, but he has been committed for trial, under a special law passed soon after the modern Babylon exposures. The police say this is the man's right name as proved by letters in his possession from New York and that he has been in the habit of crossing the ocean twice a year for several years.

A score of men have been arrested by the police this week on suspicion, but the right man still roams at large and everybody is momentarily expecting to hear of another victim.

The large sums offered by private individuals as rewards have induced hundreds of amateur detectives to take a hand in the chase, but to no avail.

Leon Rothschild has offered an income of 2 pounds a week for life for the man who gives the information leading to the arrest and conviction of the assassin.

—Boston Globe, November 18, 1888

GOSSIP SENT BY CABLE.

London, Nov 17, 1888.—Just think of it. One of the Prince of Wales' own exclusive set, a member of the Household Cavalry, and one of the best known of the many swells about town who glory in . . .

Sir George is quite a figure in London. He is the son of the late Sir Frederick Arthur, who was an influential man in his day. Sir George was conspicuous on the turf a few years ago, and was intimately associated with the Duchess of Montrose. Then he turned his attention to theatricals, and when Bancroft produced 'Fedora' he let Sir George appear as the corpse. The report is tonight that he is going to Monte Carlo for a few weeks . . . [Author's note: The Boston Globe opted not to publish this particular paragraph.]

—Chicago Daily Tribune, November 18, 1888

A BARONET ARRESTED. New York, Nov. 21.—The World's London correspondent says:—The most intense amusement has been caused among all classes of the London world by the arrest of Sir George Arthur. . .
—*Ottawa Free Press*, November 21, 1888

Greaves' news cable article was actually a composite of five separate Whitechapel investigation breaking stories, and none of them were in any of the London dailies. The correspondent even stated, "The affair [the Sir George Arthur arrest] was kept out of the newspapers . . ." Not only were they kept out of the British papers, they were in no papers, meaning each Scotland Yard story was in fact a breaking story. His only source for original Scotland Yard news was his Metropolitan Police Department informant. Further corroboration of this person being the source is in the article itself. Note the four separate references to information received directly from the police:

- It occurred to two policemen that Sir George answered very much to the description of Jack the Ripper and they watched him and when they saw him talking with a woman they collared him . . .
- The police could not hold him on suspicion of the Whitechapel crimes . . .
- The police say this is the man's right name as . . .
- A score of other men have been arrested by the police this week on suspicion . . .

Greaves' comment about visiting the club "tonight" points out that the Sir George Arthur story broke on the very day he sent the cable at the end of the week, on Saturday, November 17. The statement, "A score of other men have been arrested by the police *this week* on suspicion," (emphasis mine) shows Greaves' efficiency, collecting all Scotland Yard stories at the same time, and at the end of the week. His last Scotland Yard news cable was one week earlier, just after the Kelly murder.

The *New York World* did publish the article the very next day, along with the participating papers, but in their evening edition, the *Evening World,* they left out one particular story that their daily edition, the *Boston Globe, San Francisco Chronicle*, and *Chicago Daily Tribune* did not: the "Kumblety" story. It was an American Jack the Ripper suspect from New York:

> *Another arrest was a man who gave the name 'Dr. Kumblety of New York.' The police could not hold him on suspicion of the Whitechapel crimes, but he has been committed for trial in the Central Criminal Court under a special law passed soon after the modern Babylon exposures. The police say this is the man's right name, as proved by letters in his possession from New York, and that he has been in the habit of crossing the ocean twice a year for several years.*
> —*Chicago Daily Tribune,* November 18, 1888

No one yet knew that this Dr. Kumblety was in fact Dr. Francis Tumblety, the "celebrated Indian herb doctor" known throughout the United States and Canada since the late 1850s for his eccentric behavior and loud dress, as well as his huge newspaper advertisements promising cure-all remedies and his patent pimple banisher medicine. Greaves clearly had no idea it was the notorious doctor, merely stating in the article that Kumblety was the man's right name. This is an important point, since it demonstrates that the very first report on Tumblety's arrest on suspicion for the Whitechapel crimes was not a product of newspaper sensationalism, but mere luck on picking up the story. If there was any sensationalism it would have been Greaves' headliner story, the Sir George Arthur affair, which took up half the article and was the only story he personally got involved in by visiting the Brooks Club.

The public finally being made aware that Dr. Kumblety was Dr. Francis Tumblety the celebrated Indian herb doctor occurred the very next day on November 19, 1888, reported in at least four of the major New York papers, simultaneously. Dozens of newspapers then picked up the story. The reports explained how their respective New York City reporters discovered Francis Tumblety being arrested on suspicion. They went to the New York City Police Department, specifically the office of the detective division, headed by Chief Inspector Thomas F. Byrnes:

HE IS 'ECCENTRIC' DR. TWOMBLETY
A special London despatch to THE WORLD yesterday
morning announced the arrest of a man in connection
with the Whitechapel crimes, who gave his name as Dr.
Kumblety, of New York. He could not be held on suspi-
cion, but the police succeeded in getting him held under
the special law passed soon after the "Modern Babylon"
exposures. Dr. Kumblety is well known in this city. His
name however is Twomblety, not Kumblety . . . Ever since
his identity became known here he has been under sur-
veillance of Inspector Byrnes's officers, who rarely lose
sight of him or knowledge of his whereabouts. For twenty
years he has been widely known as the manufacturer of
Twomblety's pimple banisher, from which he professes to
gain a livelihood. His own face is covered with pimples,
and although his features are otherwise regular, his ap-
pearance on this account is somewhat repulsive. He is a
large and heavily built man, standing fully six feet in his
stockings . . . During the past few years Twomblety has
opened a branch office in London and has been making
regular trips across the ocean at intervals of five or six
months. He was last seen here about five months ago,
when he appeared on Broadway, just as he did twenty
years ago, with his leather-peaked cap, white over-gaiters
and button-hole bouquet.
—New York World, November 19, 1888

It now becomes clear as to why the *New York World*
eliminated the Kumblety story in their evening edition. The
1888 New York City directory had no one by the name of
Kumblety, so this was clearly a dead end. Dr. Kumblety
claimed to be from their own city, so they went to the perfect
source for discovering the identity of criminals, New York
City's police department. Although the *New York World*
believed at the time his last name was Twomblety, they
certainly were referring to Francis Tumblety the celebrated
Indian herb doctor.

Curiously, in his 1872 and 1889 autobiographies,
Tumblety claimed to have been introduced to Charles Dickens

at the Brooks Club, the very club that Sir George Arthur was a member of:

> *After my tour through Ireland, Scotland and the Continent of Europe, I visited London, where I was induced to prolong my stay beyond the anticipated period, through the request of parties who were anxious for me to prescribe for them. It was at this time that I had the gratification of an introduction to Charles Dickens, the immortal "Boz," and my brief acquaintance with this eminent writer constitutes one of the most pleasant episodes of my life. An extract from the copy of a letter which I wrote to a friend in New York will best detail my accidental meeting with the author of the Pickwick Papers, and its results: As I advised you, it was my intention, ere this, to be in New York, but circumstances will prevent my leaving England for a week or ten days, from this time. I have been induced to remain thus longer, through the urgent entreaties of certain parties, who are anxious that I shall prescribe for themselves and friends. Among the former is no less a person than Charles Dickens, to whom I was introduced at Brook's Club House.*

This leads to another conundrum. As the reporters invaded Chief Inspector Byrnes' office on November 18, how did the police know, with complete confidence, that Dr. Kumblety was Francis Tumblety? As evidenced by the reports, the police not only knew who he was, but they also had many details on his history readily available. The police department and the multiple news organizations would have been liable in a serious defamatory lawsuit if they claimed the wrong man as a Jack the Ripper suspect. The answer is how the New York Police Headquarters always handled criminals from across the Atlantic: continuous private correspondence about criminals involved with both cities. According to researcher Joe Chetcuti, Inspector Byrnes was interviewed in January 1886 by the *New York World*:

> *. . . Of course, it is a great help to a man in my [Inspector Byrnes'] business to keep well posted on the movements*

of all the big criminals, not only in this city but all over the United States and part of Europe. Now, here, for example, is a letter from our correspondent from London. It contains, as you see, details of the movements of several well-known American crooks who have found New York too dull a field and went to England a few months ago. . . . The same system of correspondence follows their movements there, and I can tell almost to the day where they have been. When they make up their minds to return to America I know by what steamer to expect them, and my men are ready to meet them at the steamer's pier and keep an eye on them as long as they remain in New York.

Greaves' article did state Dr. Kumblety was from New York, so Scotland Yard requesting from the New York City Police Department information on Tumblety makes sense, especially when such a request explains why Byrnes' office knew without a doubt. Byrnes stated he was informed of Tumblety's escape a week before the press had any knowledge of it, and he even had detectives waiting for Tumblety to disembark from the correct steamship.

According to the November and December London Central Criminal Court calendars, Francis Tumblety was initially arrested on November 7, 1888, an arrest for which he was being committed to Central Criminal Court, for gross indecency and indecent assault. In view of this, his earlier arrest on suspicion was some time before November 7, even as early as in October. Note the comments in the British newspaper, the *Evening Post*, February 16, 1889:

A WHITECHAPEL SUSPECT.
. . . Dr. Francis Tumblety, who was arrested in London on suspicion in connection with the Whitechapel murders, but who was released immediately when it was found there was no evidence to incriminate him. The World is probably not aware that Dr. Tumblety was afterwards taken into custody on another charge, arising out of certain correspondence with young men which was found in his possession, that he was committed for trial at the Old Bailey . . .

The *Boston Herald's* London correspondent, Arthur Warren, gave further detail about Tumblety's first arrest on suspicion, then his re-arrest for a separate charge:

> *When the London police arrested him the other day on suspicion of being the murderer he said that he belonged in New York . . . The doctor's identity was for a time concealed after his arrest, but the police, who took the liberty of hunting up his lodgings and ransacking his private effects, discovered easily who he was, and they say he has been in the habit of making two trips yearly to this side of the water.*
> —*Boston Herald*, November 25, 1888

Littlechild stated there was, "a large dossier concerning him at Scotland Yard." What they read in his file clearly caused them additional concern, and according to Littlechild it was his unusual hatred of women, as evidenced by his statement, "a fact on record." While it is true Littlechild was in charge of Special Branch, which had their own classified files—mostly on cases involving the Irish nationalist movement—his reference to Tumblety's hatred of women in the letter suggests Tumblety's dossier was a CID file. His hatred of women must have been significant enough to be written down in the file, but this was not an Irish independence issue. We know there had to have been a CID file on Tumblety, since he had been arrested in London in 1873 in an indecent assault case.

There is evidence that this initial arrest of Tumblety on suspicion of the Whitechapel murders occurred just after the double event murders on October 1, 1888. In January 1889, Tumblety claimed he was arrested because he wore an American slouch hat. Note the following report:

IS HE THE FIEND?
BY CABLE TO THE PRESS NEWS ASSOCIATION.
LONDON, Oct. 1.—A man was arrested at midnight last night on suspicion of having committed the terrible murders in Whitechapel. He is a tall man, with a dark beard. He wore an American slouch hat, by which he was traced from the locality of the last murder, where it is reported he was seen on Saturday night, to Albert Chambers on

Union street, in the Borough, South London, where he was found. The Borough is across the river and far away from the Whitechapel quarter. When arrested he was unable to give any account of himself during the previous night. He assumed a defiant attitude. The police are investigating his antecedents and movements, of which it is said he refuses to give any information. Several other suspicious persons have been arrested. The Financial News has offered a reward of £300 for the capture of the murderer.
    —The World (Evening Edition), October 1, 1888

The London correspondent of the Press News Association, or Associated Press, was the seasoned James Mclean. Mclean then followed up with:

The American Released.
    London, Oct. 4. – The American arrested yesterday on suspicion of being the Whitechapel murderer was released to-day. It was simply a case of delirium tremens. The accused tendered a name and address to the police with the understanding that it was not to be made known. Of twenty persons locked up for crimes not one of them is now in custody. The police failed to bring anything against them. Absolutely there is no clew whatever. Scotland Yard officials are frightfully at sea, while the public mind is considered agitated.

In January 1889, a reporter from the *New York World* interviewed Tumblety. Tumblety claimed he was wearing a slouch hat at the time of the murders and also claimed this is why he was arrested:

'My arrest came about this way,' said he. 'I had been going over to England for a long time—ever since 1869, indeed—and I used to go about the city a great deal until every part of it became familiar to me.
    'I happened to be there when these Whitechapel murders attracted the attention of the whole world, and, in the company with thousands of other people, I went down to the Whitechapel district. I was not dressed in a way to attract attention, I thought, though it afterwards turned

out that I did. I was interested by the excitement and the crowds and the queer scenes and sights, and did not know that all the time I was being followed by English detectives.'

'Why did they follow you?'

'My guilt was very plain to the English mind. Someone had said that Jack the Ripper was an American, and everybody believed that statement. Then it is the universal belief among the lower classes that all Americans wear slouch hats; therefore, Jack the Ripper, must wear a slouch hat. Now, I happened to have on a slouch hat, and this, together with the fact that I was an American, was enough for the police. It established my guilt beyond any question.'

While it is true that Tumblety wore a military-style cap on many occasions, there is additional evidence that, at times, he wore a slouch hat. In the 1905 Missouri Probate Court trial transcript, a witness named Daniel O'Donovan stated he knew Francis Tumblety in 1901. The attorney asked, "Will you state briefly the condition of Dr. Tumblety's clothes when you knew him, during the period you knew him?" Under oath, O'Donovan replied, "On two or three occasions during the period of time that I saw him last, he wore a slouch hat, and on one particular occasion I remember he wore a pair of cutting shoes; both the slouch hat and the cutting shoes seemed to brace up his appearance considerably . . ."

There is evidence of one location—possibly two—in England that Tumblety visited after his arrest for the Whitechapel crimes in the fall of 1888, but before he began his secret flight out of England around November 19 or 20: He may have visited his relatives. At the time of the murders, two of Tumblety's adult nieces and their respective families lived in England, both a train ride away from London. The first was Catherine Way, aged 54 in 1888, daughter of Tumblety's third-oldest sister, Judith/Julia Moore. Catherine was born in 1834 in Ireland. Julia's husband died at an early age, and according to the 1841 census, Julia had moved to Bristol with her young daughter. Catherine married Joseph Way on November 15, 1865, and was a resident of Bath, which is located west of

London near Bristol. Catherine was a resident of Bath in 1888 and was recorded as still living in Bath in 1911, but now as a widow. While Tumblety bequeathed a small fortune to two of his living nieces in 1903, Catherine received nothing, suggesting a less-than-positive relationship.

Researchers Roger Palmer and Robert Linford independently uncovered a record of oral family history at Ancestry.com pertaining to Catherine Way being visited by Tumblety. A member of Ancestry.uk stated,

> *Oral family history included a relative from America questioned in the Whitechapel murders in 1888 named Maurice Fitzsimmons. He was a man who dressed dramatically (with a cape) and was the somewhat-wild son of a doctor and uncle to Catherine, whose mother's maiden name was Powderly. The hosts of that visit were the Joseph & Catherine Way family of Bath, Somerset. Interviews with the oldest relatives showed a familiarity with the name Maurice Fitzsimons but not with Powderly. It turned out, after records research, that both surnames were connected to Catherine's family- they were the married names of two of her maternal aunts. There was also only one person in all of the connected families who was ever called doctor for any reason—Francis Tumblety, Catherine's youngest maternal uncle, also somewhat wild. That Catherine and her uncle were only a few years apart in age could account for the impression that he was her cousin. Another source of confusion could have been the waning memories of the oral historians.*

The Ancestry member also stated that Catherine Way was the daughter of Julia or Judith Tumelty Moore, who was the daughter of James Tumelty/Tumblety, a farmer, 1780 – 1850. Elizabeth Powderly, Tumblety's fourth-oldest sister, who married a Thomas Powderly, had five children, and none of them were named Catherine, so the "mother's maiden name was Powderly" recollection seems to have been a product of waning memories. It is beyond doubt that Francis Tumblety and Maurice Fitzsimmons are one and the same person: the eccentric American doctor and uncle of Catherine, known to dress dramatically, and who was indeed arrested on suspicion in 1888. Catherine Way knew who Francis Tumblety was because she was part of the group of family members challenging Tumblety's 1903 will and testament. Why then were the children of Catherine Way—and any visiting family members—lied to by her and Tumblety, and even years later, never told Maurice Fitzsimmons was Francis Tumblety? If his visit was before he was arrested on suspicion, then he would likely have bragged to his family members about the amazing Francis J. Tumblety, MD, and his encounters with the rich and famous, as he was known to do on multiple occasions. If his visit was after his arrest and he was attempting to hide his tracks, though, giving family members a fake name but still being related makes sense, especially since he was known for using aliases when evading uncomfortable situations. Snoopy Scotland Yard questioning family members, possibly finding out more about Tumblety, would certainly have been unwanted in his mind. Additionally, what resonates with Tumblety making up the Maurice Fitzsimmons persona was the reference that he was a son of a doctor, a lie Tumblety used quite often.

The fact that the descendants of Catherine Way never made the connection between Maurice Fitzsimmons and the notorious Francis Tumblety may have had something to do with the fact that Tumblety did not leave her any money in his will. Tumblety's visit to Catherine's home must not have made an impact upon Tumblety, nor with Catherine. The references to Maurice Fitzsimmons do not paint a positive picture, so even the children were not impressed. After Tumblety left, Catherine likely never discussed Maurice Fitzsimmons again. Tumblety's soon-to-be notoriety in the newspapers for being arrested on suspicion was predominantly in US newspapers. Even if family members saw an article in November/December 1888 of the American doctor Francis Tumblety being arrested, the kids would not have made the connection unless Catherine informed them. She clearly did not.

The other niece living in England when Tumblety was arrested on suspicion for the Whitechapel crimes was Margaret Brady, aged 48 in 1888, who lived with her husband, Thomas, and children near Liverpool in Widnes. She was the daughter of Tumblety's second-oldest sister, Bridget Brodigan, and she and her husband, Christopher, moved to Liverpool before Margaret was born, as evidenced by her census records stating she was born in Widnes. A Christopher and Bridget Brodigan of the appropriate age are in the 1841 census, living in Liverpool. Bridget passed away in 1853, and Christopher passed away in 1854, while Margaret was very young. Tumblety bequeathed $10,000 ($270, 000 in today's value) to her in his 1903 will and testament, referring to her as "Mrs. Thomas Brady of 20 Frederick St, Widness, Liverpool." The fact that he remembered her in his will may be the same reason why he remembered his niece Mary Fitzsimmons of Rochester, New York, in his will. Under sworn testimony, Margaret's brother Michael stated that Margaret held Tumblety's personal effects at her home on Plymouth Avenue, Rochester, New York. This is clearly because Tumblety chose a life of travel, so he needed a permanent location to store his acquired personal items, thus, through time, Tumblety gained trust in her. Throughout the 1880s, Tumblety spent many months each year in England, so he may have used Margaret Brady's home in the same way. We know Tumblety had regular contact with Margaret Brady as early as 1875. Tumblety may or may not have visited Margaret Brady in the fall of 1888, but when he arrived back in New York after he sneaked out of England, he was reported to have returned with fewer personal effects than he had been known to travel with.

The writ of habeas corpus was in effect in 1888 as it is today, meaning, when Tumblety was arrested on suspicion, the police were bound by British law. They had 24 hours to either charge Tumblety with the murders and send him in front of the police magistrate or release him. No one saw the murders, so Scotland Yard clearly had a weak case against any suspect. Instead of illegally holding Tumblety against his will and gamble that this rich man would not initiate a lawsuit as the Leather Apron suspect successfully did, they opted for a legal approach that accomplished the same goal of placing Tumblety behind bars. They released him on the suspicion case and re-arrested him on the winnable misdemeanor charge involving the "modern Babylon exposures," specifically, gross indecency and indecent assault. Within 24 hours after the re-arrest on November 7, 1888, Tumblety and his counsel pleaded their case in front of Police Court Magistrate James L. Hannay, who presided over Marlborough Street Police Court. This was Tumblety's remand hearing, which allowed Hannay to hear both sides of the case and determine if Tumblety should be remanded, or placed into custody, until the committal hearing scheduled one week later on November 14, 1888.

At the committal hearing, the prosecutors convinced Hannay that there was enough evidence to commit the case up to the next judicial level in front of a judge at Central Criminal Court, also called Old Bailey. A court date was set for November 20, 1888, and Hannay allowed bail at £300. Although no records remain, the fact that he offered bail at the committal hearing suggests he also offered bail at the earlier remand hearing as well, since it was the same case. A police court magistrate had the discretionary powers to allow bail at both hearings. On November 14, Tumblety was remanded to Holloway Prison, and two days later on November 16, 1888, he paid bail and was released. On November 19, the grand jury convened and returned a "True Bill," meaning they agreed with the magistrate that the case was strong enough to be tried at Central Criminal Court.

It was at this moment when Tumblety and his attorney, Mr. Bodkin, knew the prosecution had evidence to convict him and he was destined for prison, so this is likely when and why he decided to jump bail. The case convened at Central Criminal Court on November 20, 1888, with Tumblety absent, yet represented by his legal counsel. Bodkin successfully argued for postponement and the case was rescheduled for December 10, 1888.

Interestingly, the fact that Tumblety was released on bail on Friday, November 16, 1888, means *New York World* London correspondent E. Tracy Greaves could not have met Tumblety at any police station or at Holloway Prison. Greaves received the story from his Scotland Yard informant the next day on November 17. Further, the following November 21, 1888, article, which was authored by Greaves, shows that he did not speak to Tumblety at any time before the convening of the grand jury on November 19:

> *The Whitechapel Fiend Uses His Knife Once More. Copyright, 1888 by The Press Publishing Company (New York World).*

[SPECIAL CABLE DESPATCH TO THE WORLD.]
LONDON, Nov. 21. – Another Whitechapel murder . . .
. . . Coming at a time when people were beginning to think
that the Dr. Twomblety now in custody might really prove
to be the Whitechapel fiend . . .
    —The World (Evening Edition), November 21, 1888

Greaves believed Tumblety was still in custody awaiting
trial, but in fact he had posted bail four days earlier and had
the court case one day earlier, albeit postponed, but clearly
making plans to jump bail. Curiously, Tumblety requested
£260 1s. 6d. from his New York bank on November 20, 1888.
He reprinted his bank's response letter in his 1889/1893
autobiographical pamphlets:

> No later than November of last year Dr. Tumblety received
> a letter from Drexel, Morgan & Co., which contained the
> subjoined passage, quoted here to show the pleasant
> business relations existing between them.
>   'In accordance with your order of the 20th inst., we
> have forwarded you by this mail our sterling letter of
> credit for £260 1s. 6d., upon Messrs. Drexel, Morgan &
> Co., of New York.
>   We are, etc.,
>   J. S. Morgan & CO.'

Coincidentally, Scotland Yard senior official Lieutenant
Colonel Pearson reported to the Home Undersecretary about
deploying twelve extra constables at two train stations on
November 20, 1888, in order to "examine the belongings of
passengers arriving from America." Officially, Tumblety was
never reported as a suspect, so it would not be a surprise
that his name was absent from any correspondence. What
is certain is that Chief Inspector Littlechild, head of Special
Branch, stated Tumblety was spotted in Boulogne, France, on
or before November 23, 1888:

> Tumblety was arrested at the time of the murders in con-
> nection with unnatural offences and charged at Marlbor-
> ough Street, remanded on bail, jumped his bail, and got
> away to Boulogne.

No one in Scotland Yard but a Special Branch detective would have been assigned in France, which explains why Littlechild remembered this fact. Since Tumblety's gross indecency case was legally postponed until December 10, 1888, resulting in a warrant issued for his arrest, being searched for and sighted in France eight to ten days earlier would not have been for the gross indecency case. Scotland Yard was already stretched thin due to the ongoing Whitechapel murders investigation, so assigning additional personnel to search for a person under no warrant in a mere misdemeanor case does not make sense. What does make sense, however, is Scotland Yard's knowledge of Tumblety sneaking away to France as a result in their interest in him regarding the Whitechapel murders, as the papers had reported.

As evidenced by all the newspaper reports, other than police officials, no one knew Tumblety posted had bail on November 16, 1888, for another two weeks. Even the man who broke the Kumblety story did not know Tumblety had his liberty on November 14. Note what the very same author of the Kumblety story, E. Tracy Greaves, working out of London, stated in a follow-up article:

> Copyright, 1888 by The Press Publishing Company (New York World).
> [SPECIAL CABLE DESPATCH TO THE WORLD.]
> LONDON, Nov. 21. – . . . Coming at a time when people were beginning to think that the Dr. Twomblety now in custody might really prove to be the Whitechapel fiend . . . What effect this may have upon Twomblety's case, and whether he will still be held by the authorities, can be only a matter of conjecture. It would, however, seem to be only a proper precaution for the police department to fully investigate all the circumstances in this new emergency before giving the doctor his liberty . . .
> —The World (Evening Ed.), November 21, 1888

At noon on November 24, 1888, the steamship *La Bretagne* sailed from La Havre, France, en route to New York. Tumblety was onboard, arriving in New York Harbor on December 2, 1888. This was not known by anyone other than the police until December 1, 1888, reported for the very first time in the

New York World on December 2, 1888, and the author of this article was again E. Tracy Greaves:

> *TUMBLETY IS MISSING. The American Charlatan Sus-*
> *pected of the Whitechapel Murders Skips from London*
> *HE WAS LAST SEEN AT HAVRE*
> *Is He On His Way Home Over the Ocean to New York?*
> *HE HAD A BITTER HATRED OF WOMEN*
> *Copyright, 1888, by the Press Publishing Company (New*
> *York World).*
>   *[SPECIAL CABLE DESPATCH TO THE WORLD.]*
> *London, Dec. 1.—The last seen of Dr. Tumblety was at*
> *Havre, and it is taken for granted that he has sailed for*
> *New York. It will be remembered that the doctor . . .*

The Scotland Yard informant that Greaves used was clearly credible, since the information was correct. What will also be clear in later chapters is that Tumblety no longer sought publicity for his business in 1888, especially if the news conflicted with his persona as a prominent physician.

There has been a claim that the Kumblety story is correct, but is actually proof that Tumblety was not a suspect once they realized who he was. The pertinent sentence in the Kumblety story states, *"The police could not hold him on suspicion of the Whitechapel crimes, but he has been committed for trial in the Central Criminal Court under a special law passed soon after the modern Babylon exposures."* This interpretation claims that Tumblety was indeed arrested on suspicion for the Whitechapel crimes, but Scotland Yard quickly rejected the possibility. Because it was undeniable that he was brazenly participating in illegal "unnatural acts" with London's young men, they switched gears and re-arrested him for gross indecency and indecent assault. Reinforcing this claim is the *New York Times* article the next day on November 19, 1888, *"The Dr. Tumblety who was arrested in London a few days ago on suspicion of complicity in the Whitechapel murders, and who when proved innocent of that charge was held for trial in the Central Criminal Court under the special law covering the offenses disclosed in the late "Modern Babylon" scandal . . ."*

Taking all of the evidence into account, though, reveals a different conclusion. First, four days later, the same *New*

York Times, the only newspaper that interpreted the Kumblety story as "proved innocent," reversed itself and stated, "[Dr. Tumblety] *who is at present under arrest on suspicion of being implicated in the Whitechapel murders . . ."* With the only newspaper no longer accepting that Scotland Yard had no interest in Tumblety after November 7, this claim has little evidence for support. Still, there is further evidence conflicting with the "proved innocent" claim. The New York reporters from the *Times, World, Herald,* and *Sun,* all received the Kumblety-Tumblety revelation from the New York City Detective Division, as evidenced by their simultaneous publishing and reporting on the same stories and personal accounts by "Inspector Byrnes' officers," specifically, "Central Office Detective Timothy J. Golden." As noted, the *World, Herald,* and *Sun* did not give a "proven innocent" interpretation, nor did they attempt at any interpretation. They merely reworded the Kumblety story, while adding the discovery that the New Yorker was Francis Tumblety. The *New York World* stated, "He could not be held on suspicion, but the police succeeded in getting him held under the special law"; the *Herald* stated, "[Tumblety] was arrested in London on suspicion of being concerned in the Whitechapel murders and held on another charge for trial under the special law passed after the 'Modern Babylon' exposure"; and the *Sun* did not report on Tumblety being held for a different charge. It is more plausible that the New York City detective merely revealed that the man arrested was Francis Tumblety, but kept tight-lipped about any further details they may have received from Scotland Yard. It is more likely that the *New York Times* reporter added his own faulty interpretation, especially since they then contradicted it four days later.

Major US newspapers had their own London correspondents, and since they just learned that a New Yorker might possibly be involved in the world-famous Whitechapel murders, tasking them to dig up more details from Scotland Yard informants would have been sensible. This is exactly what we see, as evidenced by the London correspondents reporting new information, which further corroborates Scotland Yard's continued interest in Tumblety. The *Boston Herald*'s London correspondent, the well-respected Arthur Warren, stated in their November 25, 1888, issue,

One of the Whitechapel murder suspects is a curious character known as Dr. Tumblety . . . The doctor's identity was for a time concealed after his arrest, but the police, who took the liberty of hunting up his lodgings and ransacking his private effects, discovered easily who he was, and they say he has been in the habit of making two trips yearly to this side of the water."

The *New York Sun's* London correspondent, Arthur Brisbane, reported in their November 25, 1888, edition that, "An American doctor named Twomblety is now held because he is an erratic character, and because one theory is that some American medical institution wants specimens of the female uterus. Which it happens that Jack the Ripper often takes from the bodies of his victims . . ." E. Tracy Greaves, the *New York World* correspondent who broke the Kumblety story stated in the evening edition of the *World* on November 21, 1888, "Coming at a time when people were beginning to think that the Dr. Twomblety now in custody might really prove to be the Whitechapel fiend."

Even further corroborating Scotland Yard's continued interest in Tumblety in the Whitechapel murders case is the fact that three Scotland Yard officials refer to Tumblety as a suspect after the Kelly murder. The first official is Chief Inspector John G. Littlechild, head of Special Branch, stating in his letter to Sims that Tumblety was "amongst the suspects" and "a very likely one." As evidenced by his statements, he had knowledge of Tumblety's escape from England and his November 23, 1888, sighting in France, yet he still considered him an important enough suspect to bring him up to Sims 25 years later.

The second Scotland Yard official was Inspector First Class CID Walter Andrews. While in Toronto, Canada, on December 12, 1888, a Toronto reporter asked him if he knew Francis Tumblety and his connection to the Whitechapel murders. Andrews stated:

"Do I know Dr. Tumblety, of course I do. But he is not the Whitechapel murderer. All the same we would like to interview him, for the last time we had him he jumped his bail. He is a bad lot."
—*The Toronto World*, December 12, 1888

When Andrews stated, "we," he was now a representative of Scotland Yard as a whole. Regardless of Andrews' very public opinion that Tumblety was not Jack the Ripper—How embarrassing for Scotland Yard if he said the man who escaped their grasp was a serious suspect—why the desire to interview him on the case if he was not still considered a suspect? Nothing in an interview with him would have helped Scotland Yard on the gross indecency case.

The last Scotland Yard official commenting upon Tumblety as a suspect after November 7, 1888, was Assistant Commissioner Robert Anderson, the boss of not only Chief Inspector Littlechild but also everyone in CID, the detective division in charge of the Whitechapel murders investigation. Note the following report:

> . . . the London Police are evidently doing their level best to fasten the Whitechapel murders upon Dr. F. T. Tumblety. Today Police Superintendent Campbell received a telegram from Assistant Police Commissioner Anderson, . . . in reference to Tumblety. Mr. Anderson wants some information as to his life in Brooklyn . . .
> —Brooklyn Standard-Union, November 23, 1888

Assistant Commissioner Anderson would also have known if CID dismissed Tumblety as a suspect before November 7, since he was head of CID. If Tumblety were dismissed, Anderson would never have personally involved himself and requested information on Tumblety in support of the Whitechapel murders investigation, or for the gross indecency case for that matter.

The fourth government official within the British Empire was the Canadian Deputy Minister of Marine, William Smith, who mentioned Francis Tumblety as a suspect three weeks after November 7, 1888. Interestingly, *no one* knew the initial arrest date on gross indecency was November 7, 1888. *All* press reports stated that Tumblety's arrest on suspicion occurred on November 14 or later, or they did not give a date. Only *one* person got the time of the month correct, and that was in a private letter from Canadian Deputy Minister of Marine William Smith. He sent the letter, dated December 1, 1888, to his friend and colleague James Barber, who lived in Saint John, New Brunswick. The following is the pertinent excerpt:

. . . He is the man who was arrested in London three weeks ago as the Whitechapel murderer. He had been living in Birmingham and used to come up to London on Saturday nights. The police have always had their eyes on him every place he went and finally the Birmingham Police telegraphed to the London Police that he had left for London, and on his arrival he was nabbed accordingly.

Smith ran the marine department, which was responsible for the classified cable transmissions coming into Canada per the 1875 Marine Telegraph Act, and he worked in the same parliamentary halls in Central Block with the head of the federal law enforcement arm of Eastern Canada, the Dominion of Police, Lieutenant Colonel Arthur Percy Sherwood. Sherwood was the man Scotland Yard contacted about any mutual criminals, which would have included Tumblety, especially since Tumblety had an extensive background in Canada. Some have argued that Smith merely read local papers and did not receive inside information from Scotland Yard, but no papers knew that the initial arrest for gross indecency occurred at the end of the first week of November. The argument is that the arrest of a man in Birmingham was someone else, and he must have gotten this information from the local press then combined the two separate Whitechapel murders issues together. Smith may indeed have passed on information from local papers, but this does not explain how he knew the date of the initial arrest. Note, though, the following report, which conflicts with the claim that Smith combined newspaper reports:

STILL ON THE SCENT.
Additional Rewards for the Arrest of the Whitechapel Fiend.
London, Nov. 18. – On the arrival of the Birmingham train this morning, a Dr. Kumblety was arrested on suspicion of being the Whitechapel murderer.

He greatly resembles the individual seen in company with the latest victim on the evening of the last murder. A score of other men have been arrested by the police this week on suspicion of the murders . . .
—*The Daily Colonist*, November 22, 1888, Victoria, British Columbia

There has been a suggestion by modern researchers that Tumblety was arrested for the Ripper murders but only as a smokescreen in order to masquerade Scotland Yard's true interest—Tumblety's involvement in the Irish Nationalist issue. The leaders of the Irish Nationalist movement would certainly have had an interest in Tumblety, since he was a rich, well-traveled Irish American, and would have been approached for assistance, yet, the pieces of evidence conflicting with him being directly involved are many. First, Scotland Yard refused to acknowledge their interest in Tumblety as a Ripper suspect publicly. Anderson's comments were directed toward the US chiefs of police; Littlechild's comments were made privately and years later; and Andrews' comments were purposely dismissive. Even privately, Scotland Yard had little evidence on any suspect, thus arresting Tumblety on this case was short-term. Second, when E. Tracy Greaves was told by his Scotland Yard informant that "an American doctor named Kumblety" was arrested on suspicion, they forgot to tell him it was Tumblety. It was not until the next day in New York, inquiring at Inspector Byrnes' office, that the papers realized who Kumblety was. The first step in making a smokescreen is to convince the public of the smokescreen.

The third reason that conflicts with Scotland Yard using the 1888 Ripper case as a smokescreen in order to arrest Tumblety for being a Fenian was timing. Tumblety was making yearly trips to England since 1873, and was on Scotland Yard's radar soon after he arrived when he was arrested for committing "unnatural acts" with a young man in London. This ensured that Tumblety was now on file at Scotland Yard. The man in charge of the Irish Nationalist issue was the head of Special Branch, Chief Inspector Littlechild, who even comments in the Littlechild letter upon Tumblety's frequent visits and his run-ins with the police: "Tumblety was at one time a frequent visitor to London and on these occasions constantly brought under the notice of police, there being a large dossier concerning him at Scotland Yard." There were serious Irish Nationalist issues between 1873 and 1888 when Tumblety was a frequent visitor, and if he were a Fenian, Scotland Yard—already having an extensive record on him—would have watched him. If true, then why wait to arrest him in 1888, when the investigation of these events were years earlier? One suggestion is Tumblety was involved with the November 19, 1887, Trafalgar Square "Bloody Sunday" incident. Although Bloody Sunday was a demonstration of unemployed and social reformers, it was a serious headache for the government. The claim is he sneaked out and left for America after the incident, so they had to wait for him to return to England before arresting him. The problem is, Tumblety was not in England during Bloody Sunday. Tumblety's favorite transatlantic cruise ship was the *City of Rome*, which was the largest ship traveling across the Atlantic at the time. Tumblety sailed from New York for Liverpool on May 25, 1887, and left England sailing back for New York on September 26, 1887. This was over a month and a half earlier than Bloody Sunday. Note that Tumblety's travels to England do not match sporadic Irish nationalist events.

Special Branch under Littlechild was directly responsible for not only investigating illegal Irish Nationalist actions and movements, they were also responsible for stopping any future illegal Irish nationalist plans, such as kidnappings and assassinations. Forewarned is forearmed. If Scotland Yard had such an interest in Tumblety in 1888 that they used the Ripper murders as a smokescreen, then Littlechild would have been directly involved with Tumblety's arrest. He would also have had him watched after he arrived in New York, just as they did with all the known Irish Nationalist leaders in the United States. Littlechild was chief inspector of Special Branch for another five years, yet he had no idea about the history of Tumblety after his men spotted him in Boulogne, France, on November 23, 1888. Littlechild even stated it was generally believed that Tumblety committed suicide soon after, as per his letter, "He shortly left Boulogne and was never heard of afterwards. It was believed he committed suicide . . ."

Ironically, the day the news hit the streets on December 2, 1888, about Tumblety jumping bail and likely being on his way to New York City, he arrived at New York Harbor onboard the *La Bretagne*. Two of Inspector Byrnes' detectives were already at the docks waiting for Tumblety. Chief Inspector Byrnes was clearly informed of Tumblety's upcoming arrival, and he even stated this in the following article:

TWOMBLETY ARRIVES.
"Dr." Francis Tumblety or Twomblety, who was arrested
in London on suspicion of knowing something about the
horrible Whitechapel murders. . . . he had sailed from
there [Havre] for this country. Inspector Byrnes said yes-
terday that he knew of Tumblety's expected arrival in this
city a week ago and had determined to make sure that his
information was correct . . .
—*The New York Sun,* December 4, 1888

Chief Inspector Byrnes admitted he had been in correspondence with Scotland Yard about Ripper suspect Francis Tumblety. The following demonstrates that his interest in having Tumblety followed by his detectives was for the Whitechapel murders case and not the gross indecency case, knowing full well this was the formal charge against Tumblety:

> *. . . Inspector Byrnes was asked what his object was*
> *in shadowing Twomblety. "I simply wanted to put a tag*
> *on him." he replied, "so that we can tell where he is. Of*
> *course, he cannot be arrested, for there is no proof in his*
> *complicity in the Whitechapel murders, and the crime for*
> *which he was under bond in London is not extraditable."*
> *"Do you think he is Jack the Ripper?" the Inspector*
> *was asked.*
> *"I don't know anything about it, and therefore I don't*
> *care to be quoted. But if they think in London that they*
> *may need him, and he turns out to be guilty our men will*
> *probably have a good idea where he can be found."*
> —*New York World,* December 4, 1888

It should also be noted that Tumblety did not officially receive a warrant for his arrest on the gross indecency case from the Central Criminal Court judge for another six days. Assistant Commissioner Anderson contacted Brooklyn's chief of police, and when Tumblety claimed he came from "New York," not contacting the New York City Police Department about Tumblety would have been a complete surprise. With the personnel in Chief Inspector Byrnes' office having full knowledge of Francis Tumblety on November 17, 1888, when the reporters came to them and knowing of Anderson's private correspondences to the chiefs of police, it would not be a surprise if they had communicated with each other immediately after they realized their suspect was a New Yorker.

Scotland Yard's interest in Tumblety continued into New York. Not only did New York City detectives follow Tumblety's cab after he disembarked the *La Bretagne*, newspaper reporters did as well. Note the comments made by a *New York World* reporter:

> *Dr. Twomblety's cab stopped at Fourth avenue and 10th street, where the doctor got out, paid the driver and stepped briskly up the steps of No. 75 East Tenth street, the Arnold House. He pulled the bell, and, as no one came, he grew impatient and walked a little further down the street to No. 81. Here there was another delay in responding to his summons, and he became impatient that he tried the next house No. 79. This time there was a prompt answer to his ring and he entered. It was just 2:20 when the door closed on Dr. Twomblety and he has not been seen since.*

Tumblety finally received temporary residence at 79 East Tenth Street, Mrs. McNamara's boarding house. It clearly was not his first choice, but he was in a hurry to get off the streets. Knowing the Tumblety story was not done, the reporters stayed. Note that the *New York World* reporter spotted a person just as interested in Tumblety as they were:

> *. . . It was just as this story was being furnished to the press that a new character appeared on the scene, and it was not long before he completely absorbed the attention of every one . . . He could not be mistaken in his mission. There was an elaborate attempt at concealment and mystery which could not be possibly misunderstood. Everything about him told of his business. From his little billycock hat, alternately set jauntily on the side of his head and pulled lowering over his eyes, down to the very bottom of his thick boots, he was a typical English detective . . .*

Then his hat would be pulled down over his eyes and he would walk up and down in front of No. 79 staring intently into the windows as he passed, to the intense dismay of Mrs. McNamara . . .

His headquarters was a saloon on the corner, where he held long and mysterious conversations with the barkeeper always ending in both of them drinking together. The barkeeper epitomized the conversations by saying: 'He wanted to know about a feller named Tumblety, and I sez I didn't know nothing at all about him; and he says he wuz an English detective and he told me all about them Whitechapel murders, and how he came over to get the chap that did it.'

The *New York World* reporter noticed that the man who looked like an "English detective" had extensive conversations with a barkeeper, so he asked who the man was. Not only did this man, who had a serious interest in Tumblety, say he was an English detective, he stated why he "came over": to catch Jack the Ripper. Chief Inspector Littlechild stated that Scotland Yard knew Tumblety was in France no later than November 23, 1888, and possibly earlier. Chief Inspector Byrnes had two detectives waiting for Tumblety to arrive on the *La Bretagne* and was informed by Scotland Yard one week earlier that he would arrive on that ship. Numerous transatlantic ships transited to New York from England and arrived on the same day or earlier than the *La Bretagne*, and one of interest is the *SS Umbria*, the fastest cruise ship in 1888. The *Umbria* broke the record for the fastest trip across the Atlantic to Liverpool on its previous cruise. It left Liverpool, England, on November 24, the same day the *La Bretagne* left Havre, France, and arrived in New York on December 2, 1888.

Corroborating this *New York World* story about the English detective was a reporter from a competitive New York newspaper, the *New York Herald*, who also spotted the man. While the *Herald* reporter was doing his investigative job interviewing people who knew Tumblety, he independently came across the same English detective:

. . . I found that the Doctor was pretty well known in the neighborhood. The bartenders in McKenna's saloon, at the corner of Tenth street and Fourth avenue, knew him well.

And it was here that I discovered an English detective on the track of the suspect. This man wore a dark mustache and side whiskers, a tweed suit, a billycock hat and very thick walking boots. He was of medium height and had very sharp eyes and a rather florid complexion. He had been hanging around the place all day and had posted himself at a window which commanded No. 79. He made some inquiries about Dr. Tumblety to the bartenders, but gave no information about himself, although it appeared he did not know much about New York. It is uncertain whether he came over in the same ship with the suspect.
—*New York Herald*, December 4, 1888

Note that the *Herald* reporter could not have just lied and worked off the *World* reporter's article since they were published on the very same day. Also, the *Herald* reporter questioned multiple bartenders and not just one.

One claim by a number of modern researchers states that this man was an English private detective hired by the two men who gave the sureties for Tumblety's bail before he sneaked out of the country. According to the Certificate of Indictment on Tumblety, the "recognizances of defendant" were estreated, meaning Tumblety officially jumped bail and his sureties were kept. Since the men did not receive their money, they sent an English private detective across the Atlantic in order to get it back. There are a number of reasons why this explanation does not fit the evidence. First, the bartender clearly told the *World* reporter that the English detective came over to get the Whitechapel murderer, not to get money from him. Scotland Yard did hire private detectives, but in the United States they almost always hired the Pinkerton Agency, and Allan Pinkerton's office was in New York City. This, though, was clearly an Englishman, and not a Pinkerton detective. If two private men from England did decide to hire an English private detective from England, they had to have known Tumblety sneaked out of the country by November 24 in time to have a ship pull into New York, so the reporters would see him outside Tumblety's residence on December 3, 1888. This conflicts with the evidence. The very organization that contacted Chief Inspector Byrnes was the only one that knew Tumblety was in France by November 23, until it was reported on December 2, 1888. If Tumblety was sneaking out of England with full intentions not to pay his bailers back, then they would have been the last people he would have told.

Philo Smith was a partner of the Mona House in St. Louis where Tumblety occasionally stayed. Smith stated under oath in April/May of 1903 that he knew Tumblety for fifteen to seventeen years and said that no one ever got close to him to his knowledge. Smith recalled that Tumblety came to St. Louis once or twice a year. He thought Tumblety was a keen and shrewd man. He understood Tumblety to be an "Indian doctor, roots, herbs, and so on." He then continued:

> 'Also that he had been arrested as Jack the Ripper, followed to this country from abroad by Scotland street detectives. His habits were exceedingly peculiar, kept to his room most all the daytime, nighttime he was around.'

According to Smith, he first knew Tumblety in the year of the Whitechapel murders for just before. Even if he received his information about Scotland "street" detectives following Tumblety to the US from the papers, it shows that contemporary American readers believed English detectives were synonymous with Scotland Yard detectives, not private detectives from England. The New York reporters would have known this and thus would have had no reason to differentiate in the article. Even in England, Scotland Yard detectives were often referred to as English detectives:

> The Star publishes a lady's story as to the past life of Dr. Twomblety who is suspected of the Whitechapel murders. She is a friend of the Doctor's . . . According to her story the Doctor was living very quietly in Charring Cross, doing quite an excellent business with his 'pimple eradicator.'. . . When the English detectives had been baffled on every hand, and could not find anyone to answer the description of 'Jack the Ripper,' they finally swooped down on quack surgeons and cranks in every walk of life. It was in one of these general hauls that Dr. Twomblety was arrested, but he was not held by the authorities, for he easily proved that he was not a surgeon . . ."
> —Wheeling Register, December 8, 1888

Tumblety himself referred to Scotland Yard detectives as English detectives in the January 1889 interview, when he mentioned being just one of many who slummed in Whitechapel in morbid curiosity, only to find out that he was "being followed by English detectives."

Corroborating this English detective following Tumblety in New York being a Scotland Yard detective is the following article:

"JACK THE RIPPER."
English Detectives Prosecuting Inquiries in This City.

It has been known for some days past that the detectives have been quietly tracing the career in this city of Dr. Francis Tumblety, one of the suspects under surveillance by the English authorities, and who was recently followed across the ocean by Scotland Yard's men. From information which leaked out yesterday around police headquarters, the inquiries presented here are not so much in reference to Tumblety himself as to a companion who attracted almost as much attention as the doctor, both on account of oddity of character and the shadow-like persistence with which he followed his employer. The investigation in this city is understood to be under the direction of English officials now in New York, and based upon certain information they have forwarded by mail. One of the officers whom current reports connects with this local investigation is James Jackson, the well-known private detective . . .

The officials at police headquarters declined to talk about the matter or to answer any questions bearing on this supposed discovery of 'Jack the Ripper's' identity.

—*Cincinnati Enquirer*, December 14, 1888

Scotland Yard detectives referred to as "English detectives" were indeed in New York City between December 1 to December 14, 1888. In 1889, John T. McEnnis, author of *The Clan-Na-Gael and the Murder of Dr. Cronin* (San Francisco, 1889), reported:

. . . There are also employed expert cryptologists who are supposed to be able to unravel the blindest of ciphers . . .

The cipher used by Scotland Yard itself is the old movable key-word, the key generally being the name of the place to which the message is sent . . . In cabling a code cipher is used, which, of course, defies unravelment. A specimen of this stenograph received in New York last winter runs thus: "Able – desert – ocean – Chicago – manly – revolution – silver – Ireland – pretense." All that is known about this dispatch is that it certainly came from Scotland Yard to an English detective in New York and that it preceded by a few weeks Le Caron's departure for London.

—Chicago Tribune, June 30, 1889 [Author's note: Henri Le Caron, the British spy, departed for London on December 8, 1888.]

Claiming that the funding of a Scotland Yard man being sent to New York must be in Home Office records conflicts with the facts. The following is a *Chicago Tribune* reporter's interaction with Special Branch Detective H. Dutton in June 1889:

. . . They [CID] were formerly attached to each station. Now they are under the central control . . . They form a division by themselves called the 'C.O.' and are under the immediate command of the Assistant Commissioner of Police of the Home Office . . . About twenty of the men are employed on political matters solely, and of these ten have made a specialty of Irish affairs both in Ireland and America. The political detectives have the best of it. They are entrusted with the spending of the secret service moneys, and much of it of course is expended without vouchers or accounts. . .

'It is a case of fighting the devil with fire,' said Detective H. Dutton, one of the Scotland Yard men now stationed in Dublin, to the writer while in that city last winter . . .

Beside the salary there is always a liberal traveling allowance, and all expenses incurred in the line of duty are paid without question. Vouchers are seldom asked for, nor even itemized accounts. Sometimes these expense bills are heavy, especially when there are ocean voyages

*to be made. The ordinary traveling expenditure is about
£2 a day . . .*

Tumblety clearly knew he was being watched, as evidenced
by a report in the newspapers that he left Mrs. McNamara's
boarding house by December 6, 1888. The *Galveston Daily
News*, December 7, 1888, reported, "It is now certain that Dr.
Thos. F. Tumbledy, the notorious Whitechapel suspect, who
has been stopping at 79 East One Hundred and Eighth streets
last Sunday afternoon, is no longer an inmate of the house."
The mystery as to where Tumblety fled to seems to have been
solved. There is credible evidence that Tumblety left New
York City and made his way to Waterloo, New York, which is
about 40 miles east of Rochester in Western New York. In the
Waterloo Observer, December 12, 1888, it states:

*Wild rumors are afloat about villians in many villages
and cities assaulting, insulting and molesting women and
young girls on public streets after dark. All these places
have a modified prototype of the White Chapel murderer.
'Dick the Slasher.' The announcement that Dr. Tumblety
had come to New York and departed for a rural retreat, in
the fancy of many timid females he has been located in
Waterloo. And this is the more certain; since the veritable
doctor spent a summer here some ten years ago. Moreover, during the past week, a young lady was met about
seven o'clock, in the evening on a public street in the first
ward by a man who said, 'You are the girl I want,' and
tried to seize her by the neck, when she beat him in the
face with an umbrella and he fled. Also, in the lower ward,
a woman was followed for a long distance in a menac-
ing manner, and sought safety in a neighbor's house and
company home. If there is anything going on in this line
more serious than trying to frighten timid females, the vil-
lain ought to be run down and punished.*

Why this particular article should be taken seriously is
because Tumblety's sister, Elizabeth Powderly, lived with her
husband, Thomas, and her children in Waterloo, New York, in
1888. It was not the first time Tumblety came to Elizabeth's
home after receiving unwanted attention. In the fall of 1880

Tumblety was arrested in Toronto for sodomy. According to the sworn testimony of Elizabeth's son, Thomas, Tumblety visited them immediately after his Toronto troubles.

Scotland Yard detectives were reported to be in New York City in May 1889. A *New York Herald* correspondent reported "agents from the British government" having a long discussion with New York City detectives in Madison Square Park, one of these detectives being the police official who told the New York reporters that Dr. Kumblety was in fact Dr. Francis Tumblety. Curiously, Tumblety was also in that very same New York park:

Inspector Byrnes is quietly endeavoring to clear up the mystery of the assassination of Dr. Cronin in Chicago. The man Starkey, who is supposed to have been implicated in the conspiracy, is being watched in the hope that some important development concerning the case may be the outcome of the surveillance. Detectives Golden and Vallely are searching for the man Williams or Emmons, who is believed to have hired the house where Cronin met his death. Two men, said to be agents of the British government, had a long talk with Detective Golden last night upon one of the benches in Madison Square Park. As a strange coincidence Dr. Tumblety, otherwise known as "Jack the Ripper," occupied a bench on the other side of the walk near the statue of Lafayette.
—New York Herald, May 27, 1889

Was this just a strange coincidence only six months after Tumblety's escape from London? There is evidence that the local police would know to go to a city park in order to find the elusive Tumblety, because of his passion for encounters with younger males. Under sworn testimony, Tumblety's Baltimore attorney made a comment not only about Tumblety's habit of preying upon boys in the parks but also the police watching him. Simpson stated:

My candid opinion about it is that he had a habit of resorting to unnatural practices on little boys; he [was] watched very closely and frequented our parks a good deal.

The attorney questioning Simpson asked by whom was Tumblety being watched. Simpson replied,

The policemen, and he would dodge around and sometimes he would be at Patterson Park and sometimes at Druid Hill Park . . .

Simpson gave details about one event in the park, ". . . at another time he was in trouble; there was a lady, I never could find out who she was; he told me she lived on Pierce Street; he had taken a little boy out . . ." The attorney interrupted Simpson, "Do you mean Dr. Tumblety had taken a little boy out?" Simpson replied:

'Yes, sir; he had met him on the street and talked to him and bought him some candy, some confectionary and such as that and took him to the park, Druid Hill Park. He put him on the car and took him out to the park and it seems as if the little boy went home and told his mother some story; however, the little boy told his mother where Tumblety could be found; I do not know what occurred; but I drew my influence from what I heard from different policemen and what I heard about it; and I suggested to him to give the woman a hundred dollars and let her go; this also was in the year 1900.'

The unfortunate Alice Mackenzie was murdered on July 17, 1889, and at the time, most officials in Scotland Yard believed her to be a victim of Jack the Ripper. The coroner, Dr. Thomas Bond, stated that "the murder was performed by the same person who committed the former series of Whitechapel murders." Additionally, Metropolitan Police Commissioner James Monro was convinced, and he even added an extra two sergeants and thirty-nine constables to the Whitechapel District. Since Tumblety was in America at the time, this took him off the radar.

3

Amongst the Suspects

"He [Francis Tumblety] *said the trouble with young men are those cigarettes, and those confounded Street Walkers. He said, if he had his way they would all be disemboweled."*
–Richard S. Norris

When Francis Tumblety was arrested on suspicion for the Whitechapel murders and the letters in his pocket were confiscated, those documents revealed his name. Authorities would then have wired headquarters to see if they had any record on him. This seems to have occurred, as evidenced by Littlechild stating they had a large dossier on the doctor and discussing facts in that record. Because of earlier suspicions that the Whitechapel murderer was an American and Tumblety was the Great American Doctor from New York, they would have been even more interested, since he likely had anatomical knowledge. Tumblety never promoted his Indian herb doctor persona in England and claimed he had military surgical experience in France. Scotland Yard certainly was aware that Tumblety was a quack doctor, which may have been more damning. While the divisional surgeon, Dr. Bagster Phillips, believed the crime scenes showed that the killer had anatomical *knowledge*, anatomical *skill* was not apparent.

Not only did Chief Inspector Littlechild state that Tumblety was among the suspects, meaning a suspect identified by CID, but he also explained why: his remarkable and extremely bitter feelings toward women. Littlechild would never have recalled a suspect CID thought to be insignificant. Further corroborating Littlechild's bitter-hatred-explanation as to why

CID considered him a suspect were the newspaper reports. Of all the reasons reported in the papers as to why Scotland Yard suspected Francis Tumblety, the most-often stated was him being a woman-hater. Some have argued that the phrase "woman-hater" in the nineteenth century was merely a euphemism for being gay, especially since Littlechild discussed Tumblety's homosexuality. It certainly was used to refer to homosexuality, but it was also used to mean a misogynist, as evidenced by the following statement from a nineteenth-century gay man not understanding the sexual attraction to a woman, "Even their [women's] physical beauty has little or no charm for me, and I often wonder how men can be so affected by it. On the other hand, I am not a woman-hater, and have several strong friends of the opposite sex" (*Sexual Inversion*, 1897). The problem is, Littlechild never used the phrase "woman-hater." He stated, "but his feelings toward women were remarkable and bitter in the extreme, a fact on record." Littlechild meaning gay in this statement makes little sense. To take that meaning would be to say Littlechild stated that Tumblety was not gay—he was really, *really* gay. On January 17, 1889, the *St. Louis Republic* reported on an interview with a James D. Maguire, who in 1869 was recruited from his job as a young bellboy at the Southern Hotel in St. Louis by Tumblety to be his personal valet. This is very plausible, since Tumblety hired a young man in every city in which he opened an office. He was also known to attempt a sexual relationship with his new teenage hires. Maguire claimed Tumblety was a woman-hater, and further claimed, "His antipathy to fallen women has been especially marked." What is important about this particular statement by Maguire, regardless if he was telling the truth or not, was that he indeed referred to the phrase woman-hater to mean misogynist, giving further credibility to the connotation of the phrase at that time.

Follow-up research discovered that Tumblety was known for his unusual hatred of women on both sides of the Atlantic. Initially, this evidence came in the form of contemporary newspaper reports, especially out of North America. An article in the *New York World*, December 3, 1888, states, "Reasons which led some of them to believe that Twomblety is the fiend who so successfully eluded the London police are that the 'Doctor' had an inveterate hatred for women . . ." After discovering Tumblety had a history at the Fifth Avenue Hotel in Manhattan, a *New York World* reporter went to the hotel and asked questions. William Carr, a clerk of over thirty years, recalled Tumblety, which was reported in the November 26, 1888, issue: "the general impression among those who knew him about his habits was that he avoided women." San Francisco Chief of Police Patrick Crowley was reported in the *San Francisco Examiner*, November 23, 1888, to have inside information on Tumblety's treatment of women in New York, ". . . and in New York his behavior was that of a man who had no liking for women."

Supporting Littlechild's comment that Scotland Yard had a large dossier on Tumblety was an interview with the famous international detective William Pinkerton. In the *Chicago Daily Inter-Ocean*, November 19, 1888, William Pinkerton, a man who knew of Tumblety's eccentric and immoral behavior since the onset of the Civil War, commented upon his hatred of women, saying, "He was known as a thorough woman-hater and as a man who never associated with or mixed with women of any kind." Pinkerton even commented upon Scotland Yard asking him about Francis Tumblety in late 1873, when Tumblety was involved in a court case:

> 'In Chicago, along about '69, he [Tumblety] was detected in indulging in the vices to which I have referred and he had to fly that city. The next time I saw him was in England, in 1874. [Author's note: He arrested Steve Raymond on January 8, 1874.] I ran across him then, accidentally, in Liverpool, and again in London. In the latter city he made a complaint to the police that a boy whom he had employed as an office boy, had stolen his watch and chain. . . . When I met him in London, he was dressed about the same as he had been in Washington when I first saw him. The boy who stole the watch from him had been picked up by him in Liverpool and taken along to London. The police instituted a search after him. They found that the watch had been pawned, and recovered it, and afterward succeeded in arresting the boy. When the boy was in custody he confessed the theft but also made a statement to the police which caused a warrant to be issued for the Doctor's arrest. The fellow claimed to be an American citizen.

Superintendent Shaw asked me about him. I told him that the boy had undoubtedly told the truth, as the vile charac- ter the boy gave of the Doctor was just the character that he had a reputation for in the United States. Up to the time I left London—some three months after that incident—the Doctor had refused to call or, at least, neglected to call for his watch and chain, though they were very valuable. It was finally discovered that he had gone to Paris, his property being left in the hands of the police.'

The case, which was in front of the magistrate on December 1, 1873, involved a young man named Henry Carr, aged 18, who lived in Paddington. Pinkerton was indeed in England in late 1873 and early 1874, being involved in the arrest of a Steve Raymond on January 8, 1874. He left Liverpool on the *SS Republic* in early February 1874, arriving in New York on February 17. Pinkerton referred to his discussion with Superintendent Shaw as having occurred some three months before this, around November/December 1873, which conforms to the date of the case. Pinkerton also stated in a US newspaper that he sailed to Liverpool on the same ship he arrived back in, the *SS Republic*. Records show that the *SS Republic* left New York on November 8, 1873, arriving in Liverpool on November 20.

One particular event involving Francis Tumblety and his unusual interaction with women occurred not only in London, England, but also during the Whitechapel murders. The *Buffalo Courier*, December 7, 1888, interviewed a Buffalo man, C. A. Bloom, who knew Tumblety for fifteen years and reported on his peculiar change of behavior when forced to be near women. It occurred just after the murders of Elizabeth Stride and Catherine Eddowes:

During the past summer and early fall I [C.A. Bloom] *was in London, England, for three months. One pleasant day in October* [1888]*, in company with my wife and another lady, I was going down Regent street. At Oxford street I was greatly surprised to see this same Dr. Tumblety enter the omnibus. . . . But what surprised me was his actions when he found that I was in company with the ladies. When I introduced my wife to him his actions were so*

*strange that she has spoken about it several times since
. . . He seemed to be very ill at ease and never raised his
eyes from the floor after he had learned that the ladies
were with me.*

The British papers also reported on Scotland Yard's
suspicions of Tumblety partly because of his hatred of
women and his treatment of prostitutes. The *Evening Post*,
December 3, 1888, reported, "In Boston, says the American
correspondent of the *Daily Telegraph* . . . It is reported by
cable from Europe that a certain person, whose name is
known has sailed form Havre for New York, who is famous for
his hatred of women, and who has repeatedly made threats
against females of dissolute character." Another British
paper's record of Tumblety's misogyny outside of North
America occurred in Liverpool, England, thirteen years before
the Whitechapel murders, in 1875. Notice the reporter, not
knowing of Tumblety's reputation, singled out women as the
specific target demographic for his anger. It was reported in
the *Liverpool Leader*, January 9, 1875:

*There comes to us a tale of a decent woman from the Isle
of Man who sought his advice respecting a bad leg. He
told her it was due to the immorality of her parents, but
would cure it for 3 pounds. This she declined, whereon
he [Tumblety] ordered her to get out legs and all or else
he would kick her out! Other women young and unmar-
ried, have fled in alarm from his premises, and say his
language and conduct suggested danger.*

The earliest recorded time in Tumblety's life when he
expressed hatred of women was an eyewitness account in
the *Chicago Daily Inter-Ocean*, December 4, 1888, from a
Rochester, New York, resident recalling an experience with
Tumblety that occurred around 1850, "A few years after
reaching manhood, he evinced a great dislike for women,
and constantly spoke of the gentler sex as a curse to the
land." If true, this suggests he believed at an early age that
women are to be blamed for the misfortunes of men. The very
first recorded incident of Tumblety treating females poorly
occurred at the very first place he began his practice in 1856,

in London, Ontario. A local newspaper, the *London Free Press*, published a story in its May 6, 1856, issue about a local resident named Mrs. Carden being under Tumblety's care. Her claim was when he visited her home on a doctor's visit he insulted her by asking her to brush the dust from his coat. Tumblety was taken before the mayor of London, Ontario, on arraignment, and after listening to the evidence, he agreed Tumblety insulted her. The mayor fined him £5.

The next published account of Tumblety's poor treatment of females also occurred north of the US border and was republished by Tumblety himself. In his first autobiography, published in 1866, Tumblety commented upon his time in Saint John, New Brunswick, Canada, in 1860, which admits to his dangerous treatment of women:

> *My friends of the press were lavish in their encomiums, and frequently indulged their poetic fancy in complimentary effusions, among which, the following, from the St. Johns (N.B.) Albion, is a humorous sample:*

> DR. TUMBLETY.
> *Dr. Tumblety rode a white steed*
> *Into St. Johns in its time of need,*
> *Determined to cure with herbal pills*
> *All the ailing of all their ills.*
> *Dr. Tumblety had a greyhound—A beautiful animal I'll be bound—*
> *The dog looked up in the Doctor's face*
> *As he rode along at a slapping pace.*
> **Tumblety had a killing air,**
> *Though curing was his professional trade,*
> *Rosy of cheek, and glossy of hair,*
> **Dangerous man to widow or maid** . . . [Author emphasis added.]

The *Albion* reporter made reference to Tumblety putting on a "Killing air," and being a "Dangerous man to widow or maid," which conforms to his pattern of indecorous treatment of some women. One suggestion behind the meaning of the phrase in the poem is not of a life-threatening nature but that of Tumblety being a womanizer, breaking the hearts of single women. First, all accounts on how Tumblety interacted with single women from 1856 to 1902 show the exact opposite, even going out of his way to avoid them entirely. Second, the reporter at the *Albion* presented the phrase as the antithesis to his professional job of saving lives, "though curing was his professional trade." The opposite of curing is not flirting but harming. Lastly, and most significantly, his maltreatment of women in Saint John was corroborated by another account. An article in the *Boston Herald*, November 25, 1888, discusses an eyewitness account of Tumblety opening an office in Saint John, New Brunswick:

> *About the time that the war broke out, in 1860 or 1861, Dr. Tumblety made his appearance at St. John, N.B., where he immediately proceeded to cut a great dash. . . . After a while the more intelligent people got their eyes open to the fact that he was a charlatan, and pretty soon afterward stories began to go round about his indecorus [sic] treatment of some of his lady patients.*

The similarity between the *Boston Herald* and *Albion* accounts involving his negative interaction with single women while in Saint John in 1860 is striking, as if both were referring to the same misogynist events. With Tumblety consistently making it known to young men his bitter feelings toward women and his seeming obliviousness that this type of treatment is unusual in civilized society, it is not a surprise that he would place this into his autobiography. Interestingly, Tumblety took this poem out of the next version of his autobiography published in 1871/72. (The reason for this is the subject of Chapter 6 of this book.)

One eyewitness account published in the *New York World*, December 2, 1888, came from Colonel Charles A. Dunham, recalling an experience in 1861. In it, Tumblety not only expressed his hatred of women, especially fallen women, but he also gave a warning against them. While in Washington DC after the First Battle of Bull Run when General McClellan was assigned commander of the Army of the Potomac, Tumblety invited the general's officer to an illustrated lecture. Dunham stated:

> 'One day my lieutenant-colonel and myself accepted the 'doctor's' invitation to a late dinner—symposium, he called

it—at his rooms. He had very cosy and tastefully arranged quarters in, I believe, H. street. There were three rooms on a floor, the rear one being his office, with a bedroom or two a story higher. . . . Someone asked why he had not invited some women to his dinner. His face instantly became as black as a thunder cloud. He had a pack of cards in his hand, but he laid them down and said, almost savagely: "No, Colonel, I don't know any such cattle, and if I did I would, as your friend, sooner give you a dose of quick poison than take you into such danger." He then broke into a homily on the sin and folly of dissipation, fiercely denounced all woman and especially fallen women.'

Tumblety went on to Pittsburgh just after completing his first autobiography, and all accounts show his Indian herb doctor business continued with financial success. However, he got into trouble when dealing with two female patients. In the *Williamsport Sunday Grit*, December 9, 1888, it states:

IN PITTSBURGH
He called himself the 'Great American Herb Doctor' and said he could cure everything. His career here was in many respects a remarkable one. He came, he saw, he conquered, was in turn conquered and had to flee to es- cape the consequences of trouble from two of his female patients. While here he did a wonderful business, and a made a great deal of money. He spent it most lavishly, too, and was known to open wine and give away cigars by the box.

The aim of Tumblety's misogynist rage shows a direction. He did not hate all women, but the evidence points only to women who have the ability to lure young men towards a life of heterosexuality. In the mid-1870s, Tumblety struck up a relationship in Liverpool, England, with young Henry Hall Caine. In a private letter to Hall Caine, Tumblety stated:

In morals and obscenity they [Chinese women] are far be- low those of our most degraded prostitutes. Their women are bought and sold, for the usual purposes and they are used to decoy youths of the most tender age, into these

dens, for the purpose of exhibiting their nude and disgust-
ing person to the hitherto innocent youths of the cities.

While investigating Tumblety's history in New York City
after the discovery that he was arrested on suspicion for the
Whitechapel murders, a *New York World* reporter found an
attorney who knew Tumblety. The attorney, William P. Burr,
stated he argued a case against Francis Tumblety in 1880, as
reported in the *New York World,* December 2, 1888. Around
1878, soon after his relationship with Hall Caine ended,
Tumblety hired a young man named Joseph J. Lyons in
Manhattan as a sort of secretary. Ultimately, the young man
sued Tumblety for "atrocious assault" of the "most disgusting
sort." Burr reproduced to the reporter a letter Tumblety wrote
to Lyons, then Burr explained that Tumblety, ". . . never failed
to warn his correspondent [young Lyons] against lewd women,
and in doing it used the most shocking language."

A young Martin McGarry was hired by Tumblety around
1882. A *New York World* reporter approached him in December
1888, when McGarry was attempting to visit Tumblety. In the
December 5, 1888, issue, it states:

When asked about Dr. Tumblety's aversion to women,
McGarry said: 'He always disliked women very much. He
used to say to me: "Martin, no women for me." He could
not bear to have them near him. He thought all women
were impostors, and he often said that all the trouble in
this world was caused by women.'

Keep in mind, McGarry expressed to the reporter he was
a friend of Tumblety's and rejected the idea that he was Jack
the Ripper. McGarry does confirm two patterns with Tumblety,
however: his habit of expressing his hatred of women and
his belief that they cause misfortunes for men. In this case,
Tumblety called women impostors. Just as a duck decoy
impersonates a duck to lure other ducks to their death, he
saw women as man-decoys, luring impressionable young
men to the evils of heterosexuality, as highlighted in the Hall
Caine letter, which states that prostitutes exhibit "their nude
and disgusting person to the hitherto innocent youths of the
cities."

On May 12 through May 13, 1905, witnesses were deposed under oath in New Orleans in the legal battle for the estate of Francis Tumblety, an estate worth over three million dollars in today's value. Tumblety had made out his will two weeks before his death in St. Louis, Missouri, in May 1903, yet had bequeathed only a third of his estate. He bequeathed to selected family members, the Catholic Church, and his New York coachman, Mark A. Blackburn. The other family members, led by Francis' Rochester nephews James P. Tumilty and Michael Fitzsimons, sued, claiming Francis was not of sound mind and body, therefore, the St. Louis will should be deemed null and void. In so doing, all the family members would get proportional shares of the money.

One particular witness from New Orleans, Judge Harry H. Patin, aged 31 years, gave testimony of an experience with Tumblety while Patin was in his late twenties. One evening, Patin met Tumblety in an alley. Patin stated, ". . . one night I met him in the alley behind this building, Varities Alley, and he wanted to get me in a conversation with him, and he said men should not like women, and all those kind of things." Notice how Tumblety was referring to women who young men like and expressed his disagreement in the act of liking them. Patin was a young man at the time and met him—a new acquaintance—at night, in an alley. Tumblety's interest in him was certainly sexual, since this is exactly how Tumblety used to pick up young men.

Another account of Tumblety warning one of his young male interests about the evils of women, especially prostitutes, is also one that connects him to the Whitechapel murders. As in the case with the Littlechild letter, the Hall Caine letter, and the judge's testimony, this is not evidence found in the newspapers. It is actual testimony sworn under oath for a court case argued in front of the Missouri Probate Court, the testimony of Richard S. Norris, a man who worked in the police department for decades.

Norris was 43 years of age at the time of his deposition and was a telegraph operator and clerk for the New Orleans Police Department for years. He was questioned under oath by Judge Gabriel Fernandez Jr. on May 12, 1905. The deposition was later "read in evidence" to jurors at the Circuit Court of St. Louis, Missouri. Norris claimed to be a close acquaintance of Francis Tumblety for twenty years, meeting him each year in February during Mardi Gras beginning in the year "1880 or 1881." Since Francis Tumblety was in Europe during the entire 1880 Mardi Gras season, their first meeting would have been in 1881. Norris was seventeen or eighteen at the time, and Tumblety introduced himself to him at the St. Charles Theatre during the intermission of a performance and asked where he worked. After replying that he worked as a telegraph operator for Western Union, Tumblety responded by saying he was a surgeon drawing a pension from the government of England and was also a major stockholder in Western Union with $90,000 in stock. Tumblety's lie was clearly to gain young Norris' interest, because a major stockholder would have influence over Norris' bosses. Tumblety asked Norris to come to his room and write a letter for him, a request similar to the one asked of gifted writer Henry Hall Caine five or six years earlier. Norris stated [Author's note: There are discrepancies between the transcript generated from the New Orleans deposition on May 12, 1905, and what was read in evidence at the St. Louis Circuit Court. Certain typos were corrected, while sections were left out.]:

> Well, I was pleased to meet him, thoughthe [sic] was a fine man, and a stranger. He took me to Lamothe's and gave me a supper, and asked me to go to his room with him, wanted me to write a letter for him. He had a room at the St. Charles hotel at the time. I told him I was out late, that I lived uptown quite a distance and I could not go with him, because my peopleobjected [sic] to my staying out late; in fact, I was afraid of him. He had some large diamonds on him, and I thought he was a confidence man, or a burglar. I excused myself to him, and went on the side, and told my friend, "I will take a chance, I haven't got anything, and I will take a chance and write this let-ter for him", and I asked my friend to wait for me. I went up to the St. Charles hotel with him, he ordered a couple of bottles of Burke's ale; I drank a bottle, and he drank the other, and he insisted upon my drinking the other. I thought he wanted to get me intoxicated, and I refused to do it. He then opened a large trunk (but in the meantime ordered some more ale) and he pulled out a velvet vest

which had, I judge, four – three or four medals on each side – they looked to me like gold medals. He told me they were awarded to him by the English Government.

The next statement is significant specific to the Whitechapel murder case, since it not only connects Tumblety to surgical knives but also having the opinion that all prostitutes should be disemboweled:

Then there was a sprt [sic] of tray in the trunk, and there were alllsorts [sic] of large knives in there, surgical instruments—*that is, i [sic] did not know what they were at the time. Afte [sic] that he was arresyed [sic], supposed to be a bad character; it was a sort of put up job at the time, to find out what he really was. Therewere [sic] large knives in the trunk; and then he came over to me, and felt my pulse, and felt my legs. I was smoking a cigarette at the time, and he said, "Throw that away", and he handed me a cigar, saying it was bad to smoke cigarettes.* **He said the trouble with young men are those cigarettes, and those confounded Street Walkers. He said, if he had his way they would all be disemboweled.** *Now, I read and new [sic] of the White Chapel business and did know it at the time. I got a little scared of this man, and I went over to the Chief of Police, and told him of this fellow, and he told me that reminds him of the big tall man that he read of in the Chicago Herald, and Pittsburg Dispatch, as being Jack the Ripper, and I said, he answers the description. And seeing, and noticing the way he spoke, and how he acted ---- he never frequented the street in the daytime; he used to walk the streets all hours of the night. When I spoke to him about the numerous women that had been killed around White Chapel, he said, "Yes, I was there when it all happened". Well, after he told me that, I tried to shun him, and he sent me notes and letters, and even came to the office after me. He gave me a good time, took me to the theatre, and spent a good deal of money on me. He bought me several suits of clothes, and he never attempted to do anything wrong with me until one night he took me to his room, and he locked the door on me.* [Author emphasis added.]

According to the *Daily Picayune*, March 25, 1881, Tumblety "came to New Orleans on the Friday before Mardi Gras." Since Mardi Gras began on March 1st in 1881, Tumblety arrived on February 25, 1881. The "put up job" arrest of Tumblety occurred on March 24, 1881, by a private detective named D. C. O'Malley, and indeed, Norris comments upon Dominick O'Malley arresting Tumblety at the Customhouse later on in the deposition. This means Tumblety showed Norris his surgical knives in late February or March 1881. Norris then commented upon Tumblety sexually assaulting him, the details of which will be discussed in the next chapter. Norris explained that this assault did not occur in Tumblety's St. Charles hotel room, but in a later room on Canal Street.

> *He was not at the Charles hotel then, he had changed his place – I don't know for what cause he had change his place, but he had changed to Old No. 190 Canal street.*

After discussing this sexual assault, the attorney then asked, "When did all this take place?" Norris replied, "This happened in 1881 or 1880," which conforms to the date of the arrest by O'Malley. In view of this, Norris is explaining that the later St. Charles Hotel room experience and the February/March 1881 Canal Street hotel room experience all happened in the same 1881 season. Tumblety told Norris all street walkers should be disemboweled seven years before the Whitechapel victims were disemboweled.

In Norris' testimony, note how the court recorder, or stenographer, wrote out the following statement made by Norris, "Now, I read and new (sic) of the White Chapel business and did know it at the time." Taken literally, this suggests Norris had to have had the St. Charles Hotel room experience after the 1888 Whitechapel murders, but this conflicts with Norris himself stating "1881 or 1880." The MO of Tumblety sexually assaulting the young men he hired was to first gain their trust, then to force himself upon them. In view of this, it makes more sense that Norris actually stated, "Now, I read and new (sic) of the White Chapel business and did [NOT] know it at the time," meaning at the time of the assault in 1881, the Whitechapel business of 1888 was still yet to be, so he would not have connected Tumblety's Ripper-like comment to the future Ripper murders.

Both the New Orleans and the St. Louis stenographers made numerous mistakes in the final copy, so accuracy was not paramount. This leaves open the possibility that the word "not" was accidentally omitted. While the St. Louis recorder corrected minor typos made by the New Orleans recorder, a clear effort was made to transcribe the document exactly. Note two mistakes made by the recorders in the final draft in just one sentence: "Afte [sic] that he was arresyed [sic], supposed to be a bad character." The following is another case of the recorder accidentally omitting a word. Tumblety's Baltimore attorney, Robert Simpson, was asked about an event that occurred in 1900:

> My candid opinion about it is that he had a habit of resorting to unnatural practices on little boys; he watched very closely and frequented our parks a good deal.

The attorney was then asked, "Watched by whom?" Simpson then answered, "The policemen." In view of this, the recorder accidentally omitted a word. Instead of, "he watched very closely," Simpson had to have said, "he WAS watched very closely." Yet another case of the stenographer omitting a word is in the earlier section of the Norris testimony, "When we got to the counter he introduced himself, saying he was stranger here for the Mardi-Gras holidays, and asked us the privilege of treating." Notice the recorder omitted the "a" prior to "stranger," thus, the statement should be, "he was a stranger."

Norris was being deposed in 1905 and recounted events with Tumblety from 1881 to 1902, and he relayed to the court events throughout this time, responding to questions by the attorneys. He did not connect the events sequentially but through similarity in content asked by the attorneys. When Norris saw Tumblety's knives for the first time, it was in 1881. When he spoke to Tumblety about the Whitechapel murders, he was referring to a time just after 1888. He then spoke of the time Tumblety assaulted him in 1881. The following partial transcription of Norris' deposition demonstrates how he answered the attorneys' questions out of sequential order of events. Note how he used the chiefs of police he worked for to remind him when the events occurred:

Q: When was that?
A: When he was robbed?

Q: Yes; when he told you so?
A: That was a year after he was robbed; after he came back. I did remember [sic] what year that was.

Q: Was it after 1900?
A: Well, I will tell you, Gaster was just made Chief of Police at the time, because he was the one who called me in the office of the Chief of Police, and showed me the newspapets [sic]. It was the first year he was made Chief of Police.

Q: That was 1901?
A: It was the first year he was made Chief of Police. [Author's note: This was actually in January 21, 1891.]

Q: Who is that that was made Chief?
A. Mr. Gaster.

[Author's note: The following question and answer was not in the St. Louis transcript]

Q: This was 1901?
A: Yes, sir. He said, "Here is your friend who was robbed in Hot Springs", and he said, "It is a good thing you did not take a trip with him." I said, "Yes; it is a wonder he was not robbed here this Spring". He showed me his Jewelry, and he had one diamond there the size of a silver dime. I was trying to hunt up a couple of letters, but I haven't got them.

Q: Now reverting back to the purchase of those clothes at N.B. Stevens, for yourself, and for himself, what did you do when you came out of Stevens' place. Where did you go?

[Author's note: The following question and answer were handwritten. Notice how the attorney, Mr. Thompson, needed clarification of dates, since Norris combined a story from 1881 with one from 1901.]

By Mr. Thompson – That was in 1880 or 1881?
A: In 1880 or 1881.

By Mr. Thompson:- I object to the evidence on the same grounds as previously urged.

By Judge Fernandez:-
Q: Where did you go ? [sic]
A: Right to the head of the stairs with him. I would not go in the house with him; I was sort of scared of him then.

OBJECTION SUSTAINED:

Q: You mean the house where he lived?
A: Yes, sir. He told me he was paying Five Dollars a day. And he asked me wherewas [sic] the best restaurant to eat at, and I told him Lamothe's, and I met him there and ate with him.

Q: Mr. Norris, how long did your acquaintance with Dr. Tumilty last.
A: Fram [sic] May, 1881, or 1880, up to three or four years ago. I met him every year.

Q: And were you with him a considerable length of time every time he was in the City of New Orleans?
A: Sometimes I would stop and talk with him on the street ten or fifteen minutes; and then, again, I would take a ride with him. He was a pretty good spender, and that is what I enjoyed with him. He seemed to like my company.

Q: During your acquaintanceship with Dr. Tumilty, of over twenty years, you had occasion to notice his peculiarities and habits?
A: Yes, sir.

[Author's note: The following question and answer were not in the St. Louis transcript.]

Q: Well, besides those you have stated already, try and refresh your memory, and state if you can remember any others?
A: Well, I remember when he was arrested in the Customhouse by Dominick O'Malley [Author's note: This occurred on March 24, 1881], who claimed that he

was robbed by this man Tumilty. That was published in all the papers in this city. He sent for me that evening, and he told me what an awful city this was, that a man couldn't go around without being molested, that he would send over and prove who he was through the English Consul. The newspapers published that there were burglar tools found in his trunk, and the next day they contradicted it, saying they were surgical instruments. The following day, Sunday I think it was, he asked me to take a ride out to the Lake. I said, "Doctor, I feel pretty bad about that; I would not like to be seen in your company, you being accused of this; you say, you are innocent, but I don't know anything about the case. He said, I wouldn't stay in this town another day, but still, he says, I am advised to stay in town and have this man prosecuted, but I will not do it. It seems to me he had peculiar habits, every night going through all the dark streets, walking like a Street Walker. He would take the darkest streets, and the darkest spots at night, and at one and two o'clock in the morning he would walk up Camp street, and all the dark streets and dark corners. I used to watch him very close because I did not know what kind of fellow he was. He told me that all the girls must admire me, and all the [men] must admire me. I introduced him to the manager over there at the Telegraph Office, Mr. Doyle. He told Mr. Doyle that I was such good company. He asked him if all the boys were not stuck on me. I tried to get Mr. Doyle to take him.

Q: *Did he show the same disposition towards other young men that he showed to you?*

A: *No. I introduced him to several friends of mine, told them what a good time I had with him, and he spending his money, and I told them what kind of a man he was if they wanted to take a chance with him, but he seemed to shun them all for me.* [Author's note: the following section of Norris' answer was not in the St. Louis transcript.] *He wrote out a check for Seven Hundred Dollars in 1888 or 1889 – the Legislature was in session at the time and I had to go to Baton Rouge. He wrote the check out, payable to bearer, and guaranteed me that I could cash it in any bank where we would go if I would go there with him. He was very anxious to get me to go with him, and I refused to go with him.*

Q: Mr. Norris, when was it that Dr. Tumilty told you that he had been robbed?

A: At Hot Springs?

Q: Yes.

A: Well, about the first year that Gaster was made Chief of Police; I disremember that year. He said, he was robbed of between fifteen and twenty five thousand dollars.

Q: Did he tell you by whom he thought he had been robbed?

A: Yes, sir. He said by a race-horse jockey, or a stableman.

Q: What was Dr. Tumilty's appearance?

A: He was over six feet, a big fine looking man, rosy complexion; he had died [sic] his mustache; you could see that he had died [sic] his mustache.----

Q: How was he dressed?

A: In the 80's, the first few years I met him he used to wear a blue cap, wore one of those naval caps the first year I met him ---- in 1880 or 1881 --- like the naval officers wear, with a gold band around it. During all the time I knew him he always wore a cap.

Q: Did he look plain?

A: Yes, sir; very plain, and very shabby, especially in the last few years. That is the reason I shunned him, I didn't care how much money he had.

Q: Was he clean?

A: No, sir; he looked dirty; very filthy;.

Q: You had occasion to converse with him during the last few years?

A: Yes sir.

Q: You had occasion to judge as to his mind?

A: Well, I am no doctor, but from his manner --- his hobby was that women should be killed; that is, honestly, why I was afraid to go with him.

Q: *But during the last years you were with him, did you ever notice the condition of his mind; what was the condition of his mind?*

A: *Well, the last few years I no more than spoke to him and took a drink with him; I never bothered with him. He seemed during the last two years I met him to shun me a little. I used to talk to him and take a drink with him. I told him I had recently got married.* [Author's note: This was in 1895.]

[Author's note: The following question, objection by Mr. Thompson, and answer were not in the St. Louis transcript.]

Q: *Was his mind, to your notice, in a steady balance condition, healthy condition.*
By Mr. Thompson: I object to the question on the ground that it is incompetent.

By the Witness:
A: *I could not answer that. Of course, there are some things I could say and do know, and that is why I have tried to make a sort of statement to get around everything I do know; I cannot remember everything; I would have to sit down and refresh my memory. There are some things he done in the last few years I was in his company; of course, I don't suppose it has bearing upon what you want to know. I leave it to you, gentlemen. I don't know exactly what you want to prove, but I might be able to get at it that way.*

By Judge Fernandez:

Q: *Let me ask you this. When he had conversations with you, were those conversations complete and steady, or was he vacillating, changing from one subject to another?*

A: *Yes; he was ver [sic] vacillating. He told me so many different stories about that Western Union stock, Ninety thousand Dollars he had; drawing Ten thousand Dollar pension a year from the English Government.*

Q: *Did you notice his condition the last year you met him, about four years ago?*

A: *Yes, sir. I remarked to him, "Doctor, it looks like they cleaned you out since you have been robbed", and he said, "No, I still get my pension; I have a few dollars."*

Q: *Well, from the few words you had with him------*

A: *(Interrupting):—I could not understand his condition being so filthy, when he told me he had so much money, and he told e [sic] he did not care about dress.*

Q: *His moods were changeable, were they?*

A: *Yes, sir; considerably so.*

Q: *Is that all you know about this case, Mr. Norris; anything else that you can remember that might throw some light on it?*

A: *Well I took him to a sporting house one night (Hennessy was Chief of Police then), I judge about ten or twelve years ago----*

By Mr. Thompson:- I object to what occurred ten or twelve years ago, as being incompetent, irrelevant and immaterial.

By the Witness:- (continuing his last above answer) --- and I did not tell him it was a sporting house until I got right in front of the place. Then I told him there was a lady friend of mine bothering me about money matters, and threatening to send to the office, and being in the neighborhood [sic] I was going in, and wouldn't he go in with me". I told him that as a joke, and I told the girls what a peculiar man he was, and when I got him in, he began to treat to some champagne, and I told the girls I know we would both have to leave, because he "hated your kind of people --- your class of people." When we went in a couple of girls asked if they couldn't have some wine and he hollaed [sic] across the room "if I wanted it", and I said, "all right." He ordered the wine and a couple of girls went over to him, and he said, "go away from me". After drinking the wine he said to me, "Let's get out of here." We went out of the house, and he gave me an awful lecture. He said he was surprised I went to such a place, and I told him it was one of the swellest places in the City, that a nice class of young men went there, and he said, none of them were any good. A good many little things like that took place. I don't know whether it has any bearing on this case or not.

Cross Examination: By Mr. Thompson.

Q: *Mr. Norris, as I understand you, during the last four or five years that Dr. Tumilty visited New Orleans you did not associate with him?*
A: *Not but very little. I met him, and spoke and drank with him.*

Q: *You would occasionally meet him on the street, and stop and talk ten or fifteen minutes with him?*
A: *Yes, sir. I never did go to his room then.*

Q: *That was the extent, during that time, of your association with him?*
A: *Yes, sir.*

Q: *During those four or five years did he tell you all of his business affaris [sic]?*
A: *Well, no more than what I have stated here. He used to often recall that instance of being robbed.*

Q: *Did he speak to you of his family during those last four or five years?*
A: *During all the time I was acquainted with him, and, in-asmuch, as I spoke to him about his business, henever [sic] mentioned his family to me. The last time I met him on the street, I said, "Doctor, if you are still interested in the Western Union you ought to be able to get a fellow like me a first class position in the office." I told him I was connected with the Police Department, but did not like the job. He did not seem to pay any attention to me---- he seemed to forget that he was a stockholder.*

Q: *When was the last time you saw him?*
A: *I think it is about four years ago.*

Q: *Four years ago this month of May?*
A: *I disremember. It was during the Mardi-Gras season.*

Q: *During the Mardi-Gras season four years ago?*
A: *Yes sir. Now this is 1905, I did not see him Mardi-Gras a year ago. It was 1902 or 1903, the last Mardi-Gras I saw him. I disremember the exact year.*

Q: Now he died in May, 1903; probably that will refresh your memory as to when you saw him?
A: He died in May, 1903?

[Section omitted by author.]

Sworn to & Subscribed before me on this 12th day of May, 1905. —Gabriel Fernandez, Jr.

Some have claimed that the recorder's transcription of Norris' comment, "He [Tumblety] said, if he had his way they would all be disemboweled. Now, I read and new (sic) of the White Chapel business and did know it at the time," is written exactly how Norris stated, meaning Tumblety's comments about disemboweling occurred *after* the 1888 Whitechapel murders. This conflicts with Norris' statement, since he does create a sequential pattern between Tumblety's St. Charles hotel room where he stated that all street walkers should be disemboweled and his 190 Canal Street hotel room where Tumblety sexually assaulted him. Norris stated Tumblety strangely moved from the St. Charles Street hotel room to 190 Canal Street, and when the attorney asked when Tumblety assaulted him at 190 Canal Street, he stated, "1881 or 1880." Corroboration came from the opposing attorney, Mr. Thompson. Immediately after Norris finished discussing the hotel room stories about the large knives, the disembowelment, and the sexual advance, Mr. Thompson objected and moved to have *all* of the testimony be stricken from the record because the circumstances related occurred more than twenty years ago, or earlier than 1885:

Objection by Mr. Thompson: I move that all of this testimony be stricken out as being incompetent, irrelevant and immaterial to the issues presented in this case, having no tendency to show that Dr. Tumilty was of unsound mind or incapable of making a will, appreciating the objects of his bounty, managing his own affairs at the time that the will in question was executed, or at any other time. I object further, because the circumstances related, occurred more than twenty years before the decease of Dr. Tumilty, and have no relation to his condition at the time of his decease. I object to the introduction of further testimony of circumstances occurring at the time.

This is the first time Francis Tumblety is associated with surgical knives, the same kind of knife believed to have been used by Jack the Ripper. This should not be a complete surprise, since most stories reported in the newspaper about people with knives is that the weapon is on their person. Tumblety was arrested on many occasions and his personal belongings reported, yet Norris' testimony does point out that Tumblety kept them in his trunk.

With respect to Tumblety possibly being the Whitechapel murderer, the fact that Norris saw Tumblety with a collection of surgical knives and heard Tumblety say that prostitutes should be disemboweled, is monumental. There are two choices, either Norris told the truth, or he lied. Those who have rejected the idea that Tumblety was a major Scotland Yard suspect dismiss other eyewitness testimonies found in newspaper articles in two ways: they claim either the eyewitness is not credible or point out errors in the facts of the testimony, making all of the facts suspect. In view of this, it is necessary to dig deeper into who Richard Norris was.

Richard Norris was born in 1862, to John and Emily Norris. His father died before 1874. Richard had a brother, John, who was three years his senior. Richard began working as a telegraph operator for American District Telegraph Office for Western Union in 1880 at the age of 17 or 18, and worked in the telephone exchange in the Denegre Building. In 1879, the American District Telegraph Company secured the license rights from the American Bell Telephone Company and organized the first telephone exchange in New Orleans, which was located on the third floor of the Denegre Building on Carondelet Street. In the New Orleans city directories, Norris was listed as a telegraph operator from 1880 to 1886, then in the 1887 city directory he was listed as a telegraph operator at the 8th Precinct Police Station. Occasionally, subsequent city directories recorded Norris as a telegraph operator without mentioning the police department, so he may have begun working for the police department before 1887. Researchers Howard and Nina Brown discovered in the December 10, 1907, issue of the *New Orleans Times Democrat* that Richard Norris worked for the police department for twenty-three years, meaning he began in around 1884. This makes sense, because according to the city directory, his brother John began working for the New Orleans Police Department in 1884, also as a telegraph operator. Both were occasionally recorded in the city directories as being clerks as well. John began his career as a telegraph operator in 1882, and in 1896, John was recorded as a clerk and a superintendent of police. According to the *Times-Picayune*, December 9, 1896, the New Orleans Police Department began the use of the Bertillon System of measuring criminals, based upon the work of the French police officer Alphonse Bertillon (1853 – 1914); an alternative spelling, "Bertillion," was also used, as shown in the subsequent articles. This method was the precursor to identifying with fingerprints. John Norris was put in charge of the Bertillon Department. According to the *Times-Picayune*, February 28, 1918, Richard Norris became his brother's assistant in 1908. The *Times-Picayune*, February 28, 1918, states that Richard Norris was also involved in "taking thumbprints." The article states, "Superintendent Mooney Wednesday afternoon announced the retirement of Richard Norris, veteran assistant Bertillon operator, and four promotions, transfers and assignments among officials at police headquarters . . ." An article discovered by Howard and Nina Brown located in the *New Orleans States*, January 24, 1928, announced Norris' death, and it explained his excellent reputation:

> *Dick Norris is Dead; Mourned. Was Bertillion Expert of Police Department for Many Years.*
> *The older members of the New Orleans police department and thousands of citizens who have had occasion to visit the Bertillion office at police headquarters when that system of identification was first inaugurated in this city, will learn with deep regret of the death of Richard S. Norris, 65 years old, at 5:15 Tuesday morning in Hotel Dieu. Mr. Norris lived at 1932 Jackson avenue. Richard Norris, or 'Dick' Norris, as he was affectionately called by his friends, for many years was assistant Bertillion operator during the time that his brother, John Norris, was*

*head of that department. Together their work was recog-
nized throughout the world of criminal identification in the
United States as most accurate and dependable. John
Norris, head of the department, came to be recognized as
one of perhaps only a half dozen Bertillion operators in
the country whose records were accepted by the Bureau
of Criminal Identification at Washington without question.
And Richard Norris, under the tutelage of his brother,
soon came to enjoy a similar reputation . . .*

Note how Norris worked as both a telegraph operator
and a clerk at the New Orleans Police Station for years,
receiving promotions, then was transferred to an important
position in the Bertillion office. This indicates that Norris was
trustworthy. Also, Norris was married on April 24, 1895, to
Mary Gitz. Admitting he received pay from Tumblety to commit
homosexual acts was not at all helpful to his reputation,
especially since he worked with the police department. Norris
admitted Tumblety sodomized him and that Tumblety would
have to pay for future sexual acts. Tumblety was constantly
searching for the sexual company of young men, and Norris
socialized with him for twenty years, even after his marriage.
Admitting this friendship and Tumblety's sexual attraction to
him was likely more detrimental than beneficial.

The facts Norris gave about Tumblety were amazingly
accurate, especially when the US public did not know that the
misdemeanor charge Tumblety was arrested for in November
1888 (since there was not enough evidence to charge him in
the Whitechapel crimes) was gross indecency and indecent
assault, until the 1990s, eight decades after he testified under
oath. The offenses Tumblety was charged with in London
in 1888 match exactly the offense Norris described that
Tumblety committed against him. The only reference to this
misdemeanor charge in the newspaper reports about Tumblety
being arrested on suspicion stated that he was, "charged for
a trial under a special law passed after the 'Modern Babylon'
exposures." The US public likely had no idea what the Modern
Babylon exposures were, but even if they did, it referenced
the Maiden Tribute of Modern Babylon, which was about
protecting the rights of girls, or maidens. In July 1885, the
editor/investigator for the British newspaper *Pall Mall Gazette*

wrote a series of twelve articles collectively known as, the "Maiden Tribute of Modern Babylon," about the atrocious problem of child prostitution in England, specifically about girls. One article was titled, "The Violation of Virgins." Another article was titled, "How Girls Were Bought and Ruined." The phrase, "Maiden Tribute," referred to the prostitution, abduction, procurement, and sale of young English virgins. In the entire series of articles, the term "girl/girls" was used 91 times and "maiden" used 24 times, while the term "boy/boys" was never used, and "young men" was used only once.

A bill was introduced into legislation in 1881 on the issue, but stalled until the Maiden Tribute of Modern Babylon articles were published and caused public outrage. The Criminal Law Amendment Act of 1885 resulted. Even this particular law had little to do with homosexuality until MP Henry Labouchere pushed for an amendment—later known as the Labouchere Amendment—which clarified the definition of "gross indecency" as any homosexual behavior just short of sodomy.

In fact, a follow-up report from the *New York World*, the very newspaper organization that broke the Modern Babylon connection, in its December 9, 1888, issue, revealed the public's fear of Tumblety with girls. The article was titled, "Afraid of Tumblety,"

> *The school children of Public School No. 25, and the people living in the neighborhood of Sumner and Lewis avenues . . . in Brooklyn, were alarmed yesterday by the report that the notorious Dr. Tumblety, the Whitechapel suspect, has been prowling around that portion of the city insulting young girls.*

The man in question was proven not to be Tumblety, but it does show concern by the public and by the press for Tumblety being around young girls. Incidentally, a question has come up as to why a *New York World* reporter did not ask Tumblety about his gross indecency and indecent assault charge when he interviewed him on January 1, 1889, while in New York City. The answer is now clear: The reporter had no idea about this charge, and Tumblety was not going to bring the embarrassing arrest up.

Taken further, Norris would have had no idea that
Tumblety used to tell young men that they should avoid
women, especially prostitutes. Also, Norris claimed Tumblety
approached him at the theater. There are volumes of reports
of Tumblety going to the theater, even taking young Martin
McGarry to the theater. Further corroboration is twenty-one-
year-old Joseph Mitchell from New Orleans, who stated under
oath that Tumblety introduced himself at the theater.

Norris claimed that around 1900 Tumblety no longer
dressed well and was quite dirty, which was exactly right.
Norris claimed Tumblety handed him a cigar. Tumblety did
indeed smoke cigars all his life:

> S. B. Estey was called, and stated that Dr. Tumblety's
> Christian name was Francis; that he had boarded with
> him about thirteen weeks; that the last he saw of him was
> on Thursday night about 9 o'clock, when he came down
> stairs, lit a cigar and went out.
> —Morning Freeman, New Brunswick, Canada, Sep-
> tember 29, 1860

> 'It was back in the spring of 1870,' he [James Jackson]
> said. 'When I first met Tumblety in Pittsburgh. He was a
> tall, handsome man, excessively dignified and polite, with
> a military bearing. We met on the street, and after a few
> words he invited me to have a cigar at the Monongahela
> House. It was a cold, snowy evening, and, smoking our
> cigars, we walked down to his office.'
> —Cincinnati Enquirer, December 14, 1888

> . . . He dressed expensively and hardly spoke to the ac-
> quaintances of his boyhood . . . He spent money lavishly,
> buying champagne by the case and cigars by the box.
> —The Sun, June 26, 1904

While in St. Louis in 1890, notice how Tumblety used the
cigar as a type of signal for a young man he met:

> Jack The Ripper. The Mysterious Dr. Tumblety Now in St.
> Louis.
> But to his presence in this city. Last night at about
> 10 o'clock, while Donovan's Exchange, in the Chamber of

Commerce building was crowded with billiard players, a large, massively built man strolled into the place. He was six feet and an inch tall, broad shouldered, dark skinned, with an immense jet black mustache that gave to his face a fierce, almost fiendish, expression; his apparel was of the finest quality, but of peculiar fashion; his head gear consisted of a delicately textured silk skull cap, with patent leather peak; he wore a handsome chinchilla overcoat, broadcloth suit—sack coat—patent leather shoes, and cane; much jewelry adorned his person and altogether he was a man hard to place in any walk of life . . . He recognized no one, no one recognized him by word or sign. After a few minutes, he arose, walked deliberately across the hall, seated himself beside a youth and again relapsed into a study. Suddenly, and without speaking a word, he took a cigar from his pocket, gave it to the boy, and, still without a word, left the room, the boy following him.
  —*St. Louis Republic*, April 18, 1890

When Tumblety opened an office in Pittsburgh, it was reported that he was known for giving away boxes of cigars. This habit of Tumblety's was not pasted all over the newspapers, so Norris mentioning this supports him being truthful.

Another observation Norris made about possessions of Tumblety's are also corroborated. Norris stated Tumblety owned a large trunk. Note the following statement that Tumblety added in the *New York Herald* on May 8, 1869:

SAVINGS BANK BOOK STOLEN. – ON OR ABOUT THE 8th of February last a Savings Bank Book, issued by the Provident Institution for Savings in Jersey City to the subscriber as a depositor and numbered 19,354, was stolen from the trunk of the subscriber, which was in his room at his hotel, No. 5 Cortlandt street, in this city of New York, said trunk being found with the lock thereof broken and said book stolen therefrom. Any person who will give information in relation to the thief or restore said bank book to the treasurer of said savings bank, or to the subscriber at 52 Grove street, New York, will receive a suitable reward. FRANCIS TUMBLETY.

While the incident with Norris seeing Tumblety's knife collection and Tumblety saying all street walkers should be disemboweled occurred seven or eight years before the Whitechapel murders in 1888, Norris' sworn testimony was given in 1905. Norris was not working with the New Orleans Police Department at the time, but he was in 1888 and in 1905. Once the Whitechapel murders became public, he recalled telling the chief of police about Tumblety and this incident. What also made Norris suspicious that Tumblety might have been the Jack the Ripper was that he claimed Tumblety had the peculiar habit of always walking the streets alone at all hours of the night, walking like a street walker. Curious, he followed him one night and claimed that Tumblety would take the darkest streets and darkest spots and corners; this habit was corroborated by numerous witnesses, such as Eleanor Elsheimer, an old Rochester neighbor of the Tumblety family. She stated that one evening in the mid-1890s, she was walking at night in downtown Rochester and spotted Tumblety in a dark alley, hiding.

Further corroborating this story is a newspaper report in the New Orleans newspaper, the *Daily-Picayune*, dated December 17, 1888. It states:

> *It has been known for some days past that the detectives have been quietly tracing the career in this city of Dr. Francis Tumblety, one of the suspects under surveillance by the English authorities, and who was recently followed across the ocean by Scotland Yard's men . . . The investigation in this city is understood to be under the direction of English officials now in New York, and based upon certain information they have forwarded by mail.*

Although Tumblety did not request sexual favors on this first occasion, Norris describes the time he eventually did around the same time:

> *He bought me several suits of clothes, and he never attempted to do anything wrong with me until one night he took me to his room, and he locked the door on me. I don't know whether he was humbugging or not, but he did*

*make a bluff at me with one of those big knives. He said,
'You cannot get out of this room while I have this'.*

Further corroborating Norris's story is sworn testimony
from Tumblety's New Orleans lawyer, George F. Bartley.
When Bartley was twenty-one, around 1899, he worked with
Tumblety and stated that the only time he saw him was during
the carnival season, i.e., Mardi Gras in February. This is
exactly what Norris stated the time was when he would meet
Tumblety each year:

[Met Tumblety] *About six years ago* [1899]*, I believe . . .
The only time I saw him was during the carnival season.
. . . I saw his negligent appearance; his wearing apparel
was none too clean, and I immediately saw that he was a
man of rather eccentric habits . . .*

One of the last recorded incidents of Tumblety showing an
unusual hatred of women occurred in Baltimore, Maryland.
His first Baltimore attorney, Robert Simpson, stated under
oath that Tumblety had no use for women. When asked to
elaborate, Simpson stated, "If the question of women was
brought up why the first thing he would do would be to turn
his nose up. . ." Sworn testimony of his second Baltimore
lawyer, Frank M. Widner Jr., shows how his hatred brought
out fear and a concern for her safety in the woman targeted by
his negative attention. Widner stated that Tumblety visited his
office in November 1901, and stayed for an extended period
of time because of a bout of dizzy spells. The lawyer allowed
him to recline on his bench. Any time a woman would visit
the office and walk near him, Widner stated Tumblety would
shield his face with a newspaper:

*'If a lady happened to come into my office, he would
take a newspaper—he generally had a newspaper in his
hands—and hold it in front of his face to shield him from
the lady.'*

When asked, "Did these incidents actually happen?"
Widner replied, "Yes, they all happened in my office; not at

one time, but at various times." The lawyer received a phone call, and at that time, the offices had one phone in another room. He left his office with Tumblety at the seat and a woman seated in another area of the room. When he finished his call, he returned, finding the woman waiting outside his office. Widner continued:

> *'I asked what was the matter; she said she was not going to stay in there with that fellow. She said she was afraid to stay in there.'*

Even though Tumblety did not leave his seat, his peculiar actions caused her to leave the room. The lawyer stated that he knew this woman not to be a nervous type of person. The event was significant enough for him to be extra cautious of Tumblety any time he visited his office afterward. The lawyer, himself, felt uneasy with Tumblety after this. Tumblety gave him a cigar, and Widner stated that he accepted the cigar, but never smoked it, fearing his client may have tampered with it. Widner then recalled another incident.

> *'I remember one day he came into my office in the period from May 1902 to July 1902, sat himself on the edge of the chair, as he usually did, in an attitude that was really threatening. He was talking excitedly about, I should say, to the best of my recollection, the papers that Simpson had retained in this case of the United States Engraving Co., and the attitude he assumed toward me was such that I drew back my chair from my desk and assumed a position of defense, in case he should spring upon me. I was very much afraid that the man would make some movement, his attitude was so threatening, and he was so nervous . . . He had worked himself up to a state of mind that was not at all compatible with the amount involved, or with the importance of the case, because I knew I could procure the papers for him by process.'*

Recall, Dr. Brent Turvey identified anger-retaliatory behavioral patterns at the crime scenes of the Whitechapel murders. In cases of other serial killers exhibiting anger-retaliatory behavior, rape was usually involved. For example,

James Mitchell "Mike" DeBardeleben, born in 1940, was convicted for rape and counterfeiting and had been in prison since the 1980s, but was later discovered to have raped and murdered. DeBardeleben's third wife stated he told her, "all women were whores, sluts, tramps. They asked for what they got." If Tumblety was Jack the Ripper, one of his motives was likely anger-retaliatory, but in his case, he could not have raped, which will be explained in the following chapter.

4

Frank Tumblety –
His Formative Days

*"I am her son," replied young Frank Tumblety, "and I have just
come over from Ireland."*
     —Rochester neighbor, Eleanor R. Elsheimer

Psychologists specializing in violent abnormal behavior
have actually created a list of childhood indicators of a
prospective serial offender. This makes sense, since the latest
research in cognitive neuroscience shows that the personality
disorders of most serial offenders are both developmental in
origin as well as genetic. While serial offenders come in many
bitter flavors, a deeper understanding of Tumblety's life just
might be revealing. There is one, lone eyewitness account of
Francis Tumblety in Ireland. Under sworn testimony in 1905,
Michael Fitzsimons, Tumblety's nephew five years his junior,
recalled an event. He stated that in 1842/43, in Ireland, when
he was five years old and Francis was ten, he was escorted to
the local schoolhouse by Francis. Being literate would have
been a valuable asset to the alternative physicians he would
begin working for in Rochester, New York, by 1850/51.

  Francis Tumblety was, in early twentieth-century terms, a
hermaphrodite, possessing both male and female genitals. In
sworn testimony in front of the probate court in 1905, Robert
H. Simpson, the lawyer out of Baltimore, Maryland, stated he
was Francis Tumblety's attorney from 1894 to the spring of
1902. He stated he first met Tumblety at Simpson's mother's
home in 1890. His mother knew Tumblety in Liverpool,

England, years earlier. Simpson stated he was in school at
the time, so it was not until 1894 that he was in contact
with Tumblety as his counsel "a great deal." The first time he
knew of Tumblety's habit to prowl for boys and young men at
night was in 1900 when Tumblety approached him for legal
assistance. A lady who lived on Pierce Street had Tumblety
arrested by the police. Tumblety had taken her little boy to
Druid Hill Park, gave him some confectionary candy, then
sodomized him. When the boy told his mother what Tumblety
had done, he was arrested. Simpson advised Tumblety to
give the lady $100, which he did. Simpson then recalled an
incident at his office when Tumblety's trousers fell down:

> . . . *in the fall of 1902 he had a fainting spell in my office;
> he was sitting on a chair with no arms and he fell off; I
> raised the window and opened his coat and I noticed he
> wore no suspenders; he was breathing very heavily; my
> brother was present; I opened his trouser and as I say
> he wore no suspenders **and he seemed to be shaped
> like a woman;** we picked him up and in picking him up
> his trousers came down and I noticed **he had a penis
> that was scarcely as large as the end of your finger.**
> We said nothing to him about it; he was then stopping
> on Saratoga street; he staid [sic] away a couple of days;
> it seemed to worry him; he came back and asked what
> he did while he was in that condition; I told him he had
> a fainting spell and I said, you ought to go and get some
> treatment; he told me, I know what is the matter with me,
> I have heart trouble and everything becomes blank to me;
> everything turns dark; I to him, you ought to wear sus-
> penders. (Objection, accepted) That* [their conversation]
> *was in my office; I said to him then **I asked him the
> question whether or not he was a hermaphrodite;**
> the reason I asked him was I had heard it before; I had
> heard so much **from various police about him** I thought
> I would put the question to him just for curiosity; he asked
> me, What do you ask that for; I said, your trousers came
> down and we saw everything you had; he said, do not
> ever tell that to anybody; **that is a misfortune which
> has followed me all through my life;** that is true; an-
> other characteristic about him was he had a voice
> like a girl* . . ." [Author emphasis added.]

There are numerous sources corroborating Tumblety's hermaphroditic condition. When Tumblety locked Richard Norris in the room in New Orleans, and after showing him his knife collection and telling him that all street walkers should be disemboweled, Norris claimed Tumblety made physical advances on him. He stated Tumblety approached the bed:

> . . . *unbuttoned his pants, and showed me something,* ***and he told me he was not good****. He was trembling, and was very nervous. He asked me to go to bed with him,* ***that he enjoyed it just as much as a woman did****. Of course, I did not know at the time the difference between* ***a morphadite****, and never did now that he was a* ***morphadite*** *before. So he got in bed and* ***cocked his legs up****, but I did not get down and look at him; I stood off and looked at him; and he insisted upon* ***my having connection with him****. I told him I would do this to-morrow; and he did everything, coaxed me, and done everything, offered me money, and made me promise that I* ***would*** *be back the next morning at 10 o'clock.* [Author emphasis added.]

In Norris' cross-examination, it becomes apparent that Norris was open to male prostitution, or "taking a trick." He was first asked by the attorney, "Did I understand you to say that twenty years ago you examined his person sufficiently to see that he was neither man nor woman, but was what was commonly called a morphadite or a hermaphrodite?" Norris replied that he did and there was no doubt about that. Norris was then asked if Tumblety asked him to have sexual relations. Norris stated:

> *Yes, sir. I could tell you more than that. He threw me on the bed and we had quite a tussle. He threw me on top of him, but I was a pretty handy youngster myself then, was a wild fellow and took all sorts of chances, I was on the money side, saw he was stuck on me and I said, "I have got a price if you want me to do anything like that." I went over and told my friend Doyle about it, and he said, "Why don't you take a trick at him to see how it goes."*

The fact that Tumblety's penis was the size of the tip of a person's thumb is corroborated by the sworn statement made by Fred Nash, the undertaker who embalmed Tumblety's body in 1903. In so doing, it also demonstrates the veracity of Norris' testimony. At the State of Missouri Special Commissioner's Inquiries in the Tumblety 1903 will and testament case, which began on August 26, 1904, and continued to June 20, 1905, Fred Nash was sworn and cross examined about anything unusual with the corpse of Francis Tumblety. Nash stated:

> *Well, his testicle—he had only one testicle—and his penis was about the size of the end of your thumb—your thumbnail.*

Another condition Tumblety may have suffered from other than hermaphroditism is having a micro-penis, where there is no genital ambiguity between male and female organs, since there is no vagina. In certain hermaphroditic cases, the scrotum covers the vagina, and Tumblety's response to Simpson leaves little doubt that Tumblety had both male and female sex organs. Possessing both male and female sex organs is now termed as intersex, yet Tumblety clearly identified and appeared as a male. Some hermaphrodites identify as a female and exhibit mostly female features. A peculiar comment in an eyewitness testimony in the *New York World* now makes sense and seems to corroborate Tumblety as a person exhibiting some female features whether he admitted or not. Once it was discovered on November 18, 1888, that Francis Tumblety was arrested on suspicion for the Whitechapel murders and hailed from New York City, spending time in the posh Fifth Avenue Hotel, a *New York World* reporter went to the hotel searching for stories and found some. In an article titled, "He is a Mystery to All, Who and What is 'Dr' Twomblety, the Whitechapel Suspect?" published in the November 26, 1888, edition, James Pryor, the detective of the Fifth Avenue Hotel, recalled numerous experiences with Tumblety beginning in the 1860s. The reporter asked Pryor if he remembered if Tumblety had "antipathy for women." Pryor stated:

He seemed indifferent to them. I never saw him in all his walks up and down Broadway look at a woman. He never appeared to care for them, and many a time I have seen women look after him, for he was a very handsome fellow. He had the smallest hand and foot I ever saw.

Recall, Simpson stated Tumblety had the voice of a girl, and that, plus his diminutive hands and feet, make the point that Tumblety exhibited male and female characteristics beyond just his genitals. The other Baltimore attorney, Frank M. Widner Jr., was also asked under oath in 1905 about his interactions with Tumblety, although the two lawyers were not acquaintances. In court, he was asked by the attorney, "Any peculiarity in his voice?" Widner responded, "His voice was never one that would strike you as being very magnetic, or anything of that sort, but as I recall now it was rather a light voice, not very deep." The attorney asked, "Rather an effeminate voice?" and Widner responded, "Yes, I should say so." Agreeing that Tumblety's voice was effeminate—defined as a male showing characteristics typically regarded as those of a woman—supports the veracity of Simpson's comments. Further, in the *Washington Post,* November 18, 1890, the newspaper recorded Tumblety having an effeminate voice: "His eyes are steely blue, and he gazed steadily at nothing, as he spoke in a weak, effeminate voice. He was dressed in a big black overcoat and wore a German cap, and had on rubber boots." Tumblety stated that his sexual dysfunction misfortune had followed him all through his life. During childhood, he would have discovered he was different, then during adolescence, this intersex condition would have been at the forefront of his life. He was so bothered by this condition that just weeks before he died, in 1903, he refused to allow the attending physicians at the St. John's Hospital in to observe him naked. Dr. Francis Temm, the attending physician at St. John's Hospital, was asked under oath in 1905 if he knew what a hermaphrodite was. After Temm explained that it is a condition where a person "has the apparent genitals of both sexes," the attorney asked, "You say this patient [Tumblety] refused to allow you to strip him and examine him?" Temm replied, "Yes, sir. I was very glad he did, too." The attorney then asked, "He was quite a filthy fellow when you saw him there first, wasn't he?" Temm replied, "Yes sir." The judge then forced the conversation to stop, so the Temm did not answer any more questions on Tumblety's intersex condition.

Because Tumblety had predominantly male features, he may have had a particular intersex condition called Partial Androgen Insensitivity Syndrome, or PAIS. PAIS is the inability of the cell to respond to androgens, male hormones, such as testosterone. There is phenotypic grading of individuals from those with male genitals looking like immature male genitals to, progressively, individuals with the male genitals looking more like female genitals. On the other extreme, an individual possesses a vaginal channel. The phenotypical grading is called the Quigley Scale. Research on individuals with PAIS also identifies a pattern of psychological difficulties, not necessarily related to violent behavior.

This leads to an interesting problem with the issue of motives of homosexual serial offenders. Assuming Tumblety possessed both male and female features, i.e., he was neither male nor female, it then follows that his sexual attraction for young men did not make him a homosexual. Tumblety did indeed identify outwardly as a male being referred to by everyone as "he," but he knew he was different. It may not have been a case of him being a proponent of homosexuality, but one of an opponent to heterosexuality. In view of this, if Tumblety was the Whitechapel fiend, his motive would have had nothing to do with his own sexual preference but his opposition to heterosexuality and his antipathy toward a specific type of female. Besides the sworn testimony of Michael Fitzsimons recalling one event with Tumblety in Ireland as children, there is no evidence of his upbringing in order to determine if he experienced any childhood abuse or trauma. What can be investigated, though, is what his environment was like during his formative stage.

Siobhán Pat Mulcahy, a crime writer, historian, and former college teacher, lives in Ireland, and took up the challenge to discover Tumblety's family in Ireland. Mulcahy has published articles in numerous journals, and is the author of *The Peculiar Sex Life of Adolf Hitler* (2016). In 2013, she published an article in *Anglo-Celt* on the Irish origins of Francis Tumblety, and then followed through with a second article in *The Whitechapel Society Journal,* titled "Francis Tumblety, Madame X and the Voyage from Hell." Although she did not find documents showing Francis Tumblety or his direct family living in Ireland, Mulcahy found the next best thing: a woman living in County Cavan in Northern Ireland claiming to be related to Francis Tumblety. The woman told Mulcahy that she wanted to remain anonymous, not wanting to be associated with a suspect of Jack the Ripper. She explained that the family name spelling was originally "Tumulty," and the clan was from the town of Killycollie (now Bailliebourough). Other variant forms of Francis' family name in the historical records are Tumblety, Tumlty, Tumilty, Tumelty, Tumalty, Tumuelty, Timilty, and even Tumeltee. She knew of Francis' parents, James and Margaret, stating James was born around 1776, which does indeed match the birth of Francis' father as recorded on the family gravestone at a Catholic cemetery in Rochester, New York. She stated they had eleven children, Francis being the youngest, with three dying at childbirth or shortly thereafter. She then explained that James began as a traveling farm laborer, then eventually became tenant farmer, one of the occupations of the lower-class poor in early nineteenth century Ireland. At the time, Catholic tenant farmers rented small parcels of land from predominately Protestant landowners.

Is the Tumulty relative living in Cavan, Ireland, correct that they came from a poor tenant farm or did Francis come from a wealthy family, as he once claimed to an acquaintance around 1880? Tumblety's nephew Michael Fitzsimons stated under oath that Francis Tumblety was born in County Meath, which is adjacent to County Cavan, and Killycollie is next to the Meath border. A record of the Tumulty family living in Ireland has finally been discovered, recording an event nine years before Francis was even born. The 1821 Ireland census shows Francis' father, James Tumulty, aged 36 (b. 1785), as a farmer in County Meath, Donaghpatrick Parish, Tankardstown, living with his wife Margaret, aged 33 (b. 1788). The following are their children as recorded in the census. I have purposely added their names as they were later recorded and the sisters' married names:

1. Alice, aged 13 (Alice T. Fitzsimons, 1808–1883)
2. Bridget, aged 11 (Bridget Brodigan, 1810–1853)
3. Judith, aged 9 (Judith/Julia Moore, b. 1812)

4. Bitty, aged 7 (Elizabeth Powderly, b. 1814)
5. Mary, aged 5 (Mary Kavanagh, b. 1816)
6. Larry, aged 3 (Lawrence, 1818–1898)
7. Patt, aged 1 (Patrick J., 1820–1859)

The following are their children born after the 1821 Irish census:

8. Margaret Kelly (b. 1824)
9. Ann Mahoney (b. 1827)
10. Jane Hayes (1828/29–abt. 1904)
11. Francis (1830–1903)

The 1821 Irish census corroborates the claim of the anonymous living Cavan relative on numerous points, such as James being a farmer, his last name being spelled "Tumulty," his wife being Margaret, and the children. Note that the names of the children, genders, ages, and sequential order are close to later census material, city directories, and testimonies. The relative was also surprisingly accurate about location. Although the family is not recorded in County Cavan, County Meath shares a border, and next to that border is the town of Killycollie. James initially worked as a traveling farm laborer, which means he may very well have worked in the neighboring county just a few miles away.

Researcher Roger Palmer discovered further corroboration in 2014 for the family's origins in County Meath from a history book titled *History of Rochester and Monroe County* (New York and Chicago Pioneer, 1908). It states, "Michael H. Fitzsimons, who for many years was one of the prominent real-estate owners in Rochester, and, during the '70s and '80s, was a leader in its municipal government, was born in Castletown, County Meath, Ireland, on the 27th of July, 1838." Castletown is just a few miles north of the Tankardstown area.

In "The Great Famine in Cavan" (irishidentity.com), Ciaran Parker and Anna Sexton explain that for two decades leading up to the Great Famine, poor Irish farming communities were living well below the poverty level, almost to the point of economic collapse. In the early nineteenth century, rural communities in Ireland enjoyed a flax linen industry, where cottages and cabins were outfitted for spinning the strong fibers of the flax plant into linen cloth. Women living on farms would spin flax in their homes and earn extra income, as in the case with Margaret Tumulty recorded in the 1821 census. Just four years later in 1825, the rural flax linen industry collapsed because of the advent of industrialization and the mechanized production of flax linen in factories near Belfast. Entire rural communities experienced widespread economic stress. In the *London Times*, January 3, 1837, an article discussed the small town of Navan in County Meath, about 26 miles west of Dublin, where neighborhoods consisted of the poor living in the most deplorable conditions "almost as a season of famine" (*Meath Chronicle*, 1980, Rev. Gerard Rice, "Articles on the History of Navan").

It was around this time we see Tumblety's second-oldest sister, Bridget, and her husband, Christopher Brodigan, in the 1841 census living in Liverpool, England, then moving to neighboring Widnes. Their daughter, Margaret, was born in Widnes on August 11, 1842. Bridget died in 1853 and Christopher died in 1854. Soon, Margaret married Thomas Brady, a plumber in Widnes, in 1862. In his 1903 will and testament, Francis Tumblety bequeathed money to his niece, "Mrs. Thomas Brady of 20 Frederick Street, Widnes." Tumblety's third-oldest sister Judith, or Julia, married a John Moore from Dublin. Their daughter Catherine (Way) is listed in the 1871 and 1881 England & Wales censuses being born in Ireland in 1834. Researcher Roger Palmer discovered a marriage record in the *Bath Chronicle and Weekly Gazette*, November 23, 1865, stating, "November 15, at the Roman Catholic Church of St. John the Evangelist, Mr. Joseph Way, of the Hotwells, Clifton, to Catherine, eldest daughter of the late Mr. John Moore, of Dublin." Just north of Clifton in Trym, Gloucestershire, England, the 1851 census has Julia Moor as head of household, aged 40, born in County Meath, Ireland, with daughter Catherine Moor, aged 17, born in County Meath, and daughter Ann, aged 5, born in Bristol, St. Michaels.

While rural Ireland was experiencing economic stress in the early nineteenth century, northeast United States was experiencing an economic explosion, and records indicate the number of Irish immigrating to America was on the rise. New York was experiencing its own economic prosperity thanks to the Erie Canal. Tumblety's oldest sister, Alice, and her husband, Michael Fitzsimmons, immigrated to New York in or around 1843. It was at this time we see Tumblety's oldest brother, Lawrence, in the Rochester City Directory. Lawrence and Alice were not the first in Francis' immediate family to have immigrated to the United States and then to Rochester, New York. Francis' fifth-oldest sister, Mary, fourteen years his senior, had married a blacksmith named Michael Kavanagh (b. 1813) prior to 1839. The Kavanaghs were a family of blacksmiths, and a number of them had moved to Rochester by 1830. A Michael "Kavanaugh" is first identified in the Rochester City Directory in 1838. Their first child, John, was born in 1839 in New York. It seems Lawrence's short stay in Rochester in 1844 was likely because of visiting his sister Mary. In view of this, Mary, Lawrence, and Alice immigrated to New York before the Great Irish Famine. Francis, though, lived through the Great Famine as an adolescent.

With such a small amount of land, tenant farmers were extremely limited on which crop could bring in enough money to both pay rent and feed the family. The only harvest available to satisfy these needs was the potato crop and only in one major variety, the Lumper. It quickly became the singular crop produced by the poor farming community in Ireland. Producing only one major crop made up of very uniform genetics made it highly susceptible to significant crop destruction by only a single disease, and that is exactly what happened in September 1845. The late potato crop was almost entirely decimated by a new strain of potato blight fungus. Never did two successive potato harvests get destroyed, which convinced the English government that only limited relief was necessary in Ireland. They believed the early potato crop harvest in 1846 would alleviate the problem. This did not happen; in fact, the entire 1846 potato crop, both early and late harvest, failed. Exacerbating the crisis was that the British government took on a Laissez-Faire approach, as they did with all social and economic issues in Ireland. The government expected local Irish taxes to carry the burden of relief. Instead, local economic collapse occurred along with mass starvation in what became known as the Great Irish Potato Famine, or the Great Famine. While there were relief efforts, they were too little too late.

Being poor tenant farmers with an already impoverished existence, Francis Tumblety and his family experienced the full and immediate impact of potato crop destruction, and would have felt the resulting sufferance full force. Francis would have been fifteen years old when the first crops failed on his father's farm. Mulcahy discusses the physical and mental anguish young Francis must have observed and experienced in his formative years in Ireland during the crisis. According to the Cavan County Museum, as conditions hit crisis level in 1847, soup kitchens were feeding up to 16,000 people daily. Poorhouses, or workhouses, were established in urban centers and were inundated by malnourished men, women, and children coming in droves from the countryside. Ripperologist Joe Chetcuti, in his article, "Forest of the Boar," published in *Ripperologist 136*, February 20, 2014, makes a chilling comparison, demonstrating the impact upon the community where the Tumblety clan lived. He stated that the local poorhouse housed nearly 1,500 inmates, all weakened by malnutrition, and many stricken with dysentery, typhoid, and typhus, in a town of just a few thousand residents. This was a significant percentage of the population. At times, dead bodies were often seen on the roadsides. According to Mulcahy, by January 1847, when the *Poor Law* went into effect, forcing local Protestant property owners to fund the relief efforts, the property owners realized paying their way to emigrate was less costly than evicting them and forcing them into the poorhouses. The Cavan County Museum states that between 1845 and 1853, landlords in Ireland evicted 87,123 starving families.

Fifteen-year-old Francis Tumblety witnessed the mass destruction of the potato crops in 1845, beginning the most devastating period of the Great Famine, a time already filled with emotional and physical change in himself as a child undergoing puberty. While entire tenant farming families, including his own, were evicted by the landlords, he was now living a life in the poorhouses and soup kitchens facing famine and disease; Tumblety was also experiencing adolescence and dealing with a sexual orientation considered taboo.

The earliest evidentiary record of Francis Tumblety is his name listed on the passenger manifest of the ship he arrived in the United States in, the *Ashburton,* a.k.a., *Lord Ashburton,* albeit his last name is spelled differently. The *Ashburton* left Liverpool, England, on May 21, 1847, and arrived at New York Harbor on June 24, 1847, over one month in transit. It records Francis "Tumbleton" and three family members immigrating to the United States. First listed was a Jas. (James), aged 26; followed by Margaret, aged 52; Francis, aged 17; and lastly Ann, aged 20. There is corroborating evidence to suggest this was indeed Francis and a few of his family members, at least confirming the year he immigrated. Tumblety was involved in a court case in New York in the spring of 1861, as reported in the *New York Evening Express* on April 1, 1861. Tumblety took the stand, and under cross examination, he stated that the first time he was in New York City was 1847; clearly referring to when his ship arrived from Ireland. In view of this, Francis Tumblety was born in Ireland in or about 1830.

His month-long trip on the *Ashburton* was likely just as horrific as living through the Great Famine, if not more so. Mulcahy gives vivid detail of the severe suffering the men, women, and children went through as they immigrated to the United States onboard the coffin, or famine, ships. She pays special attention to the vessel *Lord Ashburton,* since Francis immigrated to New York on this ship. It was a wooden, three-masted ship built in 1843; 155 feet in length and 33 feet in width (its beam). In 1847, the Liverpool docks where the *Ashburton* left were filled with destitute Irish in hopes of gaining approval to embark on the coffin ships. Many were rejected if the health officers spotted any signs of being ill, what was generally referred to as "Irish fever." Mulcahy points out that nearly 300,000 Irish arrived at the Liverpool docks in 1847, and nearly 15,000 were sent back to Ireland. A coffin ship's diarist, Stephen de Vere, highlights the atrocious life onboard a coffin ship as it crossed the Atlantic. He used phrases such as "wallowing in filth," "huddled together, sick in body, dispirited in heart," and "breathing a fetid atmosphere." Mulcahy states how appalling life was on the *Ashburton*:

> For example, when the Lord Ashburton, arrived at Quebec on October 30, 1847 dangerously late in the season, carrying 477 passengers, 174 of them [Lord Palmerston's tenants from Co. Sligo] were almost naked: 87 of them

had to be clothed by charity before they could, with de-
cency, leave the ship. During the voyage, 107 persons
had died of fever and dysentery; 60 were ill. The Quebec
Gazette described the condition of the Lord Ashburton as
'a disgrace to the home authorities'.

The first recorded event involving Francis Tumblety in
Western New York occurred on the very day he arrived at the
doorstep of his Rochester home on the corner of South Sophia
Street and Magnolia. In a sworn deposition in May 1905,
by the daughter of James McMullen, Eleanor R. Elsheimer
recalled to attorneys when her father first met Francis
Tumblety. An attorney asked, "What was the occasion of
your father's first acquaintance with him [Francis Tumblety]?
Eleanor replied, "My father said he went up home to his
mother's, and he said that his mother had gone up to Mrs.
Tumilty's. He said he looked over the hill and saw a little boy
with velveteen knee pants, with a stick over his shoulders, and
he asked my father if Mrs. Tumilty lived there. He said I am
her son, and I have just come over from Ireland, and father
took him up there to his mother. He said he was then about
twelve years of age." The attorney then asked, "Do you know
what was his first employment in this country?" She replied,
"I heard father say that he got Frank Tumilty his first position
on the canal." In cross examination, another attorney asked,
"How old was the doctor at that time?" She replied, "Twelve
or fourteen years old, I don't know for certain." The attorney
then asked, "Your father was a grown man?" She replied,
"Yes, he was a man of twenty years of age." She also explained
that her father was married at the time, and according to
census records, this occurred around 1845. According to
the 1844/45/46 Rochester City directories, Eleanor's father,
John McMullen, was a carman (meaning he drove a wagon to
transport goods similar to a modern-day delivery driver) along
with his father, James McMullen, and both lived on the corner
of South Sophia and Bartlett since 1827. This means they did
indeed live next to the Tumilty residence at South Sophia and
Magnolia Street. The Tumiltys are not listed in the 1847/48
directory but are in the 1849/50 directory. John McMullen
was born in 1825, making him approximately five years older
than Francis Tumblety, who was born in 1830.

If Eleanor was accurate about her father being around twenty years old, along with the date of his marriage, Francis Tumblety arrived in Rochester no earlier than 1845. This, along with the Tumilty family listed in the 1849/50 directory, shows that Francis arrived in Rochester between 1845 and 1849. Recall, the earliest record of Francis Tumblety is his name listed on the passenger manifest of the *Ashburton* on June 24, 1847. In view of this, James McMullen's first meeting with Francis Tumblety must have been between late 1847 and 1849. A seeming conflict with this scenario is that Francis was recorded in the passenger manifest as being seventeen years old, not twelve to fifteen, but then again, Eleanor's father was only going by physical appearances, and Francis may have looked younger than he was. Eleanor even admitted he could have been older. In sworn testimony at the probate court trial in 1905 of the disposition of Francis Tumblety's will, Tumblety's nephew Michael Fitzsimons stated under oath that the first time he saw Francis Tumblety in Rochester was in 1848.

Conforming temporally to these events is Tumblety's 1861 sworn testimony during a court case, as recorded by a *New York Evening Express* reporter, published in their April 1, 1861, issue. In the spring of 1861, Tumblety sued the Chemical Bank for accepting a $400 forged check against his account. According to a reporter present, during cross-examination, Tumblety explained that he "came to this city [New York City] in 1847," and "after staying for a time in the city went to Rochester, where he stayed for nine years." This explains how Tumblety could have immigrated with his mother to New York City yet arrive in Rochester after her, as noted by Eleanor Elsheimer about young Tumblety inquiring to her father where his mother lived. Francis' mother probably continued onto Rochester immediately with some family members in 1847 and Francis temporarily stayed with family members who lived in New York City.

Interestingly, Francis' older brother Lawrence, twelve years his senior, immigrated to the United States prior to the 1845/46 Irish potato crop destruction. Lawrence Tumulty is in the 1844 Rochester City Directory, albeit not living at the future Tumulty residence near Magnolia Street. Francis' oldest sister, Alice, twenty years his senior, married Michael

Fitzsimmons in Ireland around 1830/31, and claimed in the 1900 census that she immigrated to the United States in 1843. The close dates suggest Lawrence immigrated with Alice and Michael. The 1845 New York City directory has a Michael Fitzsimmons living next to relatives, so the couple stayed in New York City while Lawrence continued to Rochester. Biographical data on Civil War officer and Illinois National Guard general Charles Fitzsimons, son of Alice and Michael, states he lived as a child in New York City until 1848, when the family moved to Rochester, New York (*Memorials of Deceased Companions of the Commandery of the State of Illinois Military Order of the Loyal Legion of the United States, v.2, 320 Ashland Block, Chicago*, Illinois, 1912). The 1849 Rochester City Directory shows that Lawrence had finally moved into the Tumblety homestead on South Sophia Street near Magnolia Street, and living next to him was likely his father, James. Lawrence's mother, Margaret, sister Ann, and brother Francis are not listed, because they were not the head of household. All were in Rochester in the 1850 census with the exception of James, but since he died in Rochester in 1851, he must have been in the area. Their neighbors at South Sophia, which was renamed Plymouth Avenue that year, were Francis' sister Alice Fitzsimmons, and her family.

Taking the Rochester City Directory information into account, Francis likely stayed with Michael and Alice Fitzsimmons in New York City. He may even have traveled to Rochester with them in 1847/48 when they moved to Rochester.

The aforementioned dates and locations conform to the following scenario: When Francis arrived in New York Harbor with parents James and Margaret, and sister Ann, they were greeted by Francis' sister Alice, and brother Lawrence, and possibly even their sister Mary. Within one year, the Tumblety family and the Fitzsimons family moved to Rochester, New York, together, purchasing land one mile southwest of downtown on South Sophia and Magnolia. Francis' brother Patrick Tumilty is also found in the 1849 Rochester City directory, but as head of household in his own right at a different address. Census records show he married his wife, Mary, in Ireland, thus they lived elsewhere on Rapids Street (now Brooks Avenue), located three-quarters of a mile farther southwest. There is a suggestion that the James, aged 29, who immigrated with Francis on the *Ashburton*, was Patrick James Tumilty, but was merely referred to by his middle name. While this happened quite often, a major problem with this in the case of Patrick is that his wife and children, all recorded in the censuses as being born in Ireland, were with him in Rochester in 1848. They likely immigrated together, and the family is not on the *Ashburton* passenger manifest.

It has been suggested that Francis Tumblety's father, James (b. 1776/7), came to the United States with son Lawrence prior to the rest of the family in order to earn enough money to pay for their remaining family's passage to America—this being matriarch Margaret, and children James, Ann, and Francis—on the *Ashburton* in 1847. This theory is almost plausible, since the cost of one ticket on a transatlantic ship in 1847 was £7, totaling £28 for Margaret, James, Ann, and Francis, which would have been roughly $1,500 today. However, the majority of the facts do not support James the elder traveling to America first. Recall, Lawrence was in Rochester, New York, before the Great Famine hit crisis level in 1846. Further, James was nearing seventy years of age and was close to the end of his working career as a laborer. Patrick, in his mid-twenties, would have been a better choice to survive the rough trip across the Atlantic and quickly earn the money, yet Patrick did not arrive until 1848. So far, nowhere has there been discovered a James Tumulty/Tumilty of the correct age range recorded in the passenger and immigration lists before 1847. It seems more likely that once Lawrence, Mary, and Alice were made aware of the family's crisis, they bore the responsibility of buying the tickets for their remaining relatives—if the Irish tenant landowners did not do so in the first place.

5

Dr. Francis Tumblety: The Celebrated Indian Herb Doctor

He would dash through the streets mounted on a superb white horse, followed by a troop of thoroughbred hounds, and arrayed in the most gorgeous style. Practice poured into him, he charged whatever fee he pleased and made money rapidly.
—*Evening Star,* November 27, 1888

The Doctor [Tumblety] *proceeded to open them* [letters] *leisurely and smilingly before the gaping inmates. Two or three of them were seen to contain bank bills, of what denominations was not visible. The Doctor carelessly extracted them, observing jocosely, that he called that operation "gutting."*
—*New Era,* November 3, 1857 (reprint from *Tonawanda Volksblatt,* September 31, 1857)

The very first evidence of Francis Tumblety opening an office and practicing his chosen lucrative profession as an "alternative" doctor was in the spring of 1856 in London, Ontario, Canada. He advertised himself in the local papers as the "Great Indian Herb Doctor." Tumblety was reported in the *London Free Press,* May 6, 1856, treating a local resident named Mrs. Carden. Additional evidence of Tumblety opening an office in London, Ontario, in 1856, can be seen in his 1866 autobiography, where he claimed to have received endorsements of his successful treatment from the mayor of London, Ontario, W. Baker, and from the editor of the local newspaper, *London Atlas*, Hamilton Hunter. The mayor's name was William Barker, and he was mayor only for the year of 1856. Hamilton Hunter was indeed the chief editor for the *London Atlas* in 1856.

The last record of Francis Tumblety prior to him opening a London, Ontario, office in 1856 is in the 1851/52 Rochester, New York, city directory. It shows a Franklin Tumilty as a "pedlar" living with his brother Lawrence and his widowed mother Margaret on South Sophia Street, which soon got renamed Plymouth Avenue. Francis' father, James, died on May 7, 1851, so in the four or five years after his father's death, Tumblety acquired the knowledge and skills to operate and advertise as a successful Indian herb doctor.

Tumblety's first experience with alternative medicine was not herbal, or even botanical, in nature, but sexual. When he began to operate as an Indian herb doctor, he was also selling medical pamphlets on the French cures for the "secret habits of young men." His pamphlets were nearly identical to a Dr. Lispenard's "Practical Private Medical Guide." This makes sense, because in 1851, Tumblety worked for Dr. Lispenard as a "pedlar." Lispenard operated an office on 14 Exchange Place in downtown Rochester and was also listed in the 1851/52 Rochester directory. His 1850 advertisement stated:

> *Established A.D. 1850. Great Combined Talent! Dr. E.J. Reynolds, Proprietor W.C. Lispenard, M.D., Consulting Physician & Surgeon, Rochester, N.Y. This is the only office in the city where a permanent cure of private diseases can be had without the use of mercury or a change of diet. We guarantee to cure Gonorrhea, Gleet, Syphilis, Impotency, Nocturnal Emissions, or Self Abuse, Diurnal Emissions, Female Complaints, in short, every possible form and variety of Sexual Disease. Dr. Reynolds' Patent French Safe is warranted a safe and sure preventative against pregnancy and disease. Dr. Reynolds' great work, THE PRIVATE MEDICAL GUIDE, beautifully illustrated, with nearly 800 pages. Price 25 cents. Consulting office and Operating Rooms, corner of Mill and Market streets, up stairs. All letters addressed to Dr. E.J. Reynolds, Rochester, N.Y.*

It was soon discovered that William C. Lispenard and Ezra J. Reynolds were one and the same person, and Lispenard was a pseudonym. Reynolds was born in 1827 in Columbia County, New York, just south of Albany, and moved to Rochester in late 1850, being recorded in the 1850 census as living in Albany. He actually operated his Albany office concurrently with his Rochester office at least until 1853. The French pseudonym Lispenard was used by Reynolds as an advertising strategy, since the common belief was that the French better understood sexuality, including cures for sexual diseases. The *New York World*, December 2, 1888, records a canal boat captain named W. C. Streeter, an eyewitness, who claimed around 1848 that young Francis jumped on his boat and peddled books and papers on the packets largely "of the kind Anthony Comstock suppresses now." (Anthony Comstock was a moral crusader in the late nineteenth century who began the New York Society of the Suppression of Vice in 1874 and fought against the French cures doctors.) A man who also knew Tumblety at the time, Edward Haywood, stated in the December 3, 1888, issue of the *Rochester Democrat and Republican* that he remembered Tumblety running about the canal. He stated:

> *The only training he ever had for the medical profession was in a little drug store at the back of the Arcade, which was kept by a 'Doctor' Lispenard, who carried on a medical business of a disreputable kind.*

The Arcade Gallery, or Reynold's Arcade Gallery, was the focal center of downtown Rochester. It was a four-story complex with eighty-six rooms, equivalent to today's shopping mall. It even had a lofty skylight corridor. Having an office near the much-frequented Arcade Gallery would guarantee a high level of visibility.

Lispenard, or Reynolds, moving to Rochester no earlier than 1850, conflicts slightly with Streeter's recollection of him seeing Tumblety peddling around the canals around 1848. While two years is not a significant issue, there is a reason Streeter would have seen Tumblety around the canals even before he began to peddle Lispenard's pamphlets on his boat. According to the sworn testimony of the daughter of James McMullen, Tumblety got his first job from her father, working on the canal, between 1848 and 1851. Michael Fitzsimons stated Francis Tumblety was also employed as a moulder in a foundry before he began working for a physician. By late 1851, he was working for the physician, Reynolds, peddling his French cures pamphlets. It was Tumblety's first experience at how the alternative medical business was a way to make a living, but it would not be the last. Since Tumblety was born in 1830, Reynolds was only three years older with a successful occupation, which may have impressed Tumblety to take seriously a career as an alternative doctor.

According to sworn testimony of the undertaker who embalmed Tumblety's body and a young man who was with Tumblety for a full twenty years each Mardi Gras from 1881 to 1900, Tumblety suffered from the physical sexual dysfunction of hermaphroditism. One possibility is that Tumblety approached Reynolds first as a patient and later decided to enter into the profession.

In 1856, in London, Ontario, Tumblety was not advertising as a French cures doctor but as a full-fledged Indian herb doctor. Evidence as to the source of his botanical education can be found in his Indian herb doctor advertisements, which were copied directly from another Indian herb doctor operating out of Rochester at the time, Rudolf J. Lyons. Lyons arrived with his family in Rochester in 1853 from Baltimore, Maryland, and opened an office inside the famous Arcade Gallery. While not in the 1851/52 Rochester City directory, Lyons is in the 1853 directory. He, his wife, Rose, and daughter, Lavinia, moved to 7 North Sophia Street, which was quite close to the Tumblety residence on South Sophia, so Tumblety may have met him in the neighborhood. The 1855 New York census gives further detail, showing a Doctor R. J. Lyon, aged 39 (b. 1816), occupation botanical physician, born in South America, moving to Rochester two years earlier, wife (no name), daughter Lavinia, aged 6, born in Maryland, son William H., aged 2, born in Rochester, and two servants, Mary and Ellen Lovitt. The 1860 census gave the wife's name as Rose. In the earlier 1850 census, Lyons is recorded as an herb doctor living with wife Rose and infant Lavinia in Baltimore, Maryland. His servant's name is listed as Mary Baleman. Lyons stayed in the Rochester area for six years. The 1860 census shows that Lyons had moved his family to Cleveland, Ohio, with Cleveland ads beginning in 1859.

Working for Lispenard just behind the popular Arcade Gallery, Tumblety would have seen the opening of thirty-five-year-old Dr. Lyons' office and his daily operation. A local resident claimed Tumblety worked for Lyons after peddling for Lispenard. In the *Rochester Union*, May 9, 1865, it states:

> *As Tumblety resided in Rochester many years, and is well known here to almost all our citizens, we need not tell them that the stories floating about in the newspapers are erroneous. His name is J. H. Tumblety . . . He will be remembered by many, some fifteen years or more since, as a peddler of books upon the cars, and subsequently in other avocations, not long in any one here in town . . . When one H. J. Lyons, an 'Indian Herb Doctor', had an office over the Post Office, Tumblety used to be with him, and he probably picked up the information requisite to start him in his profession there.*

The post office was in the Arcade Gallery, demonstrating that the witness was not confusing Lyons' office with Lispenard's. Renting three office spaces inside the Arcade was more expensive than on Exchange Place, meaning Tumblety watched as Lyons spent extravagantly in order to make even more money. This is exactly what Tumblety was later known for. Lyons clearly impressed him, as evidenced by Tumblety taking on the persona of an Indian herb doctor and copying Lyons' business practices.

Lyons' headquarters was Rochester until 1859. He would visit the rural western New York areas throughout the month. In the *Westfield Republican*, June 18, 1856, his advertisement stated:

> *Dr. Lyons will be absent from his office in Rochester, in order to attend to his country patients, at the following dates of each and every month: 1ˢᵗ, 2d, 15ᵗʰ, 16ᵗʰ, 17ᵗʰ, 23d, 24ᵗʰ, and 26ᵗʰ. The doctor would respectfully request all those who desire to know more about him, to call at his office, where they can procure, free of charge a pamphlet containing a short history of Medicines also; a brief sketch of his life, study and extensive travels. Remember the Doctor's Office in Rochester is in the Arcade Hall, over the Post*

Office and Appleby's Daguerrean Saloon. Ladies Room No. 74, Gentlemen's Room No. 86; Laboratory, No. 87.

Lyons called his rooms the Rochester North Street Botanical Infirmary, and stated:

The Indian Herb Doctor, R. Lyons Proprietor of the above named Infirmary has, a long laborious, but successful practice of four years in Rochester . . . A practical and thoroughly experienced Nurse has been employed, besides other servants to administer to the many wants and comforts of the Afflicted inmates.

The 1850, 1855, 1860, and 1870 censuses stated that Lyons was born in South America, which was a strategic lie for business reasons. In Lyons' advertisements, he stated he could cure diseases that botanical doctors from Europe and the United States could not, and he claimed to have received his expertise from his travels through South America. The last of Lyons' advertisements were in Michigan, which, according to the 1870 census, was his residence. In the 1880 census, Rudolph Lyons was still recorded as a physician, but he lived in Sulphur Springs, Virginia, and was divorced. He stated to the census taker that he and his mother were born in Virginia and his father in Maryland.

In the 1850s, both Lispenard and Lyons maintained their Rochester offices but would visit the rural areas in western New York throughout the month, and both needed assistance maintaining their offices and running their respective mail-order businesses in their absence. They advertised mail-order, thus, they needed someone literate to run it when they were gone. Francis Tumblety was recorded in the 1850 census as literate, which conforms to the testimony of Michael Fitzsimons stating Francis walked him to the school house in Ireland around 1842 or 1843. This means Tumblety had the ability to accomplish these tasks, and he clearly gained valuable knowledge on how to run an effective alternative doctor business. He would have had a front-row seat in learning how both doctors operated and advertised. In view of this, there would have been no need for any kind of training other than running the office. Once he had the confidence to begin his own business, he could have, and in 1856, Francis was twenty-six years old. Since his older brother, Lawrence, was home to take care of their widowed mother, Francis was free to run his business, as well as old enough and sufficiently rehearsed to be considered a doctor.

There is one eyewitness account recorded in the December 3, 1888, issue of the *Rochester Democrat and Republican,* of a man named Edward Haywood who knew Tumblety when he worked on the canals, then claimed to see him in Detroit, Michigan, in 1855:

> 'I am in my fifty-second year,' said Mr. Haywood to a World correspondent today, 'and I fancy Frank Tumblety must be two or three years older. I remember him very well when he used to run about the canal in Rochester . . . He lived with his brother, who was my uncle's gardener. About 1855 I went West. Tumblety turned up in Detroit as a 'doctor.' The only training he ever had for the medical profession was in a little drug store at the back of the Arcade, which was kept by a 'Doctor' Lispenard, who carried on a medical business of a disreputable kind.'

Some claim the 1855 date in Detroit is in error, because there have not been any corresponding advertisements corroborating him having an office in Detroit. Though there is some evidence that this did indeed occur. First, the Detroit office was not for an Indian herb doctor but a French cures doctor. Also, in 1855, Lispenard had mail-order ads in city directories from Rochester to Detroit, Buffalo, Cleveland, and Toledo. Tumblety was reported to have been peddling Lispenard's material on mass transits, such as Erie Canal boats and train cars. Beginning in 1856, and for the rest of his life, Tumblety constantly traveled. Tumblety may very well have been tasked by Lispenard to travel to these cities and pay for ads in the city directories. Interestingly, beginning in 1856, train tracks were laid between Detroit, through London, Ontario, to Toronto. Corroborating this is the sworn testimony of Tumblety's nephew, Michael Fitzsimons. He stated that Tumblety began working for the physician at age twenty, which was around 1850, when Reynolds arrived in Rochester. Lyons was not in Rochester for another three years.

During the Circuit Court case involving Tumblety's will and testament, the attorney asked Fitzsimons, "When did he leave there [Rochester] and become a traveling man?" Fitzsimons replied, "Oh, he left at intervals, I should think, when he was twenty years old." The attorney then asked, "And at the time that he left Rochester when he was about twenty what was his business?" Fitzsimons answered, "He had been in the employ of a physician." Fitzsimons makes it clear that Reynolds paid Tumblety to leave at intervals of time, which conforms with a task to visit neighboring cities.

One *Chicago Tribune* report has Tumblety in Boston, Massachusetts, in 1855, and if true, it may very well have been the same reason he began his Canadian operation in London, Ontario, one year later; he had relatives who lived in Boston. In 1855, both London, Ontario, and Boston, Massachusetts, were home to families of the Irish Tumilty clan. Not only is Francis' name absent from the Rochester City directories beginning in 1853/1854, Lawrence and Margaret's names are also absent. Francis' brother Patrick was still in the Rochester directories living with his wife and kids up until his death in 1859. Lawrence and Margaret returned to the very same address in 1857/58, suggesting their four-year absence was temporary with full intentions of returning. Recall that Margaret's husband and Francis' father, James, passed away in May 1851. If the Boston relatives came to Rochester to pay their last respects, Margaret, Lawrence, and Francis may have returned to Boston with them, only to return to Rochester at a later time.

Currently, the earliest newspaper report on Tumblety being referred to as Dr. Tumblety and him making amazing cures is in the May 21, 1856, issue of the *Troy New York Daily Times*. A small commentary is located in the "News Summary" section, stating, "A Dr. Tumblety (what a name!) is performing marvelous cures in Rochester. He cures scrofuls in fifteen minutes, and small pox before it breaks out!" Troy is in the eastern part of New York; a location that Tumblety did not open up offices in the late 1850s. In view of this, the report is likely not an advertisement targeting potential Troy, New York, customers, but a favorable commentary about happenings in Rochester. It seems Tumblety returned home temporarily just after he finished in London, Ontario, in May 1856, and just before he continued onto Toronto.

By November 1856, Tumblety had opened an office in Toronto, Canada, publicizing that he was formerly from Rochester, New York, and was planning on making Toronto his home, as he stated in an advertisement in the *Daily Globe*'s January 3, 1857, issue. The ad continued until March. Tumblety was reported to have had a young man assist him in Toronto, and Tumblety needed someone to run his office when he was on the road. This young man may have been one Charles P. Jones. In his biography published in 1884, Jones stated that he studied with Tumblety as he was attending the Toronto Medical Institute, claiming to have graduated in 1859.

We do have evidence that Tumblety opened up an office in Niagara Falls, New York, before beginning in Toronto in November 1856, and during his operation in 1857. Note the following article in the *Louisville Evening Bulletin*, October 7, 1857:

A correspondent of the New York Tribune, writing from Brantford, Canada, says:

We had a quack doctor at Toronto for several months, who seemed to make money fast. He was a young Irishman of the name Tumblety, and he called himself the Indian herb doctor. Credulity sent her dupes to him by hundreds. It was supposed he was a male Madame Restell, and when he shifted the scene to Montreal, a police detective brought him a woman of the town; he gave her drugs to produce a miscarriage, and at the latest advices here he was "under advisement." He was formerly a circus agent; his real name is Ryan, and I hear he drove a cab in Rochester.

No one could have spent any considerable time at Niagara during this summer [1857] or last [1856] or the summer before that [1855] without being struck now and then with the figure of a tall, slender, rosy-faced, dandyish looking fellow dashing through the streets on horseback, or moving rapidly about the halls and saloons of the hotels, distributing yellow and purple bills, and taking frequent and deliberate glances at himself in the mirrors. That was Tnmblety [sic]. Some time in July of this summer, he was, we heard, genteelly thrashed at Clifton,

*the little town at the Canada terminus of the Suspension
Bridge, and as we were leaving Niagara one gray evening
in August, we read a most scathing and pitiless denuncia-
tion of the impostor in one of the papers of the place. Since
then Tumblety has been dead to us, as he ought to have
been to everybody else. But the correspondent of the Tribune has revived him. We think it is rather a pity that the
authorities of Montreal couldn't resolve themselves into a
Chancery Court, and keep him "under advisement" for the
term of his natural life. He is unquestionably as rich a
scoundrel as ever cultivated a neck for the halter.*

In the August 19, 1857, issue of the *Niagara Falls Gazette*,
Tumblety placed his advertisement, which had a drawing of
him dressed in a dark overcoat, standing outdoors, holding
a book with his left hand, and pointing at a plant with the
other. In it, he stated he would treat people in Niagara Falls
from July 11, 1857, to September 14, 1857. He also stated
that his office was at 3 Frontier Mart across the street from
the New York Central train depot. This corroborates the *New
York Tribune* correspondent's comments about seeing him in
Clifton, which was on the Canadian side of the Suspension
Bridge at Niagara Falls. The Suspension Bridge, or Niagara
Falls Suspension Bridge, connected Niagara Falls, New York,
with Clifton, Ontario, Canada, (changed name to Niagara Falls,
Ontario, in 1881) across the Niagara Gorge by train in 1855.
The correspondent claimed Tumblety was in Clifton for three
summers in a row, 1855, 1856, and 1857. Tumblety did not
begin his career until 1856, but he may have visited Clifton
in 1855 when he was still been employed by RJ Lyons. The
opening of the Suspension Bridge and his enjoyment of Clifton
may have contributed to his decision to begin his Indian herb
doctor operation at London, Ontario, just a few hours' train
ride west of Clifton.

Tumblety placed ads in the *Toronto Globe* from November
1856 to September 1857, yet he was in Niagara Falls from July
to September. This is reminiscent of Tumblety's Indian herb
doctor mentor, RJ Lyons, who headquartered in Rochester but
visited outlying rural communities. He continued his Rochester
office through mail order, hiring assistants like Tumblety to run
the mail order business. It seems Tumblety was using the same

business plan and enjoying his summers in Niagara Falls. In the fall of 1857, Tumblety placed ads in Montreal and opened up an office. By August 1857, Tumblety had opened an office in Montreal on Great St. James Street but explained in his ads that he was headquartered in Toronto. This date conforms to the very first direct rail links from Toronto to Montreal, and Tumblety was known to travel by train. On September 23, 1857, Tumblety again found himself in jail, and this time it was for allegedly attempting to procure an abortion for a prostitute. His radical Irish attorney Bernard Devlin immediately petitioned for a writ of habeas corpus, and Tumblety was released on bail. A grand jury threw the case out on October 24, 1857. In January 1858, Tumblety returned to Toronto as advertised, but a *Boston Daily Globe* reporter witnessed that he opened a shop in Ottawa for three months before this:

> *The writer first met Dr. Twomblety in 1857, in Ottawa, where he opened an office and advertised himself as a specialist. His principal place of business at that time was in Toronto, from which city he travelled with two horses— one an Irish hunter, the other a cob—two dogs and a basket phaeton. He dressed in a very 'loud' manner, and had with him a private secretary.*
>
> *His first move on arrival was to make a small deposit in the local branch of the Quebec bank, and on the following Sunday, preceded by his secretary carrying a large, gorgeous prayer book, he marched up the middle aisle of the principal Catholic church of Ottawa and presented a $100 bill as his offering. During his three months sojourn he did a large business in his special line, and made lots of money.*
>
> *His meals were carried in to him from a first class boarding house, at which place his secretary and big Newfoundland dog took their meals. For the latter he paid $5 per week board. After leaving Ottawa he returned to Toronto and the writer lost sight of him for some years.*
> *—Boston Daily Globe, November 27, 1888*

It was at this time in Toronto that we begin to see evidence of Tumblety's disreputable habits. In the *San Francisco Daily Report*, November 23, 1888, a C. F. Smythe recalled seeing Tumblety in Toronto in 1858, and commented upon his "unenviable reputation." He then stated, "He practiced medicine for a short time, but his habits did not inspire the confidence of his patients, and he was forced to turn to something else. At one time he would appear half-naked and the next would strut forth decked with medals." In March 1858, in Toronto, Tumblety again found himself in court. He was brought before the police magistrate on charges that he extorted a gold watch from his patient Adolphus Binkert.

The last of his Toronto advertisements ended in February 1858, and Tumblety soon arrived in Rochester, New York, visiting family and opening an office for a few months, even temporarily opening up an office in Buffalo. Captain Streeter commented upon Tumblety's return to Rochester as a "great physician." He even commented about his older brothers arguing about him:

Frank continued to sell papers until 1850, I think, and then disappeared, and I did not see him again for ten years, when he returned to Rochester as a great physician and soon became the wonder of the city. He wore a light fur overcoat that reached to his feet and had a dark collar and cuffs, and he was always followed by a big greyhound. When a boy he had no associates, and when he returned he was more exclusive and solitary than ever. I don't remember ever having seen him in company with another person in his walks. When I met him on his return, having known him quite well as a boy, I said, 'Hello, Frank, how d'ye do?' and he merely replied, 'Hello Streeter,' and passed on. He had become very aristocratic during his absence. The papers had a great deal to say about him, and he created quite a sensation by giving barrels of flour and other provisions to poor people. Afterwards he went to Buffalo and did likewise, and I understand he visited other cities. I think Frank was born in Rochester. He had no foreign accent when I first met him, and I understood at the time that he was a Rochester boy. I remember after he became famous his two brothers quarreled [sic] because each imagined the other was thought more of by the 'doctor.'
—*New York World*, December 2, 1888

Tumblety announced in their papers that he would be distributing fifty sacks of flour to the poor:

ANOTHER OFFER—Dr. TUMBLETY publishes a card in the Express offering to give twenty barrels of flour to the poor, once in every two weeks, if another person will do likewise. Here is an opportunity for some one to come forward and ensure those who are praying 'Give us day by day our daily bread,' a considerable supply of food. We notice that the Commercial speaks of the Doctor's distribution of flour on Tuesday, as a 'beggarly advertising dodge,' and a 'miserable ostentation of charity.' It strikes us, these terms are too harsh and altogether uncalled for. Whether the Doctor sells good medicine and good advice, or not, has nothing to do with the fact that he gave the poor good flour, which they needed. Four hundred persons received ten pounds of flour each, and it was distributed by Mr. SHORT, a gentleman who has the opportunity to know those who are really suffering. That Dr. TUMBLETY may expect to gain some pecuniary advantage by his liberality, is hardly sufficient reason for speaking contemptuously of his good deeds. [Courier]
—Buffalo Daily Republic, February 25, 1859

The [Rochester] papers had a great deal to say about him, and he created quite a sensation by giving barrels of flour and other provisions to poor people. Afterwards he went to Buffalo and did likewise, and I understand he visited other cities.
—New York World, December 3, 1888

Francis Tumblety's decision to follow in the footsteps of the celebrated Indian herb doctor R. J. Lyons was a game-changer for his financial circumstances. This, above all other decisions, made him rich in just a few years. The *Brooklyn Daily Eagle*, May 10, 1865, commented to the proprietors of a Buffalo newspaper, the *Buffalo Express*, contacting the Bank of Toronto, inquiring upon Francis Tumblety. The bank replied, stating, "His check is good for $60,000 in this bank." An inflation calculator records this value at $1,648,754 today. Being rich, Tumblety now had complete autonomy of his life, giving him virtually no restrictions on travel, conducting his business, and even leisure.

On June 13, 1858, Tumblety was back in Canada, in Quebec City. The Grand Trunk Railway between Toronto and Quebec City had been completed two years earlier. In November 1858, Tumblety posted an ad in a local Perth, Ontario, newspaper, a city located just southwest of Ottawa. In the advertisement, he stated his headquarters was Toronto. His Canadian area of operation extended as far east as Quebec City, and at the time, Cunard Lines offered ocean cruises to Boston, Massachusetts, in the summer months. By late-summer 1859, Tumblety had opened an office in Boston:

> *THE INDIAN DOCTOR. – As Dr. Tumblety, of Canada, has taken up his abode amongst us with a view to permanency, we with pleasure copy the following notice from the 'Spirit of the Times,' of Woodstock, C.W., as it is applicable the present time: Invalids, and all those suffering under lingering diseases, will find it to their . . . The Doctor's office is at No. 360 Washington street Boston. [Boston Post]*
> —*Boston Courier*, August 29, 1859

Francis Tumblety corroborated this himself. In his 1866 autobiography, he referred to this antebellum period while he "resided in Boston" and mentioned his acquaintances in the Cunard Line and even the Cunard steamship *Great Eastern*, a famous oversized cruise ship at the time:

> *I first knew this by meeting with Captain Anderson, of the royal navy, but extensively and favorably known in this country, wherein he made himself a legion of friends, as the commander of the steamship Great Eastern.*
>
> *He knew me well, as also my relatives, a long time previous, while he was the captain of one of the Cunard line of packets, and while I resided in Boston, at the time the steamer came to that port. He frequently pressed me to take a trip with him to Europe, to visit my friends there, among whom I had a near relative and namesake, Tumblety, who has been connected over twenty years with the Cunard line. On one of his trips the Captain took my daguerreotype*

to my uncle in England, who has since died, in order to satisfy him that I was still in the land of the living.

Another distinguished commander in the Cunard line, Captain Moody, was also an intimate friend of my family, and he, too, I used to meet with friendly greeting, at the old Tremont, in Boston. I recall these reunions with pleasurable emotion, for they were magnetic links that connected me with dear friends far away across the stormy Atlantic. Nevertheless, it is not for the purpose of indulging pleasant reminiscences that I have introduced these personages, but simply in proof of my standing in society, for the many friends and acquaintances of Captain Anderson will understand that the person he would take by the hand must command a spotless character and a gentlemanly record.

Interestingly, the posh Tremont House Tumblety referred to was on the corner of Tremont and Bacon Streets, which is only 200 feet from his old office at 360 Washington Street. Tumblety then continued about a particular subject that he purposely avoided discussing throughout his entire life: his relatives. This rare event is explainable because it suggested that he and his family were from higher society, having long-time and highly esteemed friends. It does corroborate the possibility that Tumblety's time he "resided in Boston" before the Civil War may have had something to do with relatives.

In the Addendum part one section of Evans and Gainey's, *Jack the Ripper First American Serial Killer* (Kodansha International, 1995), the authors comment upon a *Rochester Democrat* article dated October 27, 1885, reporting on the death of Patrick Tumblety, aged 39, who lived at the corner of Plymouth Avenue and Germain Street. He was in a fatal accident in the southwest part of Rochester City, killed by a chimney falling off the roof of a small building as he was moving it onto his own premises. It stated:

Mr. Tumblety had just completed a new brick house and moved into it. The small wooden house formerly occupied by him was to be moved to the rear of the new dwelling and serve as a kitchen. Tumblety's skull fractured and he died 90 minutes later. He was employed at the gas

works, and three or four years ago became heir to a for-
tune of several thousand dollars in England, of which he
was a native, and crossed the ocean to claim it.

Patrick Tumilty's death from a falling chimney was
actually in 1859, which means the year 1885 is a typo in
Evan's and Gainey's book, but the other details in the report
are quite accurate. First, the Tumblety family did live a
few miles southwest of downtown Rochester, New York, on
Plymouth Avenue. Second, the 1865 New York census shows
Mary Tumilty, Patrick's wife, owning a brick house. Third,
Patrick was born in 1820, so he did indeed die at 39 years of
age. And lastly, the Rochester City directories recorded him
working at the gas works.

There are two interesting errors in the newspaper article.
Patrick was not from England, but Ireland, and since his
mother was still alive along with most of his siblings, he would
not have been sole heir to a fortune coming out of England if it
was a familial bequest. There is evidence that the errors were
not a reporter's mistake, but a family lie in order to hide the
fact that they were from the poor class of Irish society. The
1850 US census and 1855 New York census state that Patrick
emigrated from Ireland, yet in the 1900 census, his son,
James, claimed his father was born in England, demonstrating
that the family was sensitive about emigrating from Ireland
during the Great Famine. The common theme throughout
Francis Tumblety's autobiographical pamphlets is that his
position in society was, and always had been, upper class. So,
where did the money come from? Note that the article stated
that Patrick acquired the money three or four years before his
death at the end of 1859. This coincides with the time Francis
Tumblety began his lucrative Indian herb doctor business,
showing up in Hamilton and Toronto, Canada, in 1856/57.
Tumblety was reported to have earned over $60,000 in Toronto
alone. Further, Francis Tumblety returned to Rochester in
1858 and opened an office for about four months. He even
placed ads in the local papers. It stands to reason that Patrick
received the money from his brother Francis rather than from
some unidentified source in England.

Francis Tumblety was not done with Canada, all accounts
stating he made large sums of money in each city. He left

Boston and set up an office in Saint John, New Brunswick, Canada, in June 1859. Saint John was one of the ocean cruise stops between Boston and Quebec, which was likely how he ended up there, especially since rail connection to Saint John was years away. The earliest advertisement in Saint John papers was on June 29, 1860, in the *Morning News*. The *Morning Freeman*, July 5, 1860, also ran an ad from Francis Tumblety.

While there, trouble fell upon him fast, and on July 31, 1860, Tumblety was in front of a police magistrate on the charge of "falsely and willfully assuming titles which implied that he was a registered or lawfully recognized physician." This Medical Act Tumblety violated was passed in Canada just months before. On August 10, 1860, Tumblety was found guilty of assuming the title of MD and was fined £20. Tumblety appealed, and supreme court judge Robert Parker overturned the magistrate's decision, stating the fact that he used the title did not necessarily imply that he was lawfully recognized.

A patient then died under Tumblety's care, which was recorded in the *New York World*, November 27, 1888:

> *Just at this time one of his patients died, and under very peculiar circumstances. The man's name was Portmore, and as he was well known and had many friends, his death created a sensation. A request was made by the family for an autopsy, and when it was held it was found that Portmore's death was entirely due to the 'doctor's' atrocious treatment. So gross was the malpractice that the case was at once given to the Coroner, and a jury was empanelled to more fully investigate. There is a great deal of red tape about Coroners' juries in that part of the country, and by the time the jury had thoroughly sifted all the evidence and proved that the 'doctor' was guilty of manslaughter, he had fled to Boston.*

An eyewitness account of this event was written in a private letter from Deputy Minister William Smith to a government official named James Barber in St. John dated December 1, 1888. Smith had worked with Barber in St. John years earlier and reminded him of when Tumblety allegedly killed Portmore:

My dear Barber . . . Do you recollect Dr. Tumblety who came to St. John about 1860 and who used to ride on a beautiful white horse with a long tail, and a couple of grey hounds following after him? Do you recollect how he used to canter along like a circus man? And do you recollect that it was asserted that he killed old Portmore, the Carpenter who built the extension to my house and fleeced me to a large extent? Do you recollect how he suddenly left St. John, circus horse, hounds and all, and afterwards turned up at different places in the States and Canada? He was considered by Dr. Bayard and others an adventurer and Quack Doctor.

On the night of the inquest on September 27, 1860, Tumblety got on his white horse and rushed off across the border to Calais, Maine. In October, he sent a letter to Saint John claiming he would return to prove his innocence, but he never did. He made his way back to Boston.

Why Boston and not another US city? It may again have had something to do with extended family, since some of the Tumilty clan lived near Boston. It is at this time we see the beginnings of his lifelong interest in the slums, likely for cruising for young men. In the *Chicago Tribune*, November 22, 1888, it states:

'Dr. Kumblety's' Career
Boston, Mass., Nov 21—(Special.)—Dr. Kumblety, as the man arrested in London on suspicion of being con-nected with the Whitechapel murders calls himself, is well known in Boston. Said one today who knew the doctor: 'The fellow's name is Tumblety. About 33 years ago there came to Boston from the Canadian provinces a man who engaged an office in the Horticultural Building on Trem-ont street. He was a quack doctor, and during his stay in Boston used considerable ground gentian. I remember this fact for I sold him quite a large amount of goods from time to time. When I knew him I was a boy in my teens. His name was Dr. Tumblety. I remember him as a rather tall, fine-appearing individual. He was a most peculiar person. He wore, pinned to his vest, several large medals which he said had been awarded him in various colleges

where he had studied. He liked to display heavy jewelry.
He had every appearance as a quack doctor. I should say
he was about 30 years old when I knew him. He liked
the slums, notwithstanding the fact that he always had
plenty of money, and could have entered, if he had been
inclined, into good society.'

His second time in Boston was short-lived, and by February
1861, he began his New York City office, which became his
center of operation for years to come. When he left for another
city, Tumblety changed his office visit ads to his mail-order ads,
and he did so in June/July 1861. After the defeat of the Union
forces at the first major battle of the Civil War near Washington
DC, on July 21, 1861, Major General George B. McClellan
was appointed as commander of the Army of the Potomac by
President Lincoln. It was at this time that Tumblety began what
he called his "two year sojourn" in Washington DC, stating
in his autobiography that he partially made up his mind to
tender his "services as a surgeon in one of the regiments." On
the surface, this is a strange offer, since Tumblety was not a
surgeon and had never gone to medical school for professional
training in surgery. Tumblety clearly wanted to separate
himself from other advertising alternative doctors, as evidenced
of him adding "MD" at the end of his name as he began his
business in Canada. This was also the reason he was pushed
out of Canadian cities, the professional medical community
charging him with illegally using the title of medical doctor.
Tumblety certainly did attempt to connect himself with the
general's surgical staff at the nation's capital in 1861:

DR. TUMBLETY REDIVIDUS.
The Buffalo Courier has it from good authority that the
original Dr. Tumblety is flourishing about Washington
with the original dog, as large as life and a good deal
more natural. Also, that he had been attached to Gen. Mc-
Clellean's Staff as a Surgeon.
—*Cleveland Morning Leader*, November 18, 1861

Curiously, prior to his departure from New York, he
was seen by a *Vanity Fair* reporter with multiple pictures of
anatomical specimens posted outside his Broadway Street
office:

A CASE FOR THE POLICE – IF POSSIBLE
. . . But if one quack is thus happily thwarted in his at-
tempts to outrage decency and insult the public, why
should another be quietly suffered to hang out his disgust-
ing banners in our very midst? In a central part of Broad-
way—we forget the exact Spot, there are so many there
to confuse the eye—the passers by are daily outraged by
the exhibition of certain anatomical pictures, which look as
if they might once have formed part of the collection of a
lunatic confined in a leper hospital . . . He is generally ac-
companied by a large greyhound—a well-bred animal, but
wearing a dejected look, as if ashamed of the company
into which it has fallen. The man's name is TUMBLETY . . .
—Vanity Fair, August 31, 1861

Tumblety was interested in human anatomy immediately prior to his planned two-year sojourn in Washington DC. If Tumblety was going to claim skill in the surgical field with no professional surgical training, then a self-help crash course in anatomy prior to his offer to the general makes sense. Note a change in business practice when he arrived in Washington DC that conforms to Tumblety's desire to promote himself as a qualified surgeon. Tumblety did not begin his usual Indian herb doctor advertising campaign, a business practice he never varied since he began his traveling-advertising alternative doctor career. Advertising as an Indian herb doctor would contradict his claims of being a surgeon. The problem for Tumblety was he was not a surgeon, thus, he could not present a medical diploma to the general's medical staff, so he did the next best thing: He invited the general's officers to an illustrated medical lecture in 1861. It would have been foolhardy for Tumblety to have given an anatomical lecture without some kind of training, so Tumblety having anatomical pictures in New York is not a surprise.

Giving medical lectures illustrated with anatomical specimens of their own design was a common practice of competing surgeons in the nineteenth century. It demonstrated their skill level and legitimacy. According to Michael Sappol, curator-historian at the National Library of Medicine in Bethesda, Maryland, in the nineteenth century, "Membership in the [surgical/medical] profession was consolidated by a common culture of collectorship [of anatomical specimens] . . ." Doctor A. W. Bates, PhD, MD, at the Department of Histopathology in the Royal Free Hospital, London, England, states,

> "Anatomy teachers assembled their own collections or "museums" of material with which to illustrate lectures . . . Ownership of a museum indicated that a teacher was likely to be financially solvent and, in the 1820s, possession of a museum worth more than 500 pounds was suggested as a prerequisite for an anatomy teacher to be recognized by the College of Surgeons."

Additionally, Sappol states, "Doctors were known to keep a few specimens or a cabinet of material on display in their offices as trophies and, more broadly, as objects that advertised a medical vocation (as did diplomas . . .) The specimens served as a credential, proof that the doctor had dissected and had special knowledge of the interior of the body."

At the lecture, Tumblety revealed to the military audience his anatomical collection, specifically, his prized collection of uterus specimens—the same organ that was taken by Jack the Ripper from two of his victims. One man who saw Tumblety's uterus collection was New York City lawyer and Civil War provacatour and spy Charles A. Dunham. Dunham stated to a *New York World* reporter on December 1, 1888, that he was a colonel at the time he met Tumblety in the capital,

> *Colonel C. A. Dunham, a well-known lawyer who lives near Fairview, N.J., was intimately acquainted with Twomblety for many years . . . 'At length it was whispered about that he was an adventurer. One day my lieutenant-colonel and myself accepted the "doctor's" invitation to a late dinner—symposium, he called it—at his rooms. . . . Then he invited us into his office where he illustrated his lecture, so to speak. One side of this room was entirely occupied with cases, outwardly resembling wardrobes. When the doors were opened quite a museum was revealed—tiers of shelves with glass jars and cases, some round and others square, filled with all sorts of anatomical specimens. The "doctor" placed on a table a dozen*

or more jars containing, as he said, the matrices of every
class of women. Nearly a half of one of these cases was
occupied exclusively with these specimens'.
     —*New York World*, December 2, 1888

Dunham's position as one of the general's officers would
have been the reason why Tumblety invited him to the lecture.
The general's officers were his eyes and ears. Of the dozens
of sworn testimonies of eyewitnesses who knew Tumblety in
his later years, including judges, lawyers, physicians, and
bankers, the most consistent response was that he was very
intelligent and cunning. Less than a year before Tumblety
arrived in Washington DC, he was legally challenged in
Canada for using the title of MD. Being recognized as a
surgeon by the US Army would have given him legitimacy
to use the title of MD, effectively bypassing—at least in his
mind—the requirement for a medical diploma. If successful, it
would have been a medical profession coup.

Tumblety's plan to be embraced by the general did not
work, and he left Washington DC by the end of 1861. William
Pinkerton, of the famous Pinkerton Detective Agency, was
in Washington DC in 1861, and recalled the General forcing
Tumblety to leave:

At that time my duties in Washington were connected with
the secret service of the army, and my attention was natu-
rally drawn to him [Tumblety] *a good deal by his military*
appearance . . . I soon found out that he was a quack doc-
tor, and that he was scattering broadcast his advertise-
ments of a cure for a certain class of complaints. A little
inquiry soon showed that he had flooded the army with
his handbills and with objectionable books, so much so
that General McClellan issued strict orders that the circu-
lation of these books in the army should be suppressed,
on the ground that many of the books were calculated to
debase the soldiers, their contents being of an immoral
character and their illustrations still more so. Of course
this military acknowledgment that the doctor existed only
caused a still more wide attention to be turned upon him.
He was watched with closer scrutiny, and, at last, it be-
came known that he was in the habit of indulging in certain
vices that finally resulted in him being driven from the city.

Tumblety went back to New York for two months, but he returned to DC and decided to practice his money-making venture, beginning his Indian herb doctor advertising in Washington papers in February 1862.

Charles Dunham certainly had the ability to fill a newspaper with lies, as he did so twenty-five years earlier in his capacity as a Civil War provocateur, but in the 1888 interview about Tumblety, the *New York World* reporter sought Dunham out, hearing he had experiences with Tumblety. Tumblety indeed had a professional reason to give an illustrated anatomical lecture as he attempted to "tender his services as a surgeon." Recall that Tumblety was seen by a New York City reporter displaying images of anatomical specimens just weeks or months prior to the time he was supposed to have given the lecture. Lastly, after Tumblety completed his two-year sojourn in Washington DC in the spring of 1863, he made his way to Buffalo, New York, and a reporter from the *Buffalo Courier* stated that Tumblety was giving medical lectures, corroborating his method of promoting himself as a qualified medical professional:

> One particular week that will ever remain notable in local history was in July, 1863. . . . In fact quite an intimacy sprang up between him [John Wilkes Booth] and a Dr. Tumblety—or Tumulty. He drove around selling cure-alls for everything, giving lectures with Thespian emphasis. He frequently located himself on the Terrace, where he would draw big crowds by distributing bags of flour.
> —Buffalo Courier, May 31, 1914

Tumblety likely met his nephew Charles Fitzsimons in DC just after the Battle of Bull Run. Dunham stated that he met Tumblety in the capital a few days after that battle, which took place on July 21, 1861. An article in 1881 states that Tumblety visited the 13th New York regiment while he was in DC:

'DR.' TUMBLETY

The 'Dr.' Francis Tumblety mentioned in the UNION'S Southern Notes yesterday for having come to grief in New Orleans for picking the pocket of a government clerk,

appears to be not altogether unknown in this city . . . He then disappeared from Rochester for a time and when he was next heard from by Rochester men he was parading himself as one of General McClellan's staff at Washington. He was not on the staff, but dressed as near like an officer as he dare, and would follow the General's staff on horseback at a safe distance. When the Thirteenth Regiment was at Fort Corcoran, Tumblety came around mounted on a fine Arabian horse and when the men who knew him asked where he got it his answer was 'My friend Billy Seward gave it to me.'
—Rochester Daily Union and Advertiser, April 5, 1881

Charles Fitzsimons was a captain in the 3rd Regiment of New York Volunteers, which was mustered on May 14, 1861. The regiment reached the capital on the day of the First Battle of Bull Run on July 21, 1861, and reassigned to Baltimore, Maryland, on July 30, 1861.

It was at this time that Tumblety began to separate his name from his newspaper ads. Case in point, in the *Brooklyn Daily Eagle*, November 16, 1863; January 2, 1864; and May 11, 1865, Tumblety had his large advertisements published, but he did not put his name on them. He still used the title of Indian herb doctor, which made good business sense since the business was still very profitable. A report about his St. Louis office in 1865 stated he was earning $200 to $300 per day, which is over $4000 in today's value.

Actor John Wilkes Booth assassinated President Abraham Lincoln at the Ford's Theatre in Washington DC on April 14, 1865. One of his co-conspirators was David Herold, a twenty-three-year-old pharmacist. A mutual acquaintance and fellow conspirator, John Surrat, introduced Herold to Booth in December 1864. The secretary of war, Edwin Stanton, personally directed the manhunt for all conspirators, and the chief prosecutor for the trials was Judge Advocate General of the Army Joseph Holt. Caught in the middle of the exhaustive manhunt was Francis Tumblety. This series of events affected Tumblety to such an extent that it was the primary reason why he wrote his first autobiography in 1866. Tumblety was first arrested by local St. Louis authorities for wearing a semi-military uniform and "putting on foreign airs." He stated in his autobiography, "in short, as one of my gallant captors affirmed, 'You're thinking yourself another God Almighty, and we won't stand it.'"

Tumblety was released, and attended President Lincoln's funeral services in Springfield, Illinois, on May 4, 1865. He returned to St. Louis to what by all accounts was a thriving business. On May 5, he was arrested. Note the report in the *Chicago Tribune* on May 6, 1865:

> FROM ST. LOUIS
> *(Special Dispatch to the Chicago Tribune.)*
> *St. Louis, May 5, 1865*
> *Dr. Tumblety, a so-called Indian herb doctor, has been arrested on a charge of complicity with Harrold., The Assassin's accomplice. He was at Mr. Lincoln's funeral at Springfield yesterday, and today is in the Military Prison.*

Tumblety was arrested by officers of Peter Tallon, chief of US detectives for the state of Missouri, on a special order from Colonel J. H. Baker, provost marshal general of St. Louis, for conspiracy in the Lincoln assassination. Regarding this, Tumblety stated:

> *The last sad, solemn ceremony performed, I returned, Heaven knows in how melancholy a mood, to St. Louis, and the day after I was once again arrested, thrown into prison, and this time my office and apartments were searched, ransacked, and plundered of every article of portable value, including a considerable amount of money. I remained incarcerated in St. Louis two days, during which period I was visited by several military officers, who, to my anxious demand for the cause of my arrest, laughingly replied, 'Oh, they have such an immense amount of excitement in Washington, that Colonel Baker—under whose order the arrest was made—thinks that we ought to have a little sensation here.'*

Tumblety then claimed one of the reasons why he was arrested was because officials in Washington believed he was Dr. Luke Blackburn, the man accused of smuggling to the North linens and garments used by yellow fever patients:

After a confinement of two days, during which I succeeded in discovering that beside being charged as the identical Dr. Blackburn, of yellow-fever-plot notoriety, I was also accused of complicity in the assassination of the President, I was carried to Washington, where I was thrust into the Old Capitol Prison; and without the formality of an examination, or any effort on the part of Stanton or his underlings to establish my identity with the notorious person for whom I was arrested, I was detained there three weeks, after which I was turned loose in the same reckless manner that distinguished my arrest, no examination whatever having been made of the case; nor was I afforded the opportunity, the right of every free-born man, to meet face to face my accuser, if there were such.

A subordinate of Peter Tallon, US Detective Henry W. Huthsing, swore out an affidavit in a US district court on May 28, 1873:

I arrested him and seized all his papers and property. The property I seized consisted of gold coin amounting to between twenty-two and twenty-five hundred dollars, several gold medals, and two gold-headed canes. I took him and the property I had seized to the office of the Provost Marshal General, Colonel Baker. I then searched (Tumblety), and took from him whatever property I found on his person. I then turned him over to the Provost Marshal General, Colonel Baker, to whom at the same time, I turned over the personal property and money seized at the (medical) office and upon the person of Dr. Tumblety.

Peter Tallon himself recalled this incident in 1888:

THE WHITECHAPEL MURDER.
Capt. Peter Tallon Remembers Arresting Dr. Tumblety During the War.
    Capt. Peter Tallon of the real estate firm of D.J. Hayden & Co. entertains a clear recollection of Dr. Tumblety, who is suspected of the Whitechapel murders in London, England, when the latter was a resident of this city during the war. The Captain says that if he is not mistaken Tumblety

is the man he arrested for being suspected of complicity in the plot to murder President Lincoln, while he was Chief of the United States Police for the State of Missouri in 1864. Tumblety was taken in custody on an order from the authorities at Washington. He was held only a short time when it was ascertained that he was in no manner connected with the assassination and he was released. Tumblety subsequently preferred a claim against the National Government for false imprisonment.

    —St. Louis Post-Dispatch, December 11, 1888

Note that here, Tumblety's arrest dealt with the Lincoln assassination and not the Yellow Fever Plot Tumblety claimed in his autobiography regarding US government officials believing that he was Dr. Luke Blackburn. Conflicting with this are the actual orders for his arrest stating his name as Francis Tumblety. Corroborating this is a letter from Sir Edward Thornton, the British Minister in Washington DC, to his superior, Lord Granville, which reveals comments made by the secretary of war:

Letter from Thornton to Lord Granville, Catskill Station, 18 August 1873
My Lord,
    . . . I addressed a note to Mr. Fish, enquiring what had been the ground of Dr. Tumblety's arrest and imprisonment in May 1865. I also wrote a confidential letter to the British Vice Consul at St. Louis, requesting him to make enquiries upon the subject in that city. Mr. Cooke however was unable to obtain any information further than that Dr. Tumblety had been arrested in consequence of orders from Washington, and that the Police were ignorant of the grounds of the arrest. . . . I have now the honour to enclose copy of a note from Mr. Fish, in which he transmits communication, copy of which is also enclosed, from the Secretary of War who states that Dr. Tumblety passed at St. Louis under the alias of Blackburn and was arrested on suspicion of complicity in the assassination of President Lincoln.

It is clear that the US authorities knew Tumblety was not Luke Blackburn and arrested him just on the Lincoln

assassination and not the Yellow Fever Plot as Tumblety
also claimed. Tumblety was transported to the Old Capitol
Prison in Washington DC (now occupied by the US Supreme
Court building), held for three weeks, and was then released
and cleared of all charges. In his autobiography, he blamed
Secretary of War Edwin Stanton for what he believed was an
illegal arrest. Stanton may very well have become interested
in Tumblety in the Yellow Fever Plot, but it was not the initial
reason for his interest in him. Corroborating the arrest records
is the following series of events. Note what occurred two days
before Tumblety's May 6, 1865, St. Louis arrest:

> *New York, May 4, 1865—A boy has been arrested at
> Brooklyn and taken to Washington, whose conversation
> leads to the belief that the accused had some knowledge
> of the assassination. He was an errand boy of Booth. It
> appears that Harrold [sic] turns out to be the agent and
> confidant of the notorious Dr Tumblety, who lately disap-
> peared from Brooklyn.*
> —*Daily Ohio Statesman*, May 5, 1865

The *New York Tribune*, May 5, 1865, published the story
of the boy's arrest in Brooklyn and gave additional details.
The boy was fifteen years old and arrested at the 41st Precinct
station house on Tuesday, May 2, 1865, which was four
full days earlier than Tumblety's St. Louis arrest. The boy
informed the officers that Harold—incorrectly spelled "Harrold"
in the article—was that companion of the man known as the
"Indian Herb Doctor, who came to Brooklyn some eighteen
months since and opened an office in Fulton Street . . .
Harrold was a kind of confidential valet of this doctor . . . The
doctor got into difficulties with some of his patients, and left
the city, and is said to be in New Orleans at the present time,
and Harrold returned to Washington."

While the young man may have lied, there is little reason
to suggest this report of what transpired in Brooklyn is
false. Tumblety did indeed get into difficulties with a patient.
According to the *Brooklyn Daily Eagle*, May 10, 1864, a patient
with asthma, Fenton Scully, stated Tumblety promised him
a cure for $20, plus $14 for medicine. He got worse instead
of better, and after complaining, he claimed Tumblety kicked

him several times and knocked him down the stairs. He took Tumblety to court, but the judge dismissed the case when Tumblety produced two witnesses. How curious that it was reported that Tumblety employed two young men in 1864; a perfect match for two witnesses in his office. Further, Tumblety did indeed go to New Orleans after New York. On December 3, 1864, he boarded the steamer *George Cromwell* in New Orleans, making its way to St. Louis. Regardless if Tumblety hired Herold in Brooklyn or not, the boy's story connected Tumblety to Herold, thus, Stanton's suspicions about Tumblety being involved in the Lincoln assassination came *before* his suspicions of him possibly being Luke Blackburn.

Assuming it is true that Stanton truly did eventually connect Tumblety to Luke Blackburn, how did this happen? This initial connection seems to have come from the fact that Luke Blackburn and Tumblety's former employee, Mark A. Blackburn, shared the same uncommon last name. It is likely not a coincidence. Mark A. Blackburn worked for Tumblety in his offices between 1861 and 1873. Tumblety often listed his office under Blackburn's name, as he did in St. Louis in 1864, listing it as "Tumblety F. (J. Blackburn A Co.)."

In a letter dated May 6, 1865, to Assistant Secretary of War C. A. Dana, Colonel J. D. Baker reported Tumblety with this alias, but only made mention of Tumblety's implication in the assassination. It also mentioned young Blackburn working with Tumblety in St. Louis:

> *Sir, I have the honor to forward herewith, in compliance with your telegram of this date, Dr. Tumblety, alias Blackburn. All his papers had been carefully examined to implicate him with the assassination, or showing him to be in any way connected with Herold or any of the supposed assassins. Tumblety's papers and his own admissions show that he has tramped the continent from Quebec to New Orleans, in the character of an 'Indian Herb Doctor', has gained an extensive notoriety as an impostor and quack; has been compelled to leave several towns and cities in Canada for his rascality and tricking and is being continually and threatened by those whom he has deluded and swindled. Tumblety's principal associates in*

Saint Louis have been one J.W. Blackburn, his assistant in the 'medical profession' and one Oregon Wilson, an artist. There appears to be nothing against them, except that they belong to a class of adventurers that encumber and prey upon society.—I am Sir, Very Respectfully, Your obdt. Servant, J.D. Baker, Col. & Pro. Mar. Gen.

Ironically, the real Luke Blackburn was arrested in Canada when Tumblety was in the Old Capital Prison in Washington DC:

ARREST of DR. BLACKBURN
Montreal May 18.—Dr. Blackburn, who shipped infected clothing from Bermuda, was arrested today on a warrant from Toronto for a breach of the Neutrality Law.
—The Daily Intelligencer, May 20, 1865

Why Tumblety was incarcerated for so long without being interviewed may indeed have had something to do with the Yellow Fever Plot, and researcher Jonathan Menges has investigated extensively on the issue. Charles Dunham, the man who witnessed Tumblety at his illustrated lecture at the capital in 1861, hatched the Yellow Fever Plot in the first place. Notice, though, how he explains Tumblety's connection to the Yellow Fever Plot to the *New York World* reporter on December 1, 1888:

Colonel Dunham also said that Tumblety had not been arrested on suspicion of having guilty knowledge of the assassination conspiracy. 'He was arrested in St. Louis,' said the Colonel, 'on suspicion of being Luke P. Blackburn, lately governor of Kentucky, who had been falsely charged with trying to introduce yellow fever into the northern cities by means of infected rags. It is perfectly clear that Tumblety purposely brought about his own arrest by sending anonymous letters to the federal authorities to the effect that Blackburn and himself were identical. His object, of course, was notoriety. He knew he was too well known in Washington, whither he felt certain he would be sent, to be kept long in custody."

"It is perfectly clear" and "anonymous" mean Dunham did not have first-hand knowledge that Tumblety truly was behind his arrest for the purpose of notoriety. While being at Tumblety's lecture was first-hand knowledge, this was merely an admitted opinion we know to be incorrect, since the arrest documents say nothing about the Yellow Fever Plot. The very first time the public had learned of the Yellow Fever Plot was from an Associated Press article that was published in numerous participating newspapers beginning on April 25, 1865. It stated that Captain Smith "of the brig J. Titus" arrived in New York harbor on Monday, April 24, from Bermuda, and stated that the US consul at the port had discovered a plot to introduce yellow fever in US cities from infected clothing by Dr. Blackburn of Wilmington, North Carolina. Tumblety was in St. Louis and had attended Lincoln's funeral on May 4, in Springfield, Illinois, likely taking a train on May 3 from St. Louis. At the time Dunham hypothesized that Tumblety was the author of multiple admittedly anonymous letters, Tumblety was arrested for wearing the semi-military uniform and incarcerated for two days. When did he have the time and inclination to act upon an unusual notoriety scam claiming to be in Bermuda? Also, Tumblety pushing involvement in a plot to purposely get arrested while his business in St. Louis was unusually lucrative, raking in $200 to $300 per day (thousands in today's value), conflicts with the very reason he would have been attempting to gain notoriety.

There is a suggestion that Dunham instigated the 1888 *New York World* interview for vindictive reasons due to residual bad blood between the two since the Civil War, as evidenced by Dunham informing the public that Tumblety selfishly created his arrest for the Yellow Fever Plot merely for notoriety. There is evidence that contradicts this claim. First, it was the *New York World* reporter who was seeking out Tumblety stories out of Manhattan in late November 1888, after it was known that Tumblety frequented Broadway Avenue. The reporter stated, "In this city he [Tumblety] had a little experience with the law, and this enabled the lawyers to work out something of his." The reporter first interviewed real estate attorney William Burr, who relayed a first-hand account of Tumblety. The reporter then left "this city" and interviewed Dunham in New Jersey. Why the reporter did this, even though he claimed he was reporting eyewitnesses and stories out of Manhattan, is because he was actually still interviewing New York City attorneys. Dunham was also a New York real estate attorney working out of Manhattan. In fact, in the 1881 New York City directory, Burr's office was at 320 Broadway while Dunham's office was at 335 Broadway. William Burr, another Civil War veteran, clearly knew Dunham and knew Dunham had a tempting Tumblety story the reporter would be interested in. It was the reporter who instigated the meeting; not Dunham.

Second, Dunham gives us a clue as to why he commented upon the Yellow Fever Plot and arrest, simply because he just read it. Dunham had Tumblety's autobiography in his hand as he spoke with the reporter:

> I have here a book published by him a number of years ago, describing some of his strange adventures and wonderful cures, all lies, of course, in which the name Francis Tumblety, M.D., appears.

Tumblety wrote the Yellow-Fever-Plot-arrest claim in both his 1866 and 1872 autobiographies. It is likely not a coincidence that Dunham spoke to the reporter about the event and that he had a written account of it in his hand. In view of this, instead of Dunham attempting to reinforce a premeditated slander campaign with the 1865 arrest, nothing was premeditated, and his copy of the autobiography simply informed him—or reminded him—of another interesting Tumblety story.

After his three weeks in prison in Washington DC, Tumblety believed his reputation had been affected and decided to publish the very first of his autobiographical pamphlets, or autobiographies—the 1866 version. His autobiography was not unusual for an Indian herb doctor. His old boss, Rudolf Lyons, had his own autobiographical pamphlet. In the *Westfield Republican*, June 18, 1856, Dr. Lyons stated, "The doctor would respectfully request all those who desire to know more about him, to call at his office, where they can procure, free of charge a pamphlet containing a short history of Medicines also; a brief sketch of his life, study and extensive travels." He added this to his ad, because he was absent from Rochester working throughout the rural areas.

Besides Tumblety defending himself from the well-publicized arrest, his autobiography contained exactly what Lyons' pamphlet had: a short history on botanical medicines, a brief sketch of his life, and extensive travels.

Even after his arrest in St. Louis in 1865, Tumblety returned:

THE WHITECHAPEL SUSPECT.
Charles A. Pollack of Jefferson City Recalls a Challenge to Dr. Tumblety.

In connection with the more or less plaid career of Dr. Tumblety, the Whitechapel murder suspect, Charles A. Pollack, formerly of this city but at present residing in Jefferson City, recalls the fact that while the sanguinary doctor lived in St. Louis in 1868 he became involved in a little unpleasantness with Mr. Leonard Loring, a young medical student, which eventually became very serious, as touching the honor of both parties. Loring capped the climax by sending Tumblety a challenge, which was carried by Pollack. Tumblety received the missive with contempt and paid no further attention to it.

—*St. Louis Post-Dispatch*, December 19, 1888

Tumblety's business travels between 1865 and 1873 were primarily through what was called the panhandle route of the Pennsylvania Railroad line, which included Chicago, Cincinnati, Pittsburgh, Philadelphia, and New Jersey, and Tumblety extended it to Brooklyn, New York. He primarily used the railroads for his travels between interior US cities. Tumblety opened offices in these cities, returning to Cincinnati and Pittsburgh on numerous occasions. He bypassed Philadelphia, but since the Philadelphia mayor put out a warrant for his arrest in 1863, this makes sense. Aside from being convenient stops on the Pennsylvania Railroad line, his focus on the panhandle route seems to have been for two reasons. First, these were fresh cities with citizens Tumblety had yet to exploit. Second, all of these cities are north of the Mason-Dixon line. Tumblety likely chose these cities in order to avoid the war-torn Southern cities, and opted to stay in the Northern territory where business was good. Also, since he was arrested in 1865 for being a Southern sympathizer, avoiding these locations seems logical.

The first post-Civil War panhandle city Tumblety opened an office in was Cincinnati, Ohio, and he brought along his young Brooklyn office assistant who helped him in St. Louis in 1865, Mark Albert Blackburn. It was at this time that Mark Blackburn met his first wife, Cincinnatian Olivia (Olevia) Young, quickly marrying her in 1866. It was also the location where Tumblety wrote and compiled his first autobiography, his 1866 version, which was published in Cincinnati, Ohio.

In 1868, Tumblety opened an office in New Jersey, but continued to push for the British government to intervene on his behalf with his claim against the US government. He sent a letter to Sir Edward Thornton, the British Minister in Washington DC:

30 April 1868
Honor'd Sir,
'I am a British subject.' With my father I came from Ireland to America while still a youth. I have never sought to detach myself by American Naturalization from the govt. whose jurisdiction I was born . . . I was arrested, conveyed to Washington by order of Mr. Stanton, Secretary of War, thrust into the Old Capitol Prison, and incarcerated there several weeks . . . I do not expect ever to regain my former condition of health. In fact it is a measure owing to my feebleness that I have not long since made application for redress through you . . . I had made application to your distinguished predecessor and my case was, by his agency, making favorable progress at the time of his lamentable decease . . .
Honor'd sir, Yr very profound obedt servt,
Francis Tumblety M.D.
18 Exchange Place
Jersey City

Not getting anywhere, he then sent an extensive letter to Lord Stanley, who at that time was the secretary of foreign affairs in London. Here is an excerpt and note from Tumblety, explaining he believed his claim to be $100,000:

6 May 1868
My Lord,

Enclosed please find copies respectively of two let-
ters—the first from myself to the British Minister, at Wash-
ington, and his reply thereto,—also a pamphlet containing
an outline, in brief, of my life . . . I place my claim at what
I think would be considered upon the proofs a moderate
amount—One Hundred thousand dollars—$100,000.

Allow me to subscribe myself My Lord, your Lordship's
very humble obedient servant, Francis Tumblety M.D.

The famous private detective out of Chicago, William
Pinkerton, commented upon seeing Tumblety in 1869:

'In Chicago, along about '69, he [Tumblety] *was detected*
in indulging in the vices to which I have referred and he
had to fly that city . . .'

Tumblety had nothing good to say about Chicago after
this event. Note what he stated in 1889 to a *St. Louis Rambler*
reporter, "Now, it's different in Chicago, which I consider a
veritable modern Babylon. The Chicagoese are a grasping,
avaricious set mean and vulgar in manner, worshippers
of the almighty dollar and salted pork; may I be delivered
from Chicago." How interesting that Tumblety's opinion
about Chicago citizens matches Tumblety himself. Tumblety
participated in "modern Babylon" sexual activities, and he was
known to value the dollar. Tumblety's New Orleans attorney
stated: "To sum it all up I came to the conclusion that Dr.
Tumilty was a man who was given to impulses. I considered
him a man, also, who had a very high regard for the almighty
dollar, for this reason, that in my professional dealings with
him I noticed that."

Tumblety was making no progress with his requests for
the British government to assist him in his claim against
the US government for losses during his St. Louis arrest and
incarceration in Washington DC; in 1869, he took his first trip
back across the Atlantic to England. While he had a relative
living near Liverpool, and probably visited her, the primary
reason he went to England was likely to push his claim.

A huge business opportunity occurred on May 10, 1869, when the state of California was connected to the eastern states by the transcontinental railroad, built with government assistance from the Pacific Railway Act of 1862. Once the Civil War ended, construction resumed. While in the east, Tumblety began to take his name off his newspaper advertisements. San Francisco, with its 150,000 inhabitants, was ripe for Tumblety the Celebrated Indian herb doctor. Interestingly, he added his name again to his ad, but only once. In the *Daily Evening Bulletin*, San Francisco, Tumblety placed a full-column ad in the June 13, 1870, issue titled, ODE TO AN INDIAN HERB DOCTOR. His name was embedded inside a long poem with the line, "Medical potions of Tumblety's making." San Francisco witnesses commented upon his business being large and successful.

By November 1870, Tumblety was back in New York, but only using the title "Indian Herb Doctor" in his ads, eliminating his name completely:

'$30 Reward if the Indian Herb Doctor fails to describe diseases,' Office No. 284 Fulton Street.
　　—*Brooklyn Daily Eagle*, November 1870

'Pimples on the face removed free of charge at the Indian Herb Doctor's office, 850 Broadway.'
　　—*The Sun*, March 4, 1871

'More Testimony. The Indian Herb Doctor of 850 Broadway has cured . . .'
　　—*The Sun*, April 5, 1871, and April 22, 1871

'The Indian Herb Doctor of 263 Fulton St. Brooklyn as cured . . .'
　　—*The Sun*, May 11, 1871 to August 17, 1871

Small ad for 'The Indian Herb Doctor of 263 Fulton St., Brooklyn' Name not connected.
　　—*The Sun*, August 17, 1871

While at 263 Fulton Street in Brooklyn in 1871, Tumblety not only continued his business but he also created the next version of his autobiography, but with a different agenda. He quickly discarded it and published his 1872 version. Missing in the title of both versions was the phrase "Indian Herb Doctor." Tumblety revised his autobiography throughout his life a total of seven times, in 1866 in Pittsburgh, 1871 in Brooklyn, 1872 in New York City, 1875 in England, 1889 in New York City, 1893 in New York City, and finally 1900 in Baltimore.

6

The Great American Doctor

*Who is the Great American Doctor? . . . great is the number
of people who, accepting his assertions as facts, rush to 142
Duke-street, and there ask his advice, pay his heavy fees, and
receive bottles of medicine which is said to be so compounded
by new and infallible processes that it will effect cures where
all other doctors have despaired.*
—*Liverpool Leader,* January 2, 1875

Soon after Tumblety's arrest and incarceration with
the Lincoln assassination investigation, Tumblety changed
a particular component of his business plan—the very
component that had made him millions. He began to shed
his Indian herb doctor persona, and evidence suggests this
is the reason why he published a new version of his 1866
autobiography in 1872. The beginning of the long title of the
1866 version was:

*A Few Passages in the Life of Dr. Francis Tumblety, The
Indian Herb Doctor, Including his Experiences in the Old
Capital Prison.*

Tumblety eliminated the title "Indian Herb Doctor" from his
1872 version:

*Narrative of Dr. Tumblety: How He was Kidnapped, Dur-
ing the American War, His Incarceration and Discharge.*

A Veritable Reign of Terror. An Exciting Life Sketch, with Important Letters and Documents from Generals Lee and Sherman, Earl De Grey, Lords Stanley, Headley and Ten-terden, Sir Edward Thornton, Horace Greeley, Abraham Lincoln, and Other Notable Celebrities, Including Private Passages Concerning the Ex-Emperor Napoleon, who Endowed the Author with the Cross of Legion of Honor; Presentation and Friendly Relations with Kaiser William of Prussia . . .

Not only was the phrase "Indian Herb Doctor" taken out of the title, it was also taken out of the body of the autobiography entirely, keeping in mind the 1866 version used Indian herb doctor a total of nineteen times. The particular poem Tumblety republished in his 1866 autobiography from the St. John, New Brunswick, Canada, paper, the *Albion*, which commented upon him being a dangerous man to widow or maid, was also omitted. The theme of the poem is about his herbal treatments and cures, clearly the reason why he omitted it. Note how the poem begins: "Dr. Tumblety rode a white steed, Into St. Johns in its time of need, Determined to cure with herbal pills, All the ailing of all their ills . . ."

Tumblety even lied in his 1889 autobiography, taking the title out in an advertised poem he used in California in 1870. In his autobiography he stated:

I cannot reflect upon my sojourn in California without re-calling a little piece of pleasantry which, in the shape of an ode, appeared in a local print:

ODE TO DR. TUMBLETY.
Cures he has wrought of each disease,
With healing herbs and barks of trees—
Samples culled from mountain and glen,
Plucked from the moor or dragged from the fen,
The mandrake, elm, and bitter bog bean . . .

Tumblety made it sound like he was not the person who placed the poem in local print, suggesting the locals loved him enough to write about him, but in fact, he did place it in local print. He had it in a large advertisement, yet the "Ode" line was different:

ODE TO THE INDIAN HERB DOCTOR.
Cures he has wrought of each disease,
With healing herbs and barks of trees—
Samples culled from mountain and glen,
Plucked from the moor or dragged from the fen,
The mandrake, elm, and bitter bog bean . . .

This June 13, 1870, *Daily Evening Bulletin* advertisement, when compared to the change he made in his 1872 autobiography, is clear evidence that Tumblety was systematically eliminating his Indian herb doctor past and replacing it with an eminent physician persona. Note how Tumblety claimed he brought "MD" credentials with him to Europe, not Indian herb doctor credentials:

I did not visit Europe without satisfactory credentials, one of which will serve as a sample: OFFICE OF WILLIAMS & GUION, No. 71 Wall Street, NEW YORK, July 13th, 1869. Messrs. A. S. PETRIE & SON, London: Dear Sirs: We have the pleasure of introducing to you Francis Tumblety M. D., of this city, a passenger per steamer Nebraska, to whom we have given a letter of credit on yourselves. Any attention to Dr. Tumblety during his stay in London will be appreciated by him and also by your friends, —WILLIAMS & GUION.

Because Tumblety had no official medical credentials, he attempted to gain legitimacy by presenting a letter from a qualified medical doctor. Just as he attempted to do at the onset of the Civil War, Tumblety claimed in his 1872 autobiography that he gained legitimacy as a medical doctor and surgeon by being accepted as one from heads of states:

The credentials which I bore were passports to the most distinguished circle, and before I became a resident of the city one week I was formally presented to the veteran King William, whom I found as simple and unostentatious

*in manner, and free and familiar in conversation, as the
most unpresuming of his subjects. His Majesty at the first
expressed a desire to consult me upon matters pertaining
to the United States, and our subsequent converse was
as free and affable as between two equals in rank. I was
honored with an appointment upon his medical staff, and
the portrait upon the title-page of this work is copied from
a photograph taken in Berlin at that time, at the instance
of the king, and represents me as I appeared in the uniform of the Imperial Guard.*

Tumblety did publish an 1871 version of his
autobiography, but he quickly replaced it with his 1872
version. The most significant change was the cover image.
The 1871 version was a photo supposedly of him wearing
a Prussian helmet and dressed in a version of a Prussian
uniform with medals. As stated in the above excerpt, the 1872
version had a sketched portrait of him without a helmet that
he claimed was copied from a photo taken of him while in
Berlin in 1869. He was again in a uniform with medals, but it
was now a Hussarian Light Cavalry Uniform.

To further gain legitimacy as a surgeon in his ever-
evolving autobiographies, in his 1889 version, he added an
introduction chapter on his diplomas:

*ONE OF SERVERAL DIPLOMAS HELD BY THE AUTHOR.
(Translation.) MILITARY AMBULANCE. SIEGE OF PARIS—
HELD DURING THE YEARS 1870 and 1871—versus THE
PRUSSIAN ARMIES.*

*The Director of the Ambulance of Brittany, established
at the RUE DU QUATRE SEPTEMBRE, 14 No., presents to
Monsieur Tumblety (Francis), M. D., the Brittany Cross,
insignia of the act, as well as the DIPLOMA, in remembrance of the kind concourse and devoted services that
he rendered in the qualification of Doctor during the war.
Paris, the 29th Jan., 1872. P. HERVE DU LORIN, Cheva-
lier, Commandant of the Ambulance of Brittany.*

Seen and approved,
(Signed),
P. HERVE DU LORIN, 21, Rue d'Arcole, 21, Paris.

Certain researchers refer to Tumblety as "the Thomsonian doctor," pointing out that a man dedicated to this botanical healing profession conflicts with a killer who would ruthlessly mutilate poor, defenseless prostitutes with a surgical knife. "Thomsonian" refers to a disciple of Samuel Thomson (1769-1843), considered by the School of Modern Herbal Medicine as the father of American herbalism. He was a New Hampshire farmer and self-taught herbalist and botanist. In 1805, he created his own botanical system centered upon the plant lobelia, also known as puke weed, and decided to take up the herbalism full-time. He believed disease was caused by cold temperatures, so treatment should be to restore the body's heat by using steam baths, cayenne pepper, laxatives, and lobelia. In 1813, he secured a patent on "Thomson's Improved System of Botanic Practice of Medicine," sold his system for $20, and established Friendly Botanical Societies. These societies proclaimed his philosophy that "every man could and ought to be his own doctor, intelligently responsible for his own health." To demonstrate how effective this approach was, by 1840, an estimated three-to-five million Americans used the Thomsonian method, opting to avoid the local medical doctor. Instead of creating a special class of medical professionals, as in medical schools, Thomson believed the skills should be within each family.

It is true that Tumblety espoused certain aspects of Thomsonian philosophy throughout his autobiographies, especially his rejection of allopathic "mineral" medicine and his claim that he had an entire reformed "vegetable" medical system. For example, in the 1866 and 1872 versions of his autobiography, he extensively quoted Thomsonian A. R. Porter:

> *The world needs to go through a process of purification, in order to make it what it ought to be, and I shall always feel proud to lend a helping hand to carry on the noble enterprise. But as it is impossible to do everything at once, those which stand out most prominently deserve our immediate attention; and upon such should be unhesitatingly directed the weapons of reform . . .*

In his 1889 version, he continues to use the exact passage but makes no mention of A. R. Porter. In other words, Tumblety plagiarized Porter. In his attempt to belittle allopathic medicine, in his 1866 and 1872 versions of his autobiographies he recruits the words of Thomas Jefferson (from a published letter to Dr. Caspar Wistar, 1807):

I have lived myself to see the disciples of Hoffman, Boer-haave, Staehl, Cullen and Brown succeed one another like the shifting figures of the magic lantern, and their fancies, like the dresses of the annual doll babies from Paris, becoming from their novelty the vogue of the day, and yielding to the next novelty their ephemeral favors.

In his 1889 version, he makes no mention of Thomas Jefferson, thus, again, Tumblety plagiarized.

The following poem was published in Tumblety's 1866 and 1872 autobiographies. Note that he signed his name, as if he authored the poem:

OUR MOTTO.
We use such balms as have no strife
With Nature or the laws of Life;
With blood our hands we never stain,
Nor poison men to ease their pain.
Our Father—whom all goodness fills—
Provides the means to cure all ills;
The simple herb beneath our feet,
Well used, relieves our pains complete.
A simple herb, a simple flower,
Culled from the dewy lea—
These, these shall speak with touching power
Of change and health to thee.
    F. TUMBLETY, M. D.

He also published the poem in his *Pittsburgh Daily Post*, April 12, 1872, advertisement. A Dr. Jackson, Indian botanical physician, also used the poem in his earlier *Westfield Republican*, April 14, 1858, advertisement. In the newspaper, *The Corrector*, February 22, 1837, this poem was published by a Dr. S. Spike, operator of a Thomsonian vegetable medicine store. This poem was part of a larger poem in Samuel Thomson's, "Lobelia Speaks for Itself," in the *Thomsonian Recorder*, June 6, 1835.

Although he did indeed quote selected aspects of Thomsonian philosophy in his autobiographies and advertisements, Francis Tumblety was not a Thomsonian. Tumblety did not claim that the cause of disease was cold, as the Thomsonians claimed. In Tumblety's 1893 autobiography, he states that disease comes—at least in part—from the brain:

> The reader will readily see the importance of this subject when he considers the fact, that the brain is the organ of the mind, and at the same time it is a part of the animal system, governed by the same general laws as the other organs of the body, and by means of the spinal marrow and the nerves, is most intimately connected with all parts of the physical organism . . . By keeping this fact in view, it will be easy to understand why the state of the mind has so much influence in the production of disease, as well as in the recovery of the sick patient.
>
> The other two were placed in new, clean beds, but were told that two others had died in those beds of cholera, and that this was the means by which they were to be executed. The effect upon their imaginations was so great that in a few hours they had both taken the disease and died. No small share of the suffering and diseases of the human race have their origin in the emotions of the mind.
>
> Disease, then, is the result of the violation of these laws [of nature], which are within the province of man to discover, and within his power to obey.

Tumblety was an Indian herb doctor. According to Brian Altonen, PhD, the first Indian root doctors had absolutely no connection with the concurrent botanical Thomsonian movement. Being a botanical medical system, Indian herbal philosophy was included in the Thomsonian philosophy, but according to Altonen, "Thomsonians championed lobelia, which was not prioritized in Indian herbal remedies." Corroborating Altonen's statement, lobelia is absent from Tumblety's autobiographies and from his herbal lists that were published on two separate occasions. Ironically, when Tumblety used the Thomsonian "Our Motto" poem in his autobiography, it was taken from Thomson's article, "Lobelia

Speaks for Itself." The main subject of the article was never published by Tumblety.

Altonen explains that between 1795 and 1825 the public had a serious distrust with regular doctors for a number of reasons, and this opened up opportunities for both botanical philosophies. Many in the rural religious communities were convinced that the medical community were all atheist scientists pushing relativism and natural philosophy over dogmatic faith. Also, it was common knowledge that regular physicians relied upon mercury and painful blood-letting with the lancet, while botanical remedies were usually painless.

Advertising Indian herb doctors found their origins in a Peter Smith (1753–1818). Smith was born in Wales, the son of a physician, and educated as a physician in Princeton. He was a devout Puritan and preached in the Ohio Valley. At the same time, he treated patients with his botanical remedies. He called himself "Peter Smith, the Indian Herb Doctor," preferring to heal with herbs and roots, as opposed to allopathic remedies. He called himself an Indian doctor because he claimed his herbal and root remedies were known to the local Indians. While there is evidence of individuals practicing Indian herbal remedies prior to Smith, he was the first to publish on his Indian herbal remedies, thus creating a reference for future practitioners. Smith published a book in 1813 titled, *The Indian Doctor's Dispensatory: Being Father Smith's Advice Respecting Disease and Their Cure.*

A more significant difference between Thomson and Tumblety, and for that matter between Smith and Tumblety, was their ultimate agenda. Thomson believed he discovered a complete medical system that was "salutary and efficacious," meaning, beneficial and effective, that was a superior alternative to the allopathic chemical medical system used by the established medical community. Neither Thomson nor Smith claimed their systems were cure-alls and offered their medical systems to anyone. Tumblety, on the other hand, claimed *he* could cure any disease, using phrases like, "Provides the means to cure all ills," and, "Cures he has wrought of each disease," and published testimonies from supposed patients proclaiming complete cures under his care. Tumblety did not promote his Indian herbal system, but promoted himself. He was, for all practical purposes, a miracle medical doctor—according to his advertisements. But because his treatments were not cure-alls, his agenda was exploitation for financial gain.

As noted in Chapter 3, Tumblety received his Indian herb doctor education from R. J. Lyons, even if it was a case of working in his office and learning the trade by observing and reading his boss' pamphlets. Both men used the same poems in their advertisements. The above "Our Motto" poem was used by Lyons in his *Michigan Argus*, December 1, 1865, advertisement. The following is a second Thomsonian poem, written in a Lyons ad in the *Livingston Republican*, February 21, 1856, and in a Tumblety ad in the *Evening Star*, April 2, 1862:

> *I have come your prostrate heart to lift,*
> *Your bleeding wounds to cure,*
> *And with the treasure of Nature's Gift,*
> *Relieve the rich and poor.*

Tumblety's practice of publishing a "Sketch in the Life" autobiographical pamphlet actually came from Lyons. Lyons' *Westfield Republican*, June 18, 1856, advertisement states:

> *The doctor would respectfully request all those who desire to know more about him, to call at his office, where they can procure, free of charge a pamphlet containing a short history of Medicines also; a brief sketch of his life, study and extensive travels.*

Notice that Lyons also stated his pamphlet contains a short history of medicines and a brief sketch in his life. Instead of Tumblety borrowing Thomsonian philosophy for his autobiography, it was likely Lyons who did, and Tumblety merely copied the philosophy. Recall, Tumblety copied Reynold's French cures pamphlet word for word.

While he followed in the footsteps of Indian herb doctor Rudolf J. Lyons, he never mentioned Lyons' name in his autobiography. He purposely hid his professional tracks just as R. J. Lyons did. Lyons published that he personally discovered the Indian herbal remedies by trekking through South America, clearly to show he was a true expert and one of a kind. Even his earlier censuses stated he was born in South America. In the censuses later in his life, he finally admitted that he was born in Virginia. Tumblety never mentions how he learned the trade in his 1866 autobiography and begins by stating, "I had been practicing my profession in Canada with distinguished success, and, in the course of a prosperous career, I accumulated an equal amount of profit and of fame." In his 1889 autobiography, Tumblety makes the same comment but begins it with, "As far back as the year 1857 I had, in accordance with the principles I espoused, been practicing my profession in Canada . . ."

Tumblety's professional Canadian experience from 1857 to 1860 made him a millionaire in today's dollars, and it changed his life. Dragging this alternative medical money cow down was the local medical community constantly labeling him as a quack. While the primary agenda for Tumblety's 1866 autobiography was to "vindicate" his poor treatment by Secretary of War Edwin Stanton, his use of Thomsonian philosophy was for a different purpose. Tumblety was far from finishing his lucrative profession, and a possible reputation of being a quack was the biggest threat. In the mid-nineteenth century, the established Thomsonian system was as close to being legitimate as any alternative medicine had ever been. It made business sense to mask as a "neo-Thomsonian." Never did Tumblety give back to any botanical community, found in every city, with lectures, published papers on his own discoveries, or lessons learned; and any examples of possible altruism, such as giving flour to the poor in Rochester and Buffalo, always had a publicity angle attached to it. Tumblety was about Tumblety.

Another divergence from Thomsonian philosophy was Tumblety's emphasis on blood, which was central to Tumblety's vegetable healing philosophy. Note what he states in his 1893 autobiography:

> *The human body, consisting of bones, muscles, sinews, blood vessels, organs of reproduction, nutrition, respiration and of thought, etc., is constructed, nourished and sustained in accordance with certain laws common to organized beings. It is made up of the elements that surround us, such as animals, vegetables and water. These*

*substances, taken into the stomach, undergo the process
of digestion, and the chyle or nutritious portion enters into
the composition of the blood, and by this means is brought
in contact with all parts of the system.* [p. 126]

Tumblety had models of the circulatory system in the front
window of his offices because blood carried the *chyle*, what
was referred to in the nineteenth century as the nutritious
portion of the blood.

A further difference between a Thomsonian and Tumblety
was his continued interest in connecting himself with
surgery and surgical instruments. Recall Tumblety's attempt
to convince General McClellan that he was a good enough
surgeon to be on his staff and his claim he received a diploma
in France by the Director of the Ambulance of Brittany. Norris
recalled Tumblety's collection of surgical knives. It does make
sense that he would possess a collection of surgical knives,
since he personally traveled to Washington DC and offered
his services to join the general's medical team as a surgeon.
When Tumblety had checked into St. John's Hospital in
St. Louis in May 1903 to die, he was attended by physician
J. H. Ziegler, MD. In sworn testimony in 1905, Dr. Ziegler
stated he saw Tumblety every day from May 2 to May 28, and
Tumblety would discuss medicine with him on a daily basis.
He stated that Tumblety would quiz him on how to handle
patients in an office setting in the country and explained that
the questions Tumblety asked required medical knowledge.
He then stated that they talked about surgery, and Tumblety
asked him what kind of operations he had seen. Ziegler
stated, "He [Tumblety] would ask about an amputation; if I
had seen any amputations, and I told him I had." When asked
if Tumblety talked about tying up the arteries, Ziegler said
yes, and sewing up the flesh over the wound. If Tumblety was
only interested in botanical cures—per his advertisements—
then having an interest in the surgical operation of
amputation makes little sense.

On July 21, 1873, Tumblety began his yearly trips to
England, eventually opening an office in Liverpool in the fall
of 1874. What he did prior to opening an office is likely the
primary reason he crossed the Atlantic. In just over a month

after his arrival, Tumblety checked into a London hotel and mailed two letters to Lord Granville; the first on September 2, and the second on September 9, in an attempt to have Granville intervene on his $100,000 claim against the US government for his arrest and incarceration at the Old Capital Building after the assassination of Lincoln:

> *Langham Hotel, Langham Place, Regent Street,*
> *Sept 2nd 1873*
> *My Lord,*
>   *I beg respectfully, to call upon your Lordship's attention to a copy of a letter received from Sir Edward Thornton by me and to request that your Lordship will cause me to be furnished with a copy of any communication that Sir Edward Thornton may have made to your Lordship in this matter and also of your Lordship's reply thereto. My stay in England is protracted at much cost and I am sure I may rely upon your Lordship's direction that prompt attention shall be given hereto.*
>   *I have the honor to be Your Lordship's most obedient & humble Servant*
>   *Francis Tumblety M.D.*

AND

> *No. 58 Margaret Street, Cavendish Square*
> *Sept 9th 1873*
> *My Lord,*
>   *Having removed my quarters from 255 Langham Hotel, I beg very respectfully to call your Lordship's attention to my letter under date 2nd inst. with respect to which I am of course most anxious to learn that it has reached your Lordship's hands as I am sure I may be satisfied that is tantamount to its receiving your immediate consideration.*
>   *May I beg the favour of your Lordship's acknowledgment hereof at your early convenience.*

Even after Tumblety opened up his office in Liverpool in September 1874, he continued to push the British government to intervene on his behalf. The following is a letter to the Earl of Derby:

177 Duke Street, Liverpool, September 30, 1874
My Lord,
Earl Granville having informed me in a letter dated, Jan 9 1873 that my claim against the United States Government, for having arrested and imprisoned me on two occasions in the year 1865, would be investigated by the Claims Commission, will your Lordship be good enough to inform me if my claim was included in the award recently made by that commission.
I am, My Lord, Your Lordship's most Obedient Humble Servant,
Francis Tumblety, M.D.

Tumblety received no assistance, but his incredible persistence continued until 1876, when his lawyer sent a letter to the Earl of Derby; but on May 22, 1876, the Foreign Office responded saying there was nothing they could do.

During this time, the US economy was tanking, beginning in 1873 with a financial crisis referred to as the Panic of 1873, which was caused in large part by an excessive influx of capital in the blossoming railroad industry, plus a switch from a gold and silver standard of backing currency to a gold-only standard. This began a two-decade-long depression, known as the Long Depression, and prior to the Great Depression of the early twentieth century, it was referred as the Great Depression, being the worst economic crisis at that time. Banks from California to New York were failing. It is likely not a coincidence, but more of a response to the economic downturn, that Tumblety began shifting his business to England. It is also the time he stopped advertising in the United States. Note what he wrote to his young male interest from Liverpool, Henry Hall Caine, in September 1875. Tumblety left Liverpool and visited London:

August 31, 1875
My dear friend,
I suppose you notice the failure of some of the banks in California, I have just recd a dispatch calling me there at once, answer this note and direct it to the National Hotel Courtlandt Street New York . . . I have just this moment

got a ticket & will sail at 10 o'clock tomorrow from London by the 'Greece' of the National Line . . . —Your Affec friend, Francis Tumblety MD

After arriving in New York, he wrote back commenting upon how bad business was:

National Hotel
Courtlandt Street, Sept 29, 1875
Dear Caine,
. . . Much as I desire your company, however, I would not advise anyone to leave their homes for America at the present time, and business, in all its branches is extremely dull, both machined, and those who follow professions finding it difficult to live with any of the comforts suitable and necessary to their positions. Neither is there any hope for better times until a change takes place in the administration . . . —Yours Affectionately, Francis Tumblety M.D.

He wrote to Hall Caine again from San Francisco on December 30, 1875, requesting to meet in Philadelphia in the Centennial (1876). The last extant letter to Caine was dated March 31, 1876, when Tumblety arrived in St. Louis from California, "My Dear Friend Caine, I left San Francisco on the first of March and am now on the banks of the Mississippi River . . ." Note an Associated Press report in the *Great Falls Leader*, January 11, 1889, commenting upon this:

He calls himself 'Doctor Francis Tumblety,' and though the oddity of the name suggests that it is assumed, he had been called by it ever since he was first known in America, though the Rochester witnesses think it was there spelled Twombletey. His 'herb doctoring' finally became unprofitable in America; so he went to London . . .

According to the *Liverpool Leader*, in an article that was attempting to ridicule Tumblety, they reluctantly admitted Tumblety was reaping him over $200 a day in Liverpool, which equals $4,000 in today's value. Opening up an office in Liverpool was clearly a smart business decision.

At the end of January 1875, Tumblety left Liverpool for London and stayed there for six months, likely running away from legal issues, as he had done in the past. From November 2 to December 12, 1874, one of the many testimonials in his advertisements was by a William Carroll, stating he was cured by the Great American Doctor. Carroll was incensed, and in January 1875, he sued Tumblety for £200 at the Liverpool County Court. Tumblety's barrister successfully postponed the case for a month. Also at the same time, a patient under Tumblety's care died; Edward Hanratty. He had congested lungs and heart disease, and on January 11, 1875 he visited Tumblety's office in Liverpool at 177 Duke Street. Tumblety told Hanratty he would have no medicine until Wednesday, January 13. Hanratty and his wife picked it up, and on that night, he took the medicine, then soon died. After being questioned at the inquest, Tumblety stated that he only sold medicine and knew nothing about disease. The conclusion was that Hanratty died of natural causes, but Tumblety fled, leaving Hall Caine to handle his Liverpool affairs.

Tumblety and Hall Caine continued writing to each other; Tumblety wrote frequently, pressuring Hall Caine to finish the English version of his autobiography by adding testimonials of famous British personalities in order to combat to an English audience the negative publicity he was receiving in the *Liverpool Leader*. On March 31, 1875, Tumblety wrote Hall Caine about opening an office with him in London:

> *I know how you are situated now I think of commencing business here and I could manufacture better pills than Holloways and I would give all of them the people a box free of charge in order to introduce them, and let the people test them and judge for themselves, and all who were not satisfied with the pills £0 worth given away to the people would break down Holloway's and Brandreth's besides it would create a fresh sensation. To do this I must have a partner who can share the profits, there is no place in the world like England for good pills to make the enterprise a success the pills must be just what they are purported to be and that's all that's necessary.*

Soon after, on April 9, 1875, Tumblety wrote, "Dear Caine, . . . I have told you more than one occasion to quit Liverpool and come with me and I will guarantee you to make more money by the operation than you will in Liverpool." This statement suggests Tumblety did begin his pills operation, as in opening an office in London. Tumblety stayed in London for six months before he moved on to Birmingham, where he opened an office. At the start of August he was in London, then his letters came from Birmingham beginning August 6, 1875. In the *Birmingham Daily Post,* August 14, 1875, Tumblety placed an ad—without his name, just "The great American Doctor, from British America"—opening an office for consultation at 50 Union Passage. It was his "Our Motto" ad with the addition of his Pimple Banisher ad. According to one of his letters to Hall Caine, Tumblety left Birmingham for the US on August 31 because he needed to go to California to handle his banking. He was likely going to stay in Birmingham longer, as he noted his success in his letter. Never did Tumblety stay in one location for an extended period and not open up an office, meaning it would have been odd behavior on Tumblety's part if he did not open up an office in London. In view of this, the reports of Tumblety opening up an office in London conforms to his business practices.

One particular eyewitness account of Tumblety during this time commented upon his high-end lifestyle in the early 1870s, and his taste for young men, but then noted his change of behavior and dress by 1879:

> *Dr. Tumblety.*
>
> *Clement R. Bennett, the well-known stenographer of the Circuit Court, knew Dr. Tumblety of New York, who has been arrested in London . . . 'The first time I ever saw Tumblety was at the Jerome Park fall races in 1870. I was then living in that fashionable suburb, Fordham . . . About 1874 he roomed at the Northern Hotel, on Cortlandt Street. Here he had a magnificent suit [sic] of rooms, the floors of which were covered with well-worn leather trunks, valises, and bags. He cordially invited any young men whom he fancied, wherever he met them, in the parks, squares or stores, to call upon him at this hotel, where he was wont to say he would show them "an easy road to fortune." By his suavity he was successful beyond comprehension in enlisting and securing the attendance, at certain hours of the day and evening of good-looking young men and*

*boys, greenhorns, to "walk into my parlor." He pretended
to be a "specialist" and to have a cure for some of the ills
which flesh is heir to. On one occasion I remember him
showing me several valuable medals given him by British
and colonial societies, with a collection of complimentary
letters and testimonial from English noblemen . . . Up to
the centennial year [1876] F. T. Tumblety, M.D., the name
he was known by in New York, appeared to be in easy
circumstances. He was a noted horseback rider and was
a familiar figure in the saddle on Broadway. In stature
he was about six feet one or two inches, weighed about
180 pounds, and he is now 50 years of age. He wore
a thick, curly, black mustache, clean-shaven re cheeks,
and there is a journalist in this city who bears a striking
resemblance to Dr. Tumblety. He invariably wore a dou-
ble-breasted, buttoned-up pea-jacket, light pantaloons, a
flashy necktie, cloth gaiters on his English box-toe shoes,
a military or university cap, with a gold cord lying upon
the straight peak, and some loud jewelry. The last time I
saw him was about 1879. He was then looking shabby,
care-worn, lame, appeared to be living a dissolute and
dissipated life, and was begging for a night's lodging.'*
—*San Francisco Chronicle*, November 20, 1888

Corroborating Bennett's recollection was the fact that
Tumblety certainly did prefer the high-end hotels on Cortlandt
Street, as evidenced by his letters to Hall Caine in 1875. An
example of Tumblety and his habit of chasing young men in
the late 1870s is young Lyons:

*William P. Burr, of No. 320 Broadway, speaking of the
man yesterday, said: "I met him in July, 1880. He brought
a suit against a Mrs. Lyons, charging her with the larceny
of $7,000 worth of bonds, and I was retained to defend
her. It seems that several years before he met the son of
Mrs. Lyons while walking on the Battery. The lad had just
come from college and was a fine looking young man. He
was out of employment. Tumblety greeted him and soon
had him under complete control. He made him a sort of
secretary in the management of his bonds, of which he
had about $100,000 worth, mostly in governments, locked*

up in a downtown safe-deposit company. He employed the youth as an amanuensis, as he personally was most illiterate. On April 23, 1878, the 'Doctor,' as he was called, started for Europe by the Guion line steamer Montana. See, here is his name on the passenger-list, 'Dr. Tumblety.' . . . At this time he kept an herb store, or something of that sort, at No. 77 East Tenth street. The suit did not come to anything, and I do not know of any other law matters in which this notorious man was concerned. "I had seen him before that time hovering about the old post office building, where there were many clerks. He had a seeming mania for the company of young men and grown-up youths. . . . I had a big batch of letters sent by him to the young man Lyon, and they were the most amusing farrago of illiterate nonsense. Here is one written from the West. He never failed to warn his correspondence against lewd women, and in doing it used the most shocking language."
—Rochester Democrat and Republican, *December 3, 1888*

Note that Tumblety traveled on the steamship *Montana* in 1878, corroborating reports that he traveled to England throughout the 1870s. The attorney also stated that Tumblety had an office in New York in 1878. Tumblety's letter to Hall Caine in the fall of 1875 stated that business in New York was extremely dull, implying he had opened an office there. Neither in 1875 nor in 1878 did Tumblety place any newspaper ads as he did in the 1860s. Perhaps business in the Long Depression was so slow that placing expensive ads was no longer profitable. His advertising in England parallels this. In Liverpool, in the fall of 1874 and early in 1875, he placed huge ads, but he purposely omitted his name. Once he left Liverpool, an advertisement by Tumblety was discovered in a Birmingham newspaper, but his name was again omitted. None are found in London, yet we have a couple accounts that suggest he opened up an office there—without advertising in the local newspaper, as he neglected to do when he was working in New York. Remember, Tumblety also proposed to Hall Caine to help him open up an office in London and later requested the young man to leave Liverpool and join him, which suggests Tumblety may have opened a London office.

Tumblety's nephew, Thomas Powderly, stated in sworn testimony that the doctor had visited Powderly's mother around 1880/1881. In his testimony, Powderly referred to a case where Tumblety was in jail in Toronto for sodomy. The following newspaper articles report on this arrest, Tumblety being incarcerated in October 1881 for indecent assault against a young man named Bulger:

AN UNNATURAL CRIME.
Francis Tumblety was arrested last night by Policeman Clark on a charge of having committed an indecent assault on a youth named Bulgar. He was detained at Court-street Station.
     —*Toronto Globe,* October 15, 1880

INDECENT ASSAULT.
Francis Tumblety was up on remand this morning charged with indecent assault on the person of a boy named Bulger on the night of October 14th. His Worship, after hearing the evidence of Bulger, was of the opinion that it could only be established as a common assault, and imposed a fine of $1 and costs, which the prisoner paid.
     —*Toronto Globe,* October 19, 1880

The phrase "unnatural crime" was a nineteenth-century euphemism for sexual assault or sodomy, and in fact Powderly stated, "In jail at Toronto; arrested for sodomy." It was reported that Tumblety spent the weekend in jail. According to the 1880 census, Thomas Powderly's mother lived in Waterloo, New York, which is about forty miles east-southeast of Rochester, located between Toronto and his residence in New York City.

Around the year 1880, there was a shift in Tumblety's travel behavior: He began spending more time in the southern United States. Under sworn testimony, John Geary, the proprietor of the Geary Hotel in Hot Springs, Arkansas, stated when Tumblety told him he first visited, ". . . he told me last winter [1902] that he had been coming here for twenty-two years [since 1880]. I don't know that I was acquainted with him for the first year or so, but I knowed him about twenty years." Besides making his annual, possibly biannual, visits to England and Hot Springs, numerous sworn testimonies show him adding St. Louis (Missouri) and New Orleans to his annual itinerary. While Tumblety continued to visit the northern cities of Toronto, Rochester, Saratoga, and New York, in 1880, this notable change of staying in southern cities for weeks on end was likely around the time he stopped running an office in New York City and spending the lion's share of his time away. It is also the time he was reported as telling his young men he was a retired surgeon. Note in Richard Norris' sworn testimony when Tumblety introduced himself to Norris in around 1880:

I met Dr. Francis Tumilty, I think, in 1880, during Mardi-Gras. I was at the St. Charles Theatre, and he had a seat alongside of me. During the intermission, a fellow and I got up to go and get a drink, and he followed us. When we got to the counter he introduced himself, saying he was [a] stranger here for the Mardi-Gras holidays, and asked us the privilege of treating. He did not notice my friend much, but seemed to pay all attention to me, and wanted to know my business. I told him I was then employed by the American District Telegraph Office, in charge of the telephone exchange here, when it was up in the Denegre Building; and he told me that he was a surgeon, drawing a pension from the government, and that he was a stockholder in the Western Union.

These visits were not short. Note the comments made by George H. Lower, a court clerk in Hot Springs who knew Tumblety well for about twenty years when working for the *Daily Sentinel*, which would have been around 1883. He remembered Tumblety telling him he was going to Europe after his visit. Lower stated Tumblety would stay in Hot Springs for three to six weeks at a time. Lower got into the drug business. He stated, "He seemed very much attached to me. . . . he complained to me more about his heart than anything else, --- that his heart was wrong. 'George,' he said, 'my heart is wrong.' He said, 'I will go some day that quick.'"

A. R. Smith, proprietor of the Hotel Navarre, Hot Springs, in 1905, served one term as mayor in 1882 and recalled Tumblety coming to him requesting to carry a gun, because he believed he was being threatened. Smith believed Tumblety was not of sound mind and refused his request. He then commented about his habit of being a loner constantly on the streets, especially at night:

> I would see him on the streets frequently. As I say, he was a public character on the streets, and you would always find him on the streets just at nightfall. He spent a great deal of time on the streets. . . . I think he has been of unsound mind ever since I first met him. Well, a man of his actions, a man that would make the complaints that he did, that would write the notes that he did without any foundation whatever for any of these complaints. He would write a note of three or four pages. . . . He was a man who kept entirely to himself, had no associates. I would see him on the streets and he would be walking along talking to himself. And when I met him on the street he never recognized me, never spoke or bowed to me on the street, never seemed to notice anybody, always by himself.

John Geary of the Geary Hotel in Hot Springs stated he first knew Tumblety around 1882/83 and that he generally kept to himself. He then recalled Tumblety "taking up with tramps." He stated, "Well, he was in the habit of taking up with any kind of tramps on the streets. I would sometimes take him on a side and have a talk with him."

Just as he did with George Lower, Tumblety commented to Geary about his health problems and his belief that he may die any time. The attorney asked, "Did he complain of heart trouble?" Geary replied yes, and stated Tumblety attributed it, "from his affliction and heart disease; on the account of wasting away." The attorney asked, "And that he was losing flesh?" Geary stated, "Yes sir. . . . Oh, he said, so many things to me, that I couldn't exactly tell you that he did say. I didn't pay any attention to him. He told me that he thought he wouldn't live, and that he had heart trouble, and was liable to die at any time." Geary stated Tumblety began to come to Hot Springs in 1880, a location he chose for hydrotherapy. This change of travel behavior may have been because of his heart and kidney condition.

Martin H. McGarry was a young male hired by Tumblety in New York City in 1882. He told a *New York World* reporter on December 4, 1888, how Tumblety recruited him, which reveals a change in his business practice:

> *It was July 1882, that I applied for work at No. 7 University Place. I saw a big, fine-looking man standing on the stoop. He had on a braided English smoking jacket, black-striped trousers, Oxford ties and a peaked cap. He told me there was no work for me in the house, but if I wanted to work he would give me a trial. I asked him what he wished me to do, and he said he was in need of a traveling companion. We walked upstairs to his room, and he told me all about himself, and I afterwards found it was true.*
>
> *He was born near Dublin, Ireland, in 1835, and was the son of a wealthy Irish gentleman. He was educated at the University of Dublin, where he graduated, as he showed by his diploma. He then studied medicine in Dublin and got another diploma, which he also showed me. In 1853 he left Ireland for America, landing in New York. Here he studied surgery, and when the war broke out he was an army surgeon. He showed me his honorable discharge from the army, and a number of personal letters from General Grant speaking of his efficiency and good conduct. About this time his father died and left him a big lot of money. I don't know how much, but it kept him from having to do anything for a living.*
>
> *He took a liking to me, and that day I was employed by him. My duties were not hard. I was always to be near him. He got up at 11 o'clock when he would usually send out his jug for a pint of old ale. He breakfasted in the house and then walked around town. Usually he went up to the Morton House, where he pointed out the actors to me and told me who they were and what they did. Sometimes in the afternoons we would drop in to the matinees. In the evenings we would stay at home generally. After we had been in New York a while he said we were to go to Niagara Falls. We stopped at a French hotel where everybody knew the doctor and seemed glad to see him.*

He showed me about, and after a short time grew tired of the place and we started to Rochester.

After we saw everything about Rochester we went to Saratoga. The Doctor took rooms at No. 151 Congress street. It was the finest suite of rooms at the Springs; there was nothing at the Grand Union that could approach them. We stayed there two months and enjoyed life. He was very kind to me and sent my people presents. We came back to New York, where we spent the Winter. He had nothing to do but amuse himself, and he used to walk about town, ride, and drive through the Park, and read to me and have me read to him. He kept everything that was said about him in the newspapers. He had no associates or companions but me, and sometimes for days I would be the only one he would talk to.

After a trip to Rome N.Y. we returned to New York and went to the Hygeia Hotel on Laight street, although the Doctor still kept his rooms on University Place. He took the front parlor room and I went back to my folk, No. 300 Henry street. Although I was not boarding with him he sent the money he would have paid for my board in a package with my salary to my people.

One day he told me he wanted to see Boston, and off we started for Boston, and then visited New Haven and Philadelphia, when we stopped at the Girard Hotel in Philadelphia. It took us three weeks to see the sights in Philadelphia. The Doctor showed me everything. We came back to New York and the Doctor took it in his mind to go to Glasgow. I wouldn't go with him and he went alone. He was back in a month, and went to Mrs. McNamara's No. 79 East Tenth street to live. He telegraphed for me to come there and I lived with him for three weeks. We knocked about New York during that time and he then persuaded me to go to Queenstown with him. When we got there we went to Dublin and then after a week to Inniskillen Falls.

McGarry came to Tumblety's residence, concerned about him, and clearly had a history with him. The fact that Tumblety always hired a young man and that Tumblety traveled incessantly demonstrates the veracity of his comments. Note the change in job description of young

McGarry as compared to Tumblety's earlier young men he hired. McGarry had nothing to do with Tumblety's business, as Mark A. Blackburn did. It was for company of a wealthy man on retirement. Tumblety was certainly not running a business from an office. Note that the locations Tumblety took McGarry to were northern locations. He even took McGarry with him across the Atlantic to Ireland, Glasgow, and Queenstown. Interestingly, he never took McGarry to the southern US, but we know Tumblety had been visiting New Orleans, Hot Springs, and St. Louis yearly since 1880/81.

According to James B. Clews, Tumblety deposited his money into the Clews Bank in New York around 1884 or 1885. This may have been the time he pulled all of his cash from the various banks around the country and deposited it into one bank. It was no longer necessary to deposit his daily earnings in these city banks, since he no longer opened up offices, and wiring cash from his New York bank from any city was a simple task. This even allowed him to show off his money with only one bank receipt.

Rochester neighbor Eleanor R. Elsheimer commented upon an experience she had with Tumblety around 1885. In her deposition on May 8, 1905, Eleanor stated she did not know Tumblety personally but saw him at her parents' house. She first met him about 1885, three years before the Ripper murders. She stated that she was frightened when he turned in at their gate. She stated he was sunburned and suntanned, then continued:

> He was tall with a fierce mustache and odd looking. He had on a fur coat which looked like a spotted dog, this being strange since it was late spring.

Eleanor let him in, and he walked in and asked if John McMullin lived there. John McMullin was her father. She said, "Yes, but he isn't in." He replied, "Tell your mother that Dr. Frank Tumilty is here, and she will see me." Eleanor led her paralytic mother into the room, and they visited for about an hour. She stated that Tumblety did not pay the slightest attention to her. She felt the failure to observe her was discourteous because she was the oldest daughter and the woman of the house. She told the attorney that she was dressed in a manner as would have attracted the attention of any man. The lack of attention by Tumblety was significant enough to have the whole family discuss this afterward. His entry into their house attracted the attention of the neighbors, who actually locked their own doors because he looked like a tramp. Eleanor stated he and her mother spoke about her illness, about himself when he traveled, and he told her that he had "barrels of money, and spent barrels of money and had barrels of money left."

This is the first account of Tumblety dressing "like a tramp" during the day, which was about three years before the Whitechapel murders. The reason for his change of attire to a fur coat in May is likely for his chronic heart condition, which ultimately ended his life in 1903. Note what Tumblety stated in his 1893 autobiography on treatment for heart disease brought on by rheumatism, the very condition he had:

> A hydro mineral treatment at Neris, Plombieres or Aix-les-Bains will do wonders in checking or lessening attacks of rheumatism, and in order to avoid more certainly their recurrence it is well to follow a perfectly regular life; to avoid excesses of all sorts, to live in a perfectly dry abode exposed to sunlight, and to always wear flannel next to the skin, as it should never be forgotten that catching cold, the sudden or prolonged action of cold on the body, particularly at a moment when the temperature of the skin is raised, is especially unfavorable to anyone with a rheumatic predisposition.

While money-making was the primary motivation in Tumblety's life before 1880, living with and surviving his chronic conditions became his primary motivation after 1880.

In the 1880s up to the Whitechapel murders in 1888, there is no indication that Tumblety changed his travel habits in the US, Canada, and England. We have three accounts of him continuing his office in London, but he did not advertise. The *Evening Star*, November 27, 1888, reported:

> A few years ago the pimple-banishing enterprise was moved to London, where the doctor for a time is said to have made money. It was his queer method of spending his money which first attracted the Scotland Yard detectives to

him, and after a slight investigation he was arrested, the idea being that if he were not the Whitechapel fiend, he is a dangerous character, and is not entitled to his liberty.

In the *New York World*, November 19, 1888, it states:

During the past few years Twomblety has opened a branch office in London and has been making regular trips across the ocean at intervals of five or six months.

Never did any of his advertisements in Liverpool and Birmingham have his name associated with them; just "The Great American Doctor." When the US papers began to report on Tumblety's arrest and connection to the Whitechapel crimes in 1888, no one knew the title he used in England was the Great American Doctor, yet in an Associated Press article published in the *Bucks County Gazette*, December 13, 1888, titled "AH THERE! TUMBLETY," it refers to Tumblety as the American doctor:

. . . His 'herb doctoring' finally became unprofitable in America; so he went to London, located near the Whitechapel road and for a while did a big business. His oddity of manner, dress and speech soon made him notorious as the 'American doctor'; but he enjoyed notoriety and turned it into money, till the Whitechapel horrors caused a general overhauling of suspicious characters.

This suggests the source for the story must have been from London, thus, credible. Corroborating him opening an office are his extended stays for at least three months at a time. A fourth article does not mention Tumblety by name, but the fact that they refer to the herb doctor coming from New York is highly suggestive:

An American who used to live in New York, and who now keeps an herb shop in the Whitechapel district, was visited by a detective who asked if he had sold any unusual compound of herbs to a costomer [sic] since August.
—Bridgeport Morning News, October 8, 1888

When Tumblety opened up offices in US cities, it was not uncommon for him to change locations. At times, Tumblety had his office in Brooklyn then changed to Broadway Avenue in New York City. He even opened an office across the river in Jersey City. For the two years Tumblety first operated out of Washington DC, he was reported to have first opened up an office on H Street when his concern was attracting the attention of General McClellan, who also lived on H Street. He then opened an office at Number 11 Washington Buildings on the corner of Pennsylvania Avenue and 7th Street when he switched to promoting his Indian herb doctor business. In light of this, Tumblety likely opened up offices in numerous locations around London each time he returned annually from 1873 to 1888.

7

Reminiscences of a
Famous Physician

I was going down town Saturday evening [Rochester, mid-1890s], *and on the right hand side of Main Street as I passed the doorway I saw this man* [Tumblety]; *he was tight against the wall as he could be, with his hands down at his side looking furtively out.*

—Eleanor R. Elsheimer

Within two months of his return to New York from England on December 2, 1888, Francis Tumblety had published the next version of his autobiography, reported in the following news article out of London in the *Evening Post*, February 16, 1889:

A WHITECHAPEL SUSPECT

The New York World devotes considerable space to a notice of an autobiography just published in America by Dr. Francis Tumblety, who was arrested in London on suspicion in connection with the Whitechapel murders, but who was released immediately it was found there was no evidence to incriminate him. The [New York] *World is probably not aware that Dr. Tumblety was afterwards taken into custody on another charge, arising out of certain correspondence with young men which was found in his possession, that he was committed for trial at the Old Bailey, and that on the day fixed for the trial he failed to appear to his bail. The World describes Dr. Tumblety's book as an "unique production, a blending of poetry, history, science, and humour, a book of travels, a collection of letters, wise observations of human life, and interesting reminiscence."* Dr. Tumblety's title-page is more pretentious. *"A Sketch of the Life of the Gifted, Eccentric, and World-famed Dr. Francis Tumblety, presenting an outline of his wonderful career, professional successes, and personal intimacies with renowned personages of two hemispheres . . .*

This was his 1889 version, and the title is pretentious, exaggerating his fame and relationships with "renowned personages." While it contained much of the same content as his previous 1872 autobiography, the 1889 version added recent personal testimonies expounding upon his good character. The most significant addition—and the primary reason why he updated his autobiography—is a short chapter titled "Vindication," which was a response to what he called slanderous attacks against him recently by certain American newspapers. The only recent so-called attacks by American newspapers were those stating he was implicated by Scotland Yard in the Whitechapel murders case. Of significance is that Tumblety purposely omitted any mention of Jack the Ripper and the Whitechapel murders investigation. Instead, he blamed his connection to the case entirely on American newspaper lies:

PART III: MY VINDICATION – Chapter 1.
Now let me say a word about the attacks which certain American newspapers recently made upon me, attacks that were as unfounded as the onslaught made on the great Irish leader. While I was not in a position to defend myself, these papers continued their foul slanders . . .

Rather than producing any evidence proving his innocence, Tumblety responded exactly as he always did: He published testimonies from prominent individuals attesting to his great character. What Tumblety knew full-well was Scotland Yard's policy not to discuss the case with the press, thus, they would never challenge his statement that the American papers were entirely to blame. Because of the embarrassment of Tumblety escaping England from under their noses, Scotland Yard would likely have welcomed him blaming the American papers.

The modern claim that Tumblety was never a Whitechapel murder suspect has as its central point the belief that US newspapers were merely sensationalizing the story in order to sell papers. Tumblety's statement in his "Vindication" chapter is likely the source. Conflicting with Tumblety's claim, and the modern claim for that matter, is the above British newspaper article in the *Evening Post*. Note the article commenting upon facts they discovered on the case that the *New York World* was completely ignorant about. This information must have come from London, not America. Corroborating the British paper are Tumblety's own words from an interview he gave to a *New York World* reporter on January 29, 1889, given just weeks before his 1889 autobiography, including the "Vindication" chapter, was published:

> *"My arrest came about this way," said he. "I had been going over to England for a long time—ever since 1869, indeed—and I used to go about the city a great deal until every part of it became familiar to me.*
>
> *I happened to be there when these Whitechapel murders attracted the attention of the whole world, and, in the company with thousands of other people, I went down to the Whitechapel district. I was not dressed in a way to attract attention, I thought, though it afterwards turned out that I did. I was interested by the excitement and the crowds and the queer scenes and sights, and did not know that all the time I was being followed by English detectives."*
>
> *"Why did they follow you?"*
>
> *"My guilt was very plain to the English mind. Someone had said that Jack the Ripper was an American, and everybody believed that statement. Then it is the universal belief among the lower classes that all Americans wear slouch hats; therefore, Jack the Ripper, must wear a slouch hat. Now, I happened to have on a slouch hat, and this, together with the fact that I was an American, was enough for the police. It established my guilt beyond any question."*

Tumblety was not blaming the American press as he did in his autobiography, but Scotland Yard detectives. In effect, he was admitting they considered him a suspect. How curious that his 1889 autobiography, which stated absolutely nothing about "English detectives," was published just weeks later. Others have claimed that Tumblety's alleged involvement in the Whitechapel murders was his own doing, inflating Scotland Yard's suspicions of him in order to gain free publicity or international notoriety. Why then did he not embellish his connection to the Whitechapel murders in his autobiography as he did with the Lincoln assassination? Besides, he was decades away from his old advertising days; in fact, it is in the 1889 version that he proclaimed his retirement in his "Farewell" chapter:

> I have now accomplished a task which I consider due to my professional position, and to my standing in the high social circle into which it is my pride to find myself initiated . . . If certain journals have been unscrupulously and dastardly in their assaults, without a single peg to hang an accusation on, I can gratefully say that I have had nothing but the fairest treatment from the major portion of the press, both in this country and abroad.

Tumblety hated any attacks against the public image he had cultivated for the last two decades as a prominent physician of the highest social class. His response to this particular slanderous London affair in 1888 was more enduring and extensive than just a few rebuttal comments in a new autobiography published just two months after his escape. It was the very reason he wrote yet another autobiography four years later, his 1893 version. Immediately after his 1889 version was published, began a four-year-long period of well-publicized essay contributions from him and financial gifts donated by him. In the late-nineteenth century, the famous Supreme Court justice, scholar, and writer, Oliver Wendell Holmes, wrote philosophical essays published in the newspapers, such as an 1890 essay titled, "Over the Tea Cups." Tumblety did the very same thing, writing a self-help essay in the *Burlington Weekly Free Press*, June 9, 1892, titled, "A Parent's Duty to the Young," where he passed on advice in parenting. He signed the article, "Dr. F. Tumblety," in a clear attempt to give the impression of his expertise. He wrote yet another personal article, published in the *Cecil Whig*, June 11, 1892, titled, "How to Live Long," which was initially published in the *Chicago Herald*. In the article, he even quotes Oliver Wendell Holmes:

> *"No one would guess from the latest products of Dr. Holmes' pen or from his genial spirit that he had been for two years an octogenarian. After all, care is necessary to the prolongation of life, not anxious care, to avoid harmful transgression . . . Holmes uses his great knowledge of the laws of health and life to keep himself not merely alive, but in good working condition."*

Tumblety placed special emphasis on the publicity power of the *New York Herald*. In the July 22, 1891, issue of the *Herald*, an article reported that Tumblety donated a check for $323.75 to assist an American stowaway named Frank Sherman. It was a donation applauded by the paper. On August 22, 1891, the *New York Herald* published an article titled, "Dr. Tumblety's Kindness," which stated:

> *He sends to the Herald Money to Pay for Baths for Four Thousand Persons*
> *To the Editor of the Herald: I cordially indorse the Herald's opinion that cheap baths are a blessing to the poor. Enclosed please find my check for $200. Please purchase tickets and supply the needy with them, and oblige—*
> *Francis Tumblety, M.D.*
> *—Bar Harbor, August 19, 1891.*

In the *New York Herald*, June 6, 1893, was an article titled, "Help the Ice Charity." It was the *New York Herald's* appeal for funds for the Free Ice Charity. In the article, "Francis Tumblety, MD" was listed as giving $100.

> *Late Sunday evening Dr. Francis Tumblety gave notice that he would have $100 at the Herald office on Monday morning and he was as good as his word. It is interesting to note in this connection that Dr. Tumblety was also the very first subscriber to the fund last year. He is a firm believer in the efficiency of charity to save life and refresh*

the sick, and consequently doubles his subscription for the work of the coming season.

Tumblety was even known to publicly brag about his charities. In sworn testimony in 1905, Eleanor R. Elsheimer stated Tumblety told her mother that he gave $200 of ice for poor people around the year 1893. In the same conversation he told Eleanor's mother that he had spent barrels of money in his travels and that he still had barrels of money. He then added that any person who ever asked him for money in his will would never get it, as he was a practical man. The expert newspaper advertising doctor took a page out of his decades-old playbook and received assistance from the newspapers, reminiscent of the highly publicized barrels of flour he gave to the poor in Rochester and Buffalo, New York, before the Civil War.

Corroborating the claim that Tumblety was attempting to fill his 1893 autobiography with his altruistic charities is the 1893 autobiography itself, just as the flour charity made it into his 1866 autobiography. Note just a few of the responses to the above charities in his autobiography:

Extract of a letter received from Dr. F.E. Shepardson: Dear Doctor, I am pleased to see the good that you are doing. There is no doubt but what your money was well spent, and that the recipients of your generosity appreciated your kindness. (p. 98)

Extract of a letter . . . July 21, 1891: Dear Dr. Tumblety, I was delighted in reading in today's Harold your manly and democratic letter, enclosing your check for the amount of $323.75 for the release of the young man Sherman. (p. 99)

The Ice Charity. From the New York Herald: The Herald's appeal for fund for the Free Ice Charity had met a ready and sympathetic response . . . Late Sunday evening DR. FRANCIS TUMBLETY gave notice that he would have $100 at the Herald office . . . (p. 111)

My Dear Doctor, It has been a long while since I had the pleasure of seeing you, but your name, I find, is always amongst those who do charity for the love they bear their fellow creatures. The Ice Fund has already profited by your aid. No nobler charity has ever been established than this. (p. 111)

If the boys who sell Evening Telegrams in Park row to- night have shiningly clean faces and lilywhite hands it will tend to show that they have taken advantage of the kindness of Dr. Francis Tumblety and the Herald, and en- joyed a real soap and hot water bath. (p. 103)

After the publication of this version in 1893, his publicized altruistic behavior abruptly stopped. A personal hidden agenda connected to any altruistic action is powerful evidence of selfish behavior and especially if it had been a pattern all his life. Recall Tumblety's Buffalo and Rochester flour charities, which gave him excellent publicity.

Tumblety exhibited changes in his behavior upon his escape from England, some of which were instantaneous and some that were gradual. The most obvious and immediate changes were in his travel habits. Since 1873, Tumblety made it a point to travel to England and Toronto at least once a year. These trips stopped after the Whitechapel murders, and it is not difficult to see why. If Tumblety were ever caught in England or Canada (although a sovereign nation in 1888, Canada was still part of the British Empire), then the warrant for his arrest for gross indecency and indecent assault could have been executed, and he would likely have been extradited back to England.

Incidentally, there are indications that Tumblety traveled south of the border into Mexico on occasions. Richard Norris stated that around 1880 or 1881 Tumblety invited him to go to Mexico:

"He [Tumblety] stopped over at H. B. Stevens to buy a coat for himself, and then he bought me a suit. He then asked me if I would go to Mexico with him. I told him I would see my folks, but never mentioned a word of it, of course, to my people. I left him at his door that day very angry with me because I would not go in with him. He met me the next evening—in fact, he sent me a letter, telling

*me that he would guaranty me a good time if I would go
to Mexico. . ."*

This is the first time we have record of Tumblety inviting
one of his young male interests to Mexico, but then again,
knowledge of his travels plans rarely made the papers. This
actually did occur near the same time that he invited Norris to
Mexico with Martin McGarry in 1882. McGarry spoke of many
cities and countries, but he did not state Mexico. Interestingly,
Martin's discussion of their itinerary reveals that they only
traveled to northern cities in North America. Tumblety stayed
in the north with McGarry possibly because he was with Norris
in the south. In view of this, McGarry would likely not have
accompanied Tumblety to Mexico. There is evidence Tumblety
was in Galveston, Texas, a city located in the close to Mexico:

*In the Galveston flood Dr. Tumblety was among the vic-
tims. He floated about on a chicken coop until rescued by
a tugboat, but his health was permanently impaired.*
—St. Louis Dispatch, June 28, 1903

The well-read and well-traveled Francis Tumblety would
have known about the thriving homosexual community in
Mexico, especially in Mexico City. According to Wayne Dynes,
chief editor of the *Encyclopedia of Homosexuality, Volume II*
(1990), when Mexico gained its independence from Spain in
1821, this ended homosexual oppression, and then the short
French occupation in 1862 to 1867 introduced the sexually
permissive Napoleonic Code. This meant that Mexico was
openly permissive to sexuality and allowed for a subculture
of homosexuality. Concurrent to this, the Latin influence in
Mexico, specific to gender relationships, created a misogynistic
male-dominated attitude labeled "machismo." According to
Dr. Julia Monarrez Fragoso, research fellow at the University
of Texas El Paso, it was not uncommon to see physical abuse
and excessive violence against women, even involving offender
rapes, strangulation, and mutilation. Fragoso states that
"sexual femicide," or the rape and killing of women, is the
"logical consequence of the patriarchal system that maintains
male supremacy through" the rape and killing of women.
Mexico would have been appealing to an extreme misogynist
homosexual like Tumblety.

Coincidentally, a serial killer named Francisco Guerrero murdered twenty-one prostitutes in Mexico City from 1880— near the time Tumblety asked Norris to come to Mexico—to 1888. Guerrero was compared to Jack the Ripper not only because he was caught while the Whitechapel crimes were being committed but also because he mutilated and murdered prostitutes. The murders showed extreme cruelty and hatred; in other words, anger-retaliatory. A personality profile of Guerrero showed psychopathy, lack of remorse, and an "inflated self-esteem." Interestingly, this sounds very similar to the narcissistic woman-hater Francis Tumblety, with the exception of Guerrero sexually molesting his victims. Then again, it was physically impossible for Tumblety to have performed intercourse, let alone psychologically, as his sexual interests were males. If Tumblety was visiting Mexico City in the 1880s, he would have had first-hand knowledge of this killer before coming to England in 1888.

After returning from England, Tumblety stayed in the US but continued his ubiquitous habit of frequenting major cities. By studying numerous eyewitness testimonies, this travel pattern seemed to be surprisingly consistent. It began in 1880 or 1881. The cities he visited included Rochester and Saratoga Springs, New York; the New York City area; Baltimore, Maryland; Hot Springs, Arkansas; St. Louis, Missouri; New Orleans, Louisiana; and Washington DC. While it was his nature to constantly travel, it is clear he traveled to Rochester to visit his brother and family, and to Saratoga Springs and Hot Springs for hydrotherapy.

His actions while visiting these cities reveal his hidden agenda. These locations were perfect for his sexual drive to prey upon older boys and younger men. He was witnessed time and time again roaming the streets of the slums of cities, being arrested for "unnatural acts," in New York City, Chicago, Cincinnati, Baltimore, St. Louis, New Orleans, and Washington DC. Since he retired from the alternative doctor business, he had even more free time, so it is no surprise the frequency for arrests for indulging his illegal habit increased. For example, in the evening on June 4, 1889, Tumblety was arrested in New York City for assault and battery on a young man named George Davis. He approached Davis and "engaged in conversation," which angered Davis, who called Tumblety "a vile name." This caused Tumblety to strike Davis with his cane. Tumblety was reported to have been "flashily dressed and sparkling with diamonds." In November 1890, Tumblety was arrested in Washington DC for being a "suspicious character." Again, Tumblety was dressed well and the case was dropped. Regardless of the disposition of both cases, this was clearly Tumblety's nightly habit. Recall, Tumblety frequented parks hoping for opportunistic sexual encounters, such as in New York City's Madison Square Park and Baltimore's Patterson Park and Druid Hill Park.

It was around this time that Richard Norris took Tumblety to a sporting house in New Orleans, recalling a time when Tumblety was still in a presentable condition. Norris stated:

> *I took him to a sporting house one night, Hennessy was Chief of Police then . . . and I did not tell him it was a sporting house until I got right in front of the place. Then I told him there was a lady friend of mine bothering me about money matters, and threatening to send to the office, and being in the neighborhood I was going in, and wouldn't he go in with me." I told him that as a joke, and I told the girls what a peculiar man he was, and when I got him in, he began to treat to some champagne, and I told the girls I know we would both have to leave, because he "hated your kind of people—your class of people." When we went in a couple of girls asked if they couldn't have some wine and he hollered across the room "if I wanted it", and I said, "all right." He ordered the wine and a couple of girls went over to him, and he said, "go away from me". After drinking the wine he said to me, "Let's get out of here." We went out of the house, and he gave me an awful lecture. He said he was surprised I went to such a place, and I told him it was one of the swellest places in the city, that a nice class of young men went there, and he said, none of them were any good.*

David C. Hennessy began as chief of police in New Orleans in April 1888, when he was appointed by the newly elected mayor Joseph A. Shakespeare. The city council officially appointed Hennessy chief of police the following spring. He was then assassinated on October 16, 1890. When Tumblety was in the papers for the Whitechapel murder, Norris approached "the Chief of Police," which would have been Hennessy. At this time, Norris explained to Hennessy that he felt threatened by Tumblety because of his connection to the Whitechapel murder case. Norris met up with him in February 1889 during Mardi Gras, which is likely the time he was so threatened. His next experience with Tumblety was when Norris took him to a sporting house. "Well I took him to a sporting house one night—Hennessy was Chief of Police then—I judge about ten or twelve years ago." Why was he not threatened by Tumblety when this had to have occurred either February 1889 or February 1890, both being so close to the Whitechapel murders? When the London casual prostitute Alice Mackenzie was murdered on July 17, 1889, Scotland Yard, and the public, believed it to be another Jack the Ripper victim. The comfortability Norris had with Tumblety while Hennessy was chief of police may very well have been after the Mackenzie murder, thus, the visit to the sports bar may have been in February 1890.

Tumblety was in Hot Springs, Arkansas, staying at the Plateau Hotel in April 1891, and was robbed:

COUPLE OF BURGLARIES
The Plateau Hotel Guests Worked For $8,000
Special to the Arkansas Gazette
HOT SPRINGS, April 18. Thieves went through the Plateau Hotel last night, securing about $8,000 in money and diamonds, Judge A.M. Duffie, of this city, and that well-known mysterious individual, Dr. Frank Francis Tumblety, being the victims. The thieves secured a gold watch and a considerable sum of money from Judge Duffie, and $2,000 in cash and diamonds valued between $5,000 and $7,000 from Dr. Tumblety. It was well known that Dr. Tumblety had the money and valuables and carried them on his person, besides valuable papers. No clue to the identity of the thieves.
—*Arkansas Gazette*, April 19, 1891

While there have been some recent theories that Tumblety was behind his own robbery, the recently discovered sworn testimonies suggest it was a local theft. John B. Brooks, a physician at Hot Springs, recalled Tumblety eventually getting his possessions returned. Brooks stated:

I remember of his losing some diamonds here. He was boarding at the Plateau Hotel. He lost some diamonds and a watch. They were found about a year and a half after they were lost, and I think he afterwards recovered his watch. He told me once about this watch, the trouble he was having with the man who had it in his possession, that this man wanted $100 to give up the watch.

Brooks recalled that his watch was in the possession of a "lawyer named Page" who claimed a "colored woman" found it. When questioned if Tumblety ever spoke of this theft and if he told him who robbed him, Richard Norris stated, yes, and recalled Tumblety telling him he lost fifteen to twenty-five thousand dollars to either a race-horse jockey or a stableman.

It was also around this time he shifted his residence from New York City to Baltimore, although according to his New York banker, James B. Clews, he would still visit the bank periodically. His Baltimore attorney, Robert Simpson, commented upon this change, stating under oath that he first met Francis in 1890 and would occasionally see him. Simpson stated he saw Tumblety more often after 1894, and it was in 1898 that the frequency of Tumblety's visits to his office increased significantly. The *Evening Star*, May 13, 1897, reported on an incident with Tumblety in Baltimore, where Tumblety was arrested for fitting the description of someone passing three forged checks:

Identity Established.
[Tumblety] was arrested in Baltimore this morning by Capt. Freeburger because of a request sent him by Inspector Holtinberger. He was suspected of being the man who passed three forged and worthless checks in this city a few days ago. The description of Dr. Tumblety answered that given of the swindler, with the exception of his heavy, bushy mustache, and Inspector Hollinberger thought he had probably had his mustache trimmed. Such did not prove to be the case, however, and he was discharged from custody.

Regardless of Tumblety's guilt or innocence, this does show Tumblety had been spending more time in Baltimore by 1897. Tumblety's Baltimore attorney, Robert Simpson, recalled under oath two events in 1900 when Tumblety came to him for professional advice, demonstrating that Tumblety's Baltimore time was more than just a quick visit. Recall, Simpson advised Tumblety to pay off the mother of a boy he took to Druid Hill Park. The other Baltimore event in 1900 also involved a young man. Tumblety had a large mark on his head and another under his eye. Simpson stated:

> He [Tumblety] *told me that he had gotten some money and he was trying to assist a young man and the young man had struck him and beaten him and taken his money. He wanted to know what to do, whether to have him arrested or what. After I closely questioned him, I found out he was in a community over here, what is called Chestnut Street, which is a very low place in the City, very low, inhabited by a lot of very low characters; however, he said the young man told him to go ahead and swear out the warrant, that he could fix him. I suggested to him to have no more to do with him.*

Tumblety's behavior seems to have changed again in the mid-1890s. The Rochester neighbor of the Tumblety family, Eleanor R. Elsheimer, recalled under oath in 1905 his visit to her home, which occurred soon after giving money to the *New York Herald*'s Ice Charity in 1893. Recall, when Tumblety was arrested in New York City for striking George Davis with a cane in 1889, he was "flashily" dressed.

Eleanor recalled seeing Francis one Saturday night in downtown Rochester around 1895 to 1897 in an alley/ stairway acting very peculiar:

> I *was going down town Saturday evening, and on the right hand side of Main Street as I passed the doorway I saw this man; he was tight against the wall as he could be, with his hands down at his side looking furtively out. It was a dark place but the light shone in. . . . he looked so queer.*

The attorney questioning Eleanor asked, "His hands were down at his side?" She replied, "Yes, and his head back against the wall." She believed his behavior was irrational. The attorney then asked, "Has it been the talk, or not, in your family of his actions?" She replied, "My father referred to him as being off, it was common talk. Whenever he was mentioned we all laughed."

Tumblety's nephew Michael Fitzsimons, or Fitzsimmons, stated under oath that Tumblety would use Mary Fitzsimons, Michael's sister, as a "receptacle for articles and anything he wished to keep." She lived at the longtime Tumblety residence on Plymouth Avenue along with his brother Lawrence. Fitzsimons stated that once Lawrence died in February 1898, "or soon after," Tumblety no longer visited Rochester. It may not have been a coincidence that Tumblety's attire changed to dressing like a homeless person in that same year. His Baltimore attorney, Robert Simpson, stated that his dressing down and not bathing began in 1898. Adolf Marx, owner of a cigar, tobacco, and confectionary store in Hot Springs, who lived there for twenty years, stated under oath that he knew Tumblety for about fifteen years, from around 1887 to 1902. He commented upon Tumblety's health and condition:

> Well, he was complaining often. He always pointed to his heart when he came in, and would say that he had heart trouble. He spoke very often of his heart trouble, and would say that he knew it would not be long before he had to go. That is all of what he complained. He didn't look as well as he did before. His clothes was not clean, his coat was shiny and soiled, and his beard, anybody could see that he had dye or blacking on his beard; was sometimes hanging in little rows of his hair. . . . He had whiskers like that and a mustache. I always noticed that when he came up there, he always was here during winter months, and in summer I never saw him; and whenever I saw him he always wore those clothes. I do not know as to the color of them. I noticed he had two or three coats on all the time.

From 1889 to 1893, Tumblety had a reason to be seen in public in expensive and clean clothes, the same reason he gave to charity: He was publishing his 1893 autobiography

promoting his persona of a high-end prominent physician.
There is evidence that he dressed rather plain beginning
around in 1881. The following conveys Richard Norris'
responses to the attorney's questions at his 1905 deposition:

Q: *How was he dressed?*
A: *In the 80's, the first few years I met him he used to
wear a blue cap, wore one of those naval caps the first
year I met him—in 1880 or 1881—the naval officers
wear, with a gold band around it. During all the time I
knew him he always wore a cap.*

Q: *Did he look plain? A: Yes, sir; very plain, and very
shabby, especially in the last few years. That is the
reason I shunned him, I didn't care how much money
he had.*
Q: *Was he clean?*
A: *No, sir; he looked dirty; very filthy.*

Tumblety's brother Lawrence—a person he continued to
visit—seems to have been his emotional anchor, and according
to Eleanor Elsheimer, her father told her Tumblety visited
Rochester each year or sometimes every other year. The
specific Rochester family member who transported his body
to Rochester for burial is likely Mary Fitzsimmons, the one
who received $10,000 from Tumblety in his will. This seems to
have been Francis' last request to Mary, to be buried with his
mother, father, and next to Lawrence. Tumblety told Richard
Norris in 1898 why he dressed filthily:

*"I remarked to him, "Doctor, it looks like they cleaned
since you have been robbed", and he said, "No, I still get
my pension; I have a few dollars." I could not understand
his condition, being so filthy, when he told me he had so
much money, and he told me he did not care about dress."*

Tumblety was a man acutely aware that his ostentatious
and eccentric attire was part of the recipe for his business
success years earlier, yet he no longer cared about how he
dressed. He reacted angrily when he was treated poorly by
others, yet he continued to maintain a decrepit look. He
seemed to live a life of contradiction, bragging about his

friendship with the rich and powerful and showing off his bank receipt on one hand and seemingly oblivious to his filthy appearance on the other. One suggestion as to why he dressed so poorly was he refused to spend the money. The mother superior at the St. John's Hospital convinced Tumblety to buy a new set of clothes. He did, but instead of wearing them, he continued to wear his filthy clothing as the new set hung by his bed.

While Tumblety no longer cared about his attire and bathing, he did continue to care about not looking old. Tumblety blackened his mustache and hair up to the end of his life. Case in point, late one evening in 1901, Tumblety walked into the office of Daniel O'Donovan, proprietor of the US Engraving Company in the City of Baltimore. According to O'Donovan, Tumblety was wearing what he thought was a cap with a peak similar to an officer on a merchant steamship and a short, thick overcoat, very much like a seaman. O'Donovan stated, "He gave me the impression from his clothes, which by the way were very dirty and greasy, and 'illy' kept, of being a sailor in hard luck." He said on one occasion that Tumblety wore a slouch hat. He said he was very eccentric looking with a florid face and an intensely black mustache, later realizing it was dyed. O'Donovan believed Tumblety would have been taken as a tramp. This is corroborated by numerous witnesses, including Richard Norris; "He was over six feet, a big fine looking man, rosy complexion; he had dyed his mustache; you could see that he had dyed his mustache." Tumblety was darkening his mustache hairs because they were white. Mr. B. McDavid, barber at the Arlington Hotel, Eastman Barbershop, Hot Springs, stated under oath, ". . . his [Tumblety's] hair and mustache were perfectly white, but he kept them blackened with a preparation made of lard and charcoal that made him look very fierce; blacked his skin and hair with it, and it made him look very peculiar, fierce; different from most people." Mr. Greaves, proprietor of the Waverley Hotel in Hot Springs, Arkansas, stated, "His [Tumblety's] hair was blackened, and his mustache was blackened, so that he really looked offensive. He would not clean himself."

Tumblety walked into Daniel O'Donovan's office in early October 1901 and bought a sheet of paper, an envelope, and a two-cent stamp, then asked if he would write a letter for him. He insisted it be written in pencil, not pen. O'Donovan agreed, and Tumblety dictated a short letter to a lady in Baltimore, referring to both her and himself as authors and writers, then thanking her for the kinds words of encouragement of a recent publication of his. O'Donovan thought the letter was "rather peculiar in nature." Instead of signing the letter himself, he asked O'Donovan to sign it. On a few occasions, Tumblety was reported to have someone else write a letter for him and even sign it.

Four or five days later, on the first Saturday in October, Tumblety returned with a handwritten letter and asked for it to be typed. It was a letter of endorsement written to Tumblety "of some person of note in the north." Tumblety was creating a fake letter from a famous person to him. Tumblety then showed O'Donovan letters from famous persons and royalty. He left, then came back again three days later with another letter. This continued, and on the fourth visit, Tumblety asked him to write a derogatory article on a place called the Riverview, stating it was a dangerous place infested with bad characters unfit for most people to associate with. He offered $200, but O'Donovan turned it down. Tumblety then pulled out of his pocket a diamond ring, another precious stone, and diamonds and rubies in order to show that he had the funds to pay him. Tumblety then brought in a manuscript and letters and asked him to print a revised edition of his autobiography with the title, *Reminiscences of a Famous Physician.* O'Donovan agreed to a price, and Tumblety paid a portion of the $40 price up front. O'Donovan delegated the job to a subordinate clerk named Charles T. Kaiss. Tumblety would come to the office on numerous occasions to work with Kaiss, having him add more letters. Just as he did during the writing of his 1893 autobiography, Tumblety wrote an essay in the *New York Sun* wishing all a Happy New Year for 1901 and wanted this added into the book. This essay was presented as evidence in court.

O'Donovan stated that Tumblety was very erratic and incoherent at times. Within a week, he came to the office and insisted the book be finished by the end of the week, since he had to go to New York. O'Donovan stated that Tumblety's concern was the stock market dropping because of the possibility that Bryant would be elected as president. It was not finished by the end of the week. Even though Tumblety constantly pushed to have them finish the book early, O'Donovan pointed out that they did finish it within the promised time of November. Due to typographical errors, Tumblety did not accept it. After dozens of corrections, Tumblety still would not accept it, so Kaiss threatened to sue. Kaiss actually attempted to sue, but because Tumblety had no fixed place of residence and no one knew about him, he decided against it. Kaiss then sold the manuscript and copies to a junk dealer. Tumblety eventually came back now wanting the book, but the building the books were stored in burned down and all of the copies were destroyed. It not being available, Tumblety demanded his $40 deposit back or he would sue. This is exactly what he did and brought a suit against him before Magistrate Daniel Bride through his Baltimore attorney Robert Simpson. O'Donovan stated he was served in March 1902 but ignored the suit and did not appear in court. Because of this, Tumblety won by default. O'Donovan then claimed his attorney opened the case back up and it was "eventually carried to the City Court, where it is supposed to be still resting." Tumblety would come to his office on numerous occasions to collect, but O'Donovan refused since the case was not done. O'Donovan recalled that Kaiss finally gave Tumblety $10 of the $40, even though the case was still pending.

Tumblety's second Baltimore attorney, Frank Widner Jr., stated that around the second week of October 1901, Tumblety approached him complaining about the case. Widner was a young lawyer and in practice for only three years. Widner stated he brought Tumblety to his other lawyer, Robert Simpson, and went over the case with them. He stated Simpson informed him that he entered into an agreement with the attorney for O'Donovan to re-try the case. Widner believed this to be the wrong approach and would be at the trial with them. Widner convinced Tumblety at this re-trial to withdraw the suit, dismiss Simpson, then hire him to appeal at the Baltimore City Court. He tried to procure the case documents from Simpson, but Simpson would not release them until he got paid, which ultimately prolonged the case. Tumblety told Widner, "Leave him (Simpson) alone, I will attend to him."

Widner stated that Tumblety would get entirely irrational, even threatening and losing emotional control, when discussing their inability to procure the documents from Simpson. He also recalled that Tumblety would have mental lapses in his office at times. Widner knew Tumblety was in New Orleans in early 1902, because he sent a letter to him from a New Orleans address dated January 4, 1902. Tumblety did not return to Widner's office until about May 1902. Widner noted Tumblety looked even more feeble with a loss of vitality. He stated Tumblety remained in Baltimore until July 1902. He then returned to Baltimore in September 1902 and was even more irrational. Widner presented to the court a note from Tumblety dated October 2, 1902, *"Dear Sir: I trust that the inclosed may instruct you. The Simpsons have stuffed you full of rot falsehoods. I will go to your office at 10 AM Monday. Please don't keep me waiting for you till noon. –F.T."*

Simpson stated that Tumblety continued to visit him, and in December 1902 Tumblety was in very poor condition. Tumblety told him around January 1903 that he was going to Hot Springs; he thought the treatment would do him some good.

According to numerous witnesses, his stay in New Orleans was always during Mardi Gras season in February, but this did not occur in 1903. Richard Norris stated that he saw Tumblety during Mardi Gras season each year since they first met in 1881, but this ended in 1902. Just as Simpson claimed, by late winter Tumblety was in Hot Springs, Arkansas, a clear choice for the therapeutic springs. John Geary of the Geary House in Hot Springs, Arkansas, claimed to see Tumblety in February or March 1903 "and possibly a little later" when Tumblety stayed in the Geary House for five or six weeks.

John B. Brooks was a practicing physician in Hot Springs, Arkansas, for thirty years and was a surgeon in the Army in the Civil War, 146th Illinois Regiment. He saw Tumblety in Hot Springs for twenty years, beginning around 1883, but did not begin to speak with him until around fifteen years later (1888). He never visited his office. He stated he saw Tumblety in Hot Springs about two months before he died, "in a very debilitated condition." He recalled years earlier when he lost some diamonds at the Plateau Hotel and Tumblety told him he recovered his watch. Brooks stated Tumblety would keep company with "the worst looking tramps that he could pick up. . . . He would pick up the worst looking specimens, regular hobos in appearance. He would always take the dark side of the street where there were no lights."

By April 1903, Tumblety was in St. Louis, but not yet at St. John's Hospital. He was at the Mona House on 290 ½ North in St. Louis between Pine and Olive Streets. The proprietor of the Mona House, Philo Smith, knew Tumblety for years and stated under oath that Tumblety was capable of handling his own affairs until the last two years. "Failed more rapidly than any person I have ever met. The last time in particular, very feeble and sick all the time he was there. If my memory serves me right, he left my house and went to the hospital."

Sister Mary Theresa was the superioress at St. John's Hospital on May 2, 1903, when Tumblety checked himself in to die. She stated under oath that when Tumblety signed in he recorded "F. Townsend, Washington." Once he finally admitted who he was, she wrote "Francis Tumilty" underneath it. Sister Theresa stated that when he arrived he was a very sick man, dressed poorly, but he could get around. She admitted that Tumblety was a "peculiar man." She eventually convinced him to go downtown and buy a new suit, because he would not be able to stay until he did so.

She explained that in the first fourteen days of his stay he would speak to her of his travels, people he had met, places he had visited, and his general condition. He had drawn money from Henry Clews while he was at the hospital, and she stated he kept it on his person. This, she stated, was when she found out his real name was Francis Tumblety. Tumblety eventually showed her his bank statement from Henry Clews, New York, and told her soon he would make a will.

Sister Mary Theresa also recalled that the room Tumblety occupied once caught fire and stated "Dr. Tumilty" set it on fire. This was not the first time Tumblety would be near a fire. In 1867, Tumblety was working out of the famous Lindell Hotel in St. Louis as Blackmore and Company, and in that year the Lindell Hotel caught fire.

Tumblety entered St. John's on May 2, 1903, and wrote out his will on May 16, witnessed by A. V. L. Brokaw:

Francis Tumblety hereby makes publishes and declares this to be his last will and testament.

I give and bequeath to Mrs. Thomas Brady, No. 20 Frederick St. Widness Liverpool, England, the sum of Ten Thousand Dollars.

I give and bequeath to Mrs. Jane Hayes, Valejo [sic], California, the sum of Ten Thousand Dollars.

I give and bequeath to Mrs. Barrett, (niece) of Gibbs Street, Rochester, N.Y., the sum of Five Thousand Dollars.

I give and bequeath to Mrs. Jane Moore (my niece), Gibbs Street, Rochester, N.Y., the sum of Five Thousand Dollars.

I give and bequeath to Mrs. Mary Fitzsimmons, Plymouth Avenue, Rochester, N.Y., the sum of Ten Thousand Dollars.

I give and bequeath to Mark A. Blackburn, formerly my coachman, the sum of Five Thousand Dollars.

I give and bequeath to James Cardinal Gibbons, of Baltimore, Md., the sum of Ten Thousand Dollars to be use by him for such charitable purposes as the said Cardinal Gibbons may deem wise and proper.

I give and bequeath to John Ireland, Archbishop of St. Paul, the sum of Ten Thousand Dollars, to be used by him as he thinks fit for charitable purposes.

I witness whereof I have hereto attached my signature this 16ᵗʰ day of May, 1903

    Dr. F. Tumblety.

We hereby certify that we the undersigned, witnessed the signature of Francis Tumblety to the foregoing instrument and that the said Tumblety declared to us at the time he signed the same that it was his last will and testament.

    A.V.L. Brokaw,
    T.D. Cannon.
    State of Missouri, City of St. Louis.

Missing from this will and testament was the phrase, "revoking all other wills made by me." Tumblety was fully aware that he did not bequeath all of his estate. The sworn testimony of T. D. Cannon, the St. Louis attorney called to St. John's hospital on the morning of May 16, 1903, by Father Conway to write Tumblety's will, made it clear why it was considered complete even though the disposition of the remaining balance was not done:

> *I met Dr. Tumblety in the hallway of St. John's Hospital. I walked him to his room. . . . That is the will of Dr. Francis Tumblety that I wrote on the morning of the 16th of May, 1903. He read it over himself, and I read it over for him, and he signed it in my presence and in the presence of Dr. A.V.L. Brokaw, and he announced when he signed it that it was his last will . . . I said to him "let me see that memorandum", because I did not understand the spelling of Spanish words [the word "Valejo"]. Then he handed me the memorandum and I simply tore up the sheet I used and started this one over again "Francis Tumilty hereby makes, publishes and declares", and of course spelled the word properly afterward. When we got down to the disposition of $65,000.00, when we got down to the end of this $65,000.00, or disposed of $65,000.00, he said "well, now, the rest I am not satisfied, I am not positive about how I desire to distribute that yet", and he said something about giving it to charity. There was a balance remaining of this statement. He talked about that balance and finally said "well, we will let that go today, until I make up my mind about it"; and I said to him, then, "Doctor" having this memorandum in this way, I asked "Had I not better go back to the office and write that out on the typewriter?" and he said "No, that is good enough; I don't want so much red tape"; and I thereupon wrote in this "In witness whereof," and put down this little short attestation clause, and I said to him "Now, Doctor, I have to have two witnesses. I can be a witness myself". . . . Dr. Tumilty signed that. I saw him sign it. Dr. Brokaw signed that, and I saw him sign it, and I signed that in the presence of them.*

Further evidence of Tumblety's end-of-life stay at St. John's Hospital, as well as his increasing shabbiness, lies in the testimonies and records of Dr. Justin Steer and Dr. J. H. Ziegler. Dr. Steer went to St. John's Hospital at the request of Dr. Temm for consultation around May 11 or 12, 1903. Steer stated Tumblety had chronic Bright's Disease and valvular disease of the heart. Dr. J. H. Ziegler, a physician employed as a nurse at St. John's Hospital, was with Tumblety about ten to fifteen times a day every day and had frequent conversations with him. Tumblety spoke to him about his travels, having stocks in a railroad in the East with Henry Clews, but mostly about medicine. He said Tumblety was very coherent. Dr. Ziegler even wrote a letter for Tumblety while being dictated to. Tumblety also told him he had just received $500 from Henry Clews, buying a new suit of black clothes. He stated he wore his old dirty clothes until Sister Mary Theresa compelled him to get a suit of clothes. He stated Tumblety got a new suit but did not wear it. He stated Tumblety broke his nose, but he was not there to witness it, since it happened at night and he worked the dayshift.

Reverend J. J. Conway was the chaplain at St. John's and was also a professor of ethics and political economy at St. Louis University. Prior to May 16, most of his conversations with Tumblety were on spiritual affairs. Tumblety also spoke to him about the disposition of his property in his will, combining his spiritual questions with how best to bequeath his estate. He told Tumblety it was a proper thing to dispose of his property to his relatives. Tumblety showed him his bank statement from Henry Clews of $138,000 or $140,000 and some stock in a railroad in the East—Long Island, Reverend Conway thought. He said to Tumblety after Tumblety asked if he should write a will, "Doctor, I think so, because you are very ill and you may not recover." He believed after his discussions that Tumblety was above average intelligence and was very capable of attending to his affairs.

Before Tumblety died, Sister Mary Theresa sent a letter to Henry Clews, the owner of the New York bank Tumblety kept his money in, because she believed her patient was very near death. The will had already been made, but she did not know this.

Francis Tumblety died on May 28, 1903, and according to Dr. Ziegler, he had a fall that broke his nasal canal three days before this. There was an earlier claim that Tumblety fell while going for a walk outside the hospital grounds, but this was not the case, as Sister Mary Theresa stated that he fell at night while attempting to sleep standing near his bed. The attending physician, Dr. Francis Temm, stated to the attorney that he believed the fall hastened Tumblety's death.

Tumblety's will was admitted to probate. Because he was not a resident of the state and also did not name an executor, St. Louis Public Administrator Gerrard P. Strode was assigned as executor. Tumblety's relatives, primarily from Rochester, claimed he was a resident of New York, so they fought to have the will probated in New York. Strode hired attorney Tom D. Cannon, the same attorney who executed the will, to argue the case in the New York courts and won. The courts directed Tumblety's New York banker, Henry Clews, to transfer his $140,000 to St. Louis in Strode's charge. In the meantime, Cannon requested over $7,000 of Tumblety's estate for his work on the case but was challenged by the family. He was awarded $4,000.

On January 16, 1904, a petition was filed by family members contesting the will. Spearheading the petition were Tumblety's nephews James P. Tumilty and Michael Fitzsimmons:

State of Missouri, City of St. Louis
Be it remembered that heretofore, to-wit: on the 16th of January, A. D. 1904, there was filed in the office of the Clerk of the Circuit Court, City of St. Louis, within and for the City and State aforesaid, a petition in cause No. 31430, Series A, of the causes in said Court, wherein James P. Tumilty et al., are plaintiffs and Jane A. Hayes, et al., are defendants, to-wit: The said petition (as amended by leave of Court on March 2nd, 1904) is in words and figures as follows; to-wit;- State of Missouri, City of St. Louis – [names of all parties involved, how they are related to Francis Tumblety, and rephrased the entire will].
In the Circuit Court, City of St. Louis, Missouri. February Term, 1904.
The plaintiffs aforesaid contest the validity of the instrument in writing aforesaid, and admitted to probate as aforesaid, as the last will of Francis Tumblety, deceased and aver that at the time of the pretended execution of said paper, the said Francis Tumblety was not of sound mind and disposing memory, and was not capable in law of making a valid will. That at the time of the alleged execution of said instrument, Francis Tumblety was suffering from general debility; that his nerves were shattered,

that his strength had failed; that he was forgetful and of unbalanced mind and was, therefore, unable to have a due and proper understanding of his property and was incapable of knowing what disposition he desired to make of amid property. Wherefore, the plaintiffs state that the instrument aforesaid is not the last will of the said Francis Tumblety, deceased, and pray that an issue to such effect be made, and that the probate of said will be set aside and that said instrument shall be declared imperfect and of no effect, and for such other decrees as to the Court may seem just and proper. – John S. Leahy.

For the State of Missouri, the Circuit Court of Appeals acted as the State Supreme Court. The family members claimed Tumblety was not of sound mind and disposing memory, thus, not capable of making a valid will. Probate proceedings, such as the State of Missouri Special Commissioner's Inquiry, began taking testimonies on August 26, 1904, and continued until June 20, 1905. The *Rochester Democrat and Chronicle,* June 27, 1905, stated,

The trial was preceded by costly depositions, and probate proceedings were begun respectively in this city, and the decedent's residence, Baltimore . . .

The attorneys for the family members contesting the will introduced witnesses from St. Louis; Hot Springs, Arkansas; Rochester, New York; and Indiana. Additionally, sworn depositions were taken in Baltimore on March 16, 1905; in Rochester, New York, on May 8, 1905; and New Orleans on May 12, 1905. Their argument was that Tumblety lived as a tramp, or street walker, wearing filthy clothing and having lapses of memory in the last year or two of his life and thus, was not of sound mind and body.

On June 24, 1904, a second will was admitted to probate in Baltimore, Maryland, claiming to have been executed by Tumblety on October 3, 1901. It was submitted by the executor of the will, Major Joseph R. Kemp, through his attorney, Robert Simpson. In sworn testimony, Major Kemp stated he became acquainted with the Simpson brothers and William Duvall, a witness in the will, in 1895. Kemp was introduced to Tumblety in 1898 and became friends because of their mutual military background. Kemp claimed Tumblety told him in 1901 he was thinking of making a will because his health was bad and was growing worse. Kemp recommended Simpson write his will. He then said Tumblety handed him the will:

> *I, Francis J. Tumblety of the City of Baltimore, State of Maryland, do make this my last Will and Testament revoking all other wills made by me.*
>
> *After the payment of all my just debts and funeral expenses, I give, devise and bequest my whole estate as follows:-*
>
> *I give and bequeath to Cardinal James Gibbons, one thousand dollars for charitable purposes.*
>
> *I give and bequeath to the Home for fallen women of Baltimore City, on North Exeter Street, one Thousand Dollars,*
>
> *I give and bequeath to my dear friend, Major Joseph R. Kemp, of Baltimore City, all my jewelry consisting of one diamond breast pin, three diamond rings, one chain and watch.*
>
> *All the rest of my estate of whatsoever kind and nature and wheresoever situated, I give, devise and bequeath to only my blood relations, per stirpes, this relationship to be determined by my hereinafter named Executors.*
>
> *I constitute and appoint Henry Clews & Co., Bankers of New York City, as one Executor and my friend Major Joseph R. Kemp, of Baltimore City, as the other, of this my Last Will and Testament, and desire that they give bond for the safe performance of their duty.*
>
> *IN TESTIMONY WHEREOF, I have hereunto subscribed my name and affixed my seal, this third day of October, 1901.*
>
> > *Francis J. Tumblety (Seal)*
>
> *Signed by Testator making his mark, published and declared by the above testator as and for his last Will and Testament, in the presence of us who at this request in his presence and the presence of each other, have hereunto subscribed our names as witnesses.*
>
> > *Robert H. Simpson,*
> > *Chas. A. Simpson,*
> > *William A. Duval.*

While Kemp recommended Tumblety go to Simpson, he recalled Simpson later saying he believed Tumblety likely did not have enough money, since Tumblety never paid him. Kemp stated under oath that he attempted to sell Tumblety stocks, which suggests Kemp knew Tumblety had money. Kemp claimed he first saw the will around November 1901 and observed Simpson put it in the safe. Simpson stated under oath that he allowed Tumblety to sign the will with an X, because of his nervous condition and shaking hands.

Some have argued that their delay in admitting the will and testament to probate court is suspicious, but it was the Baltimore Orphan's Court that caused the delay. Under sworn testimony, Joseph Kemp's second attorney, Thomas R. Clendinen, explained that Kemp and Robert Simpson came to him for assistance. Simpson, acting as Kemp's attorney, actually submitted the will to the Baltimore Orphan's Court on August 18, 1903, just three months after Tumblety's death. The Orphan's Court then prevented it from being probated. Clendinen stated:

> . . . the nature of the opposition, to answer your question categorically, was that the will in St. Louis being a later will ipso facto abrogated the will admitted to probate here.

Note that the court did not block the 1901 will from being probated because of any fake issues, but because they were aware of the 1903 St. Louis will, thus, it was not the *last* will and testament. Thomas R. Clendinen successfully argued that, under Maryland law, the Baltimore will and testament must be submitted to probate "for the purpose of determining the rights of either party." Actually, submitting an earlier will and testament even when a later one has been executed to probate is common practice even today, just in case the later will is concluded to be null and void. The Orphan's Court agreed, and the 1901 Baltimore will was submitted to probate court.

At the June 1905 court proceeding, the attorneys for the contestants challenging the will introduced over 45 testimonies and depositions to the jury in an attempt to prove Tumblety was not of sound mind and body, while the attorneys for the defendants introduced only one, Henry Clews, representing Tumblety's New York City bank. Clews said that he considered

Dr. Tumblety's mind unaffected and thought him a shrewd business man. Family members in court were Michael H. Fitzsimmons and Annie Barrett "of 123 Gible street." The defendants won. Note the statement in the *Rochester Democrat and Chronicle*, June 27, 1905:

> *The proceeding was before the jury in the Circuit Court of St. Louis, of jurisdiction akin to the New York Supreme Court, and was tried from Tuesday last to Thursday afternoon, when Judge McDonald instructed the jury to find for the defense . . .*

Attorneys for the contestants immediately requested a motion for a new trial. In the *Rochester Democrat and Chronicle*, June 29, 1905, it states:

> *Motion for a new trial of the action to have the will of the late Dr. Francis Tumblety declared invalid was argued in St. Louis yesterday before Circuit Judge McDonald. Decision was reserved. The plaintiffs, contesting the will, are nearly all residents of Rochester, and are represented by Attorney George B. Draper. They dispute the figures of counsel for the legatees, as to probable value of the inheritances, should the will stand. The proponents claimed there would not be more than $20,000 to distribute among the Rochester heirs not named in the will, but the latter say there would be double, or several times that amount, even if the will should stand, upon appeal. The case will be taken to the Supreme Court of Missouri, yesterday's motion being preliminary to appeal. The estate will be tied up two years, or more, by the litigation.*

In April 1907, Michael Fitzsimmons, the only relative still pushing for a new trial, died, which opened the way for probating a compromise agreement between opposing parties. One more hurdle stood in the way of a compromise agreement: Joseph R. Kemp's request to include the 1901 Baltimore will. This the motion for a new trial ended, Joseph R. Kemp filed a petition on March 9, 1908, to the St. Louis Probate Court:

> *Probate Court of City of St. Louis, In the Matter of the Estate of Francis J. Tumblity [sic], deceased., No. 29083.*

Now comes Joseph R. Kemp and shows to the court that Francis J. Tumblity [sic], deceased, departed this life in the City of St. Louis . . . Your petitioner further shows to the court that the said Francis J. Tumblity [sic], on the 3rd day of October 1901, at Baltimore City in the State of Maryland, made and executed a last will and testament, and by said will appointed this petitioner one of the executors thereof; that thereafter, on the 24th day of June 1904, the said will was duly admitted to probate . . . Your petitioner shows to the court that said will disposes all the estate of whatever kind belonging to said Francis J. Tumblity [sic]; that the will executed in the City of St. Louis does not dispose of all of said estate, but only a part thereof; that said latter will does not by its terms revoke prior wills, and that the legacies and bequests contained in said latter will are not in conflict with the legacies and bequests contained in said first will except in one instance.

Kemp's attorney then motioned the court to direct the administrator, Gerrard Strode, to execute the 1901 will after executing the 1903 will:

. . . after the payment of the claims proved against said estate in the Probate Court of the City of St. Louis, the expenses of his administration and the legacies provided in said will executed on the 28th day of May, 1903, to pay over the balance of said estate to your petitioner for distribution in accordance with said will executed in said Baltimore City on the said 3rd day of October 1901.

The petition to the St. Louis probate court makes it clear that the validity of the 1901 will and testament was never in question by the Baltimore courts. Kemp's attorney was not challenging the validity of the 1903 St. Louis will and testament as the family members were. He was challenging its completeness, claiming Tumblety's final wishes were only completely satisfied with the addition of the 1901 Baltimore will. He argued that the 1903 St. Louis will did not dispose of all the estate, but with the inclusion of the 1901 Baltimore will, his entire estate would have been disposed of in accordance to Tumblety's wishes. Second, the 1903 will did not contain the phrase, "revoking all other wills made by me," thus, the 1901 will was legally in play. Third, with the exception of one instance, the two wills were not in conflict. In view of these three points, argued Kemp's attorney, the 1901 will and testament must also be included.

On April 3, 1908, Kemp's motion was denied. The conclusion of the court was that the 1903 will and testament was complete disposing of Tumblety's entire final wishes, thus, the 1901 Baltimore will and testament would be ignored. The denial of Kemp's motion allowed for a compromise agreement between the family members, ending the court battle. The *Baltimore Sun* recorded this on April 17, 1908, and ironically, the attorney the reporter interviewed was the very same lawyer who drafted the 1901 Baltimore will with Tumblety—Robert Simpson:

> *Estate of Dr. F.J. Tumblety To Be Distributed At Last.*
> *Mr. Robert H. Simpson, who was attorney for the late Dr. Francis J. Tumblety, an eccentric character of his day, said yesterday that all the heirs and legatees have reached an agreement by which the estate will be distributed through the Probate Court of St. Louis. Cardinal Gibbons and Archbishop Ireland are among the legatees, and each will receive $10,000 for charitable purposes. There are 28 legatees, including relatives and those mentioned in two wills left by Dr. Tumblety – one executed in Baltimore and one in St. Louis. The will executed in this city is dated October 3, 1901, and was admitted to probate here . . . . Although to all appearances without means, Dr. Tumblety left $145,000 cash on deposit with Henry Clews & Co., the New York bankers. The money was turned over to the public administrator of St. Louis.*

A stunning surprise in the 1901 Baltimore will was that Tumblety, a Whitechapel murders suspect who had a bitter hatred of prostitutes, bequeathed one thousand dollars to the Home for Fallen Women of Baltimore City, on North Exeter Street. According to the directory of the *Charitable and Beneficent Organizations of Baltimore, 1892*, the Home for Fallen Women of Baltimore City (5 N. Exeter Street) was

"To provide a temporary refuge for women who have left the path of virtue, and to try and lead them back to a respectable living." The knowledge of this created a backlash amongst modern researchers who believed Tumblety was not even considered a suspect by Scotland Yard. In *The Prince of Quacks*, author Tim Riordan argues that the Baltimore will was merely a joke between Simpson and Kemp. He claims that the first time Simpson met Tumblety was just three years before this, in 1898, being introduced to him and Major Joseph R. Kemp by a mutual friend, William Duvall.

Actually, Simpson knew Tumblety for over a decade. William Duvall did not introduce him to Tumblety in 1898; it was Simpson's mother in 1890, in his home, when he was a law student. In testimony, sworn under oath, Simpson stated this fact and explained that his mother knew Tumblety when she lived in Liverpool, England, years earlier. Tumblety did not dress like a vagrant in 1890, but instead wore expensive, albeit eccentric clothes. Simpson elaborated, stating he saw him periodically until 1894, and once he began his practice, he saw Tumblety quite often because Tumblety came to him for counsel.

To argue against the veracity of the Baltimore will and testament that Simpson wrote for Tumblety, Riordan states, "He [Tumblety] left Baltimore in October 1900 and did not return until October 1, 1901. During his absence, Simpson had thoroughly botched the case against the United States Engraving Company. Within days of returning to Baltimore, Tumblety hired a new lawyer, Frank Widner, Jr. Is it likely that he would ask Simpson to draw up a will while looking for a new lawyer?" This is not what transpired. Tumblety's Baltimore will was dated October 3, 1901. Under sworn testimony, Frank Widner Jr. stated that on or about October 1, 1901, Tumblety walked into his office building, disjointed, looking for his attorney Robert Simpson. Tumblety had forgotten Simpson's name in his incoherent state. Widner had never met Simpson, thus, could not help him. Tumblety then left the building and did not return for another ten days, on or about October 10, 1901, and complained to him about the US Engraving case,

"He left my office that afternoon and did not return until some ten days later, when he came to my office and made

a statement to me that he had found the attorney he was looking for, and that his name was Robert H. Simpson, on the fourth floor of the Law Building. He then made to me a statement of a case that was on trial, or had been brought before, upon which suit had been before Magistrate Bride of the City of Baltimore, and stated that Mr. Simpson had brought this suit and that judgment had been rendered.... and that he was dissatisfied with the manner in which Mr. Simpson had conducted this case, and that he came to me to retain me in this case."

Actually, Widner's recollection of the second meeting is mistaken, thus, Riordan was incorrect when he stated Simpson botched the case *before* the will was signed on October 3, 1901. While Widner likely met Tumblety on November 1, 1901, as evidenced by Tumblety's letter to him dated January 2, 1902, their discussion about the case could not have occurred. The timeline for the creation and destruction of Tumblety's autobiography is inconsistent with Widner's testimony. Kaiss did not complete the first printing of the autobiography until the end of November 1901, and then it took weeks and multiple visits by Tumblety to complete the required corrections. Tumblety ultimately rejected the corrected copy then left for an extended amount of time; enough time to convince Kaiss that Tumblety was not returning and to consider suing him. Kaiss then sold all copies to a junk dealer. O'Donovan stated the sale to the junk dealer was one month after the completion of the corrected copy, which would extend the timeline to around the end of December 1901. After this, Tumblety returned to accept it. When Tumblety found out the manuscript had been sold then destroyed, he demanded his money back, but O'Donovan rejected this demand. O'Donovan stated,

". . . . [Tumblety said] he would sue me for it. I told him to go ahead and sue, I did not want him to take any more of my time. He kept coming into my office for, I guess, three months."

This extends the timeline to near March 1902, which corresponds with when O'Donovan stated he was served with papers informing him of the lawsuit and court date. O'Donovan stated this occurred in March 1902. In view of this, Simpson could not have botched the case in 1901 since it happened in 1902, so Tumblety would not have been angry with him for the reason Widner claimed.

Under cross examination, Joseph R. Kemp was asked by the defense attorney when Tumblety told him he needed to make out a will. Kemp replied, "That was in 1901, in July – June, July or August, somewhere along there." This would have given Simpson and Tumblety ample time to draft and sign the will.

Widner also stated that after Tumblety died, he had several talks with Simpson, who,"told me that he had a will in his possession that was drawn for Dr. Tumblety, and that he thought it was worthless, that the old doctor did not have any money, and that they treated the matter when they drew the will as more of a joke than anything else." Although Widner claimed Simpson stated he thought the will was "more of a joke," he admitted that Simpson said the will was "drawn for Dr. Tumblety." Even if Simpson believed the will was more of a joke because he believed Tumblety was broke, Widner's comments make it clear that Tumblety took it seriously, thus, it reflected the wishes of Tumblety at that particular time. Once Simpson realized Tumblety had the money, his reason for believing it was a joke vanished. It was Simpson's legal responsibility to execute the will even if a later one had been executed for the purpose of determining the rights of all parties involved. Interestingly, when challenged by the attorney, Widner refused to answer any question "as regards any compensation I may expect, or intended to ask of Dr. Tumblety's estate for the services rendered by me."

Notice that Tumblety did not bequeath his estate in 1901 in the same manner as in 1903. This decision to slightly alter his will on how to distribute his estate from 1901 to 1903 is supported by yet another attempt to make out a will, which occurred in 1902. In sworn testimony in 1905, Joseph Mitchell, aged 25, from New Orleans, stated that Tumblety met him at the Grand Opera House about two o'clock in the evening in 1902 in May or June and asked if he would work for him as an errand boy for thirty dollars per month. Mitchell agreed and worked for Tumblety for four months. Mitchell claimed Tumblety would pay him in New York if he would go with him. One Saturday night, Tumblety received a huge gash on his head when two "fellows" held him up and hit him with a lead pipe. Tumblety stayed in a house where "hoboes" stayed. Mitchell and a lady from the house stayed with Tumblety as he was in bed. Tumblety sent young Mitchell after Father Gaffney at eleven o'clock at night in order to make out his will. Mitchell stated:

> *He wanted to make his will that evening and I got a piece of paper and started writing. He said he had one hundred and thirty two thousand dollars, and he was going to leave twenty thousand dollars to Mrs Hayes, I believe in California, if I am not mistaken; twenty thousand dollars to a nephew in Rochester; and twenty thousand dollars to a cousin of his in New Jersey, I believe he said, and twenty thousand dollars he was leaving some friend up in New York; and he told me he would put me down for twenty thousand dollars, making it one hundred thousand dollars, and he said he would have Thirty Two Thousand Dollars to give around to Sisters and the Poor Houses, and different things in the city here, and he told me I could get Father Gaffney and let him divide up as equally as he could.*

Father Gaffney came and told Tumblety that he was not dying. Tumblety was persistent and asked Father Gaffney to bring an attorney named Bernard McCloskey from the Hibernia Bank Building with him the next day to make out his will. McCloskey came and took down the information, but Tumblety was then convinced to withdraw the will. Tumblety did indeed have relatives in New Jersey, demonstrating the veracity of Joseph Mitchell's claim. Note that the disposition of this will was also different than his 1903 will. All three do have a consistent pattern in that he was giving to a local cause in the city from which he was writing his will.

What cannot be dismissed is that Tumblety had full knowledge that he was bequeathing $1,000 ($27,000 in today's value) to a home for women, particularly of the kind that he had an extreme hatred for. In his 1902 unexecuted will and his 1903 will, Tumblety purposely omitted members of his own extended family he did not care for, yet he bequeathed a large sum to the women he had hated all his life? One suggestion is that Tumblety had an innocent change of heart about women and prostitutes near the end of his life. That he chose this particular local charity because he was most unfair throughout his life to women who could decoy young men. The problem with this line of thinking is that one month after Tumblety had this will executed, he was in the office of his second Baltimore attorney, Frank Widner, holding a newspaper in front of his face when women walked by, and even threatened one particular woman so much that she left the room. These are not the actions of a man who has had a change of heart.

The obvious possibility is that Tumblety recalled his maltreatment of "fallen women" in the past and chose redemption by bequeathing a large sum of money to their kind. This is very threatening to Ripperologists who reject the idea of Tumblety being Jack the Ripper, as both Tumblety and Jack the Ripper were known for the maltreatment of women to an extreme degree—all the more reason for Tumblety to seek redemption in this way. The irony of Tumblety being aware of this charity plus the fact that he believed all night walkers should be disemboweled cannot be overstated.

Some have suggested that this act of redemption was because of guilt, but this does not fit Tumblety's personality profile. Chapter 9 will focus upon Tumblety's complete lack of remorse, meaning he did not have the capacity to feel guilt. Following Tumblety's lifelong pattern of committing seemingly altruistic actions because of a hidden, selfish agenda, his charity to the home for fallen women was likely for selfish reasons.

One question is, why did Tumblety bequeath his "former coachman," Mark Albert Blackburn, $5,000, while not bequeathing any money to the numerous other young male interests in his life? Martin McGarry knew Tumblety in a positive light for at least ten years, and Richard Norris knew him for twenty years. Tumblety did promise a number of young men that he would remember them in his will, such as Joseph Mitchell from New Orleans for $20,000 and John W. Jones from Hot Springs for $10,000, yet he did not. Sometime after 1900, Jones had a daughter named Frances and told

Tumblety that he named the girl after him. Tumblety was so appreciative that he would buy her fruit and confectionaries and have it sent to their house.

Tumblety's relationship with Blackburn seems to have been strong enough for Tumblety to trust him, thus, Tumblety may have put him in his will because of a combination of affection for him and Blackburn's loyalty in return. Tumblety initially hired Blackburn at the beginning of the Civil War when he had an office in Brooklyn. When Tumblety made an extended trip to Washington DC around June 1861, he continued his mail-order business out of Brooklyn, so seventeen-year-old Blackburn was likely his Brooklyn office boy running the business. The Brooklyn City Directory ending in May 1865, has Tumblety's office listed as M. A. Blackburn, physician, at 181 Fulton. Later, in 1865, Blackburn—now twenty years old—seemed to have accompanied Tumblety to St. Louis. Tumblety's business was listed in the city directory as Tumblety F. (J. Blackburn & Co.). Mark did have a brother, James, ten years his senior, so there is a possibility Mark stayed in Brooklyn while his brother accompanied Francis to St. Louis. Mark Blackburn then followed Tumblety to Cincinnati in 1866 and opened an office, and while there, he met and quickly married his first wife, Olivia Young. Before 1870, the two were separated, and Blackburn followed Tumblety to Pittsburgh. Their office in the 1870 city directory was listed as M. Blackburn. Blackburn married his second wife, Elizabeth Hauff, in Jersey City, Hudson County, New Jersey, on October 9, 1871, when Tumblety had an office in Jersey City. While it seems that Tumblety had made a partner out of Blackburn, this would have been out of character for such a domineering narcissist. Recall, his 1903 will had Mark A. Blackburn listed as a former coachman; a subordinate. Also, Tumblety was recorded to have made large sums of money when Blackburn was associated with him, yet Blackburn seems not to have been well-off, recorded in the census records having low-paying jobs up to 1900.

Just as John W. Jones did, Blackburn named his second son (first was named Joseph), born around 1872, after Francis Tumblety. Tragically, Francis Blackburn died soon after the age of three. Regardless, Tumblety would have been extremely appreciative that Blackburn named his child Francis. It may not be a coincidence that both men named their children after Francis Tumblety, and Tumblety connected both of them to his will and testament.

Mark A. Blackburn was listed in the 1876 Brooklyn City Directory but was no longer recorded as a physician; instead, he was listed as a watchman. This suggests that their relationship ended before 1876, which makes sense, since Tumblety began his extended stays in England in the summer of 1873. There is one apparent connection between Tumblety and Blackburn after the mid-1870s. In February 1880, Mark and Elizabeth had a baby boy, and they again named their child Francis. Sadly, this Francis also passed away in childhood. This may just have been a case of distraught Mark and Elizabeth renaming their child after their first Francis who had recently passed. If Tumblety knew, he still likely would have appreciated it.

Blackburn was not in Tumblety's 1901 will and testament, but he was in his 1902 and 1903 versions. Although Tumblety no longer considered New York as his residence in the last few years of his life, he did still visit New York to meet up with his bankers. Tumblety may have seen Blackburn in late 1901 or early 1902. Tumblety remembering him in his will suggests he knew Blackburn was still alive. Numerous eyewitness accounts of Tumblety in the last few years of his life comment upon his mind being as sharp as it once was. A recent encounter with Blackburn may have been enough to jar his memory of the prosperous times when Blackburn worked for him.

Now, with a window into Tumblety's life just before the Whitechapel murders and after, until his death, thanks to the discovery of over forty sworn testimonies, it is clear that Tumblety's behavior permanently changed when he returned from London in 1888. In the early 1880s, he dressed well but was fully aware that his kidney and heart disease could end his life at any moment. He continued to harbor a bitter hatred of women, especially prostitutes, even blaming them for the curse of the land. Immediately after he returned from London in1888, and for the next four years, his single-minded agenda was to create a revised autobiography publicly explaining to the world he was a well-bred, caring healer, someone who could never have murdered unfortunates. Soon after his 1893 publication, he permanently transitioned into a destitute-looking and filthy street walker, preferring to be in the city slums at night, an environment not unlike the Whitechapel streets. At the end of his life, Tumblety bequeathed a large sum of money to the women he hated most: prostitutes. While his hatred never stopped, having a strong belief that the next phase in his existence—the afterlife—was about to begin, how prudent would it have been to seek redemption from the Almighty.

8

Motive and the Four Systems
of Medical Treatment

. . . he [Tumblety] *was suffering from kidney and heart
disease, and that he was constantly in dread of sudden death.*
—*Toronto Mail,* November 23, 1888

Dr. Brent Turvey, PhD, explained that with respect to
offender signature typologies, anger-retaliatory behavior is
evident with the Whitechapel murders. Tumblety's bitter
hatred of seductive women, especially prostitutes, fits this
behavior unusually well. He blamed women for the ruination
of the world and the curse of the land, including disease.
Regardless if he contracted syphilis or not, Tumblety was
convinced he had a chronic disease, stating he was constantly
in dread of sudden death. Corroborating this is the sworn
testimony of a Hot Springs, Arkansas, acquaintance named
George W. Lower. Lower stated that he had known Tumblety
since around 1885, just a few years before the Whitechapel
murders. The attorney asked Lower about Tumblety,
complaining to him about his head injury or his kidney
condition. Lower replied,

> *I think it was his head, but he complained more of his
> heart than anything else. He would make that remark, 'I
> will go off that quick some time,' snapping his fingers.*

It is not a stretch of the imagination to see Tumblety
flipping his switch and retaliating against women. He would

have known that the East End unfortunates were a forgotten people. It was in 1880 that Tumblety stopped his lucrative business in the US as a newspaper-advertising alternative doctor, opting for annual trips to Hot Springs, Arkansas, and Saratoga Springs, New York, prioritizing health over money. In the eight years before the Whitechapel murders, Tumblety's chronic condition progressively worsened, and his hatred of seductive women and prostitutes festered. Recall the credible eyewitness account seven years before the murders, of Tumblety proclaiming that all night walkers should be disemboweled; in light of his beliefs, he may very well have retaliated.

While both contemporary and modern theories have been put forward as to why the murderer took the uteruses from two separate victims, very little has been discussed as to why Jack the Ripper also selected the kidney and the heart. Francis Tumblety is the only Jack the Ripper suspect connected to these three organs, and only these three. Tumblety was reported to value his collection of uterus specimens over all other organs in his Civil-War-time anatomical collection, and in the same year as the murders, he feared his kidney and heart disease might cause him sudden death. His preoccupation with these three organs is clear.

What is less obvious about Dr. Turvey's findings in connection with the murders is the second motive he identified at the Whitechapel crime scenes: reassurance-oriented behavior, specifically, power-reassurance. Turvey states that what underlies this behavior is a lack of confidence, such as a deep-seated personal inadequacy. Turvey explains that a serial offender collecting souvenirs fits into reassurance-oriented behavior; collecting a "token of remembrance that represents a pleasant experience." This would include collecting organs. He also explains that the Whitechapel murders show a need for the offender to shock the public and a desire to put his "work on display," a characteristic desire of Tumblety's and another behavior that fits under the category of reassurance-oriented. In the case of the Whitechapel murders, the offender certainly did murder these women off the beaten path, but they were along, or very near, a patrol constable's beat.

With the murders that occurred outdoors along a police constable's beat, the offender knew he had only minutes to accomplish his task, thus, the act of displaying his victim is less likely, espccially when there is a logical alternative explanation. Recall, the victims had deep throat cuts, were lying in a prone position, and had abdominal mutilation (in most cases, and the condition of the other two can be explained by the offender being interrupted). The mutilation and position of the bodies might not represent offender signature but offender MO, meaning he did this in order to accomplish his lethal agenda. A killer with anatomical knowledge would know that cutting the throat soon stopped the heart and would cause less blood spray when eviscerating. The victims lying on their backs would allow quick access to the organs. Thus, the abdominal mutilation was incidental if the main goal was collecting specific organs. The depth of the throat cut and the light attacks to the face, though, were quick expressions of hatred.

A surprising correlation between the crime scenes may very well show both reassurance-oriented and anger-retaliatory behaviors if the offender was both gay *and* a misogynist, as in the case with Tumblety. While Jack the Ripper murdered at least five casual prostitutes, he only took one inanimate trophy: Annie Chapman's wedding ring and keeper ring, both made of cheap brass. According to Metropolitan Police Criminal Investigation Department report #52983, September 19, 1888, the deceased was in the habit of wearing both rings, and the ring finger bore marks of them having been forcibly removed. The report suggested the offender took them believing they may be gold. This suggestion seems strange, since a prostitute working in the rough Whitechapel District would be aware that having something of wealth on her finger would be cause for a probable and possibly brutal mugging. These rings are unique in that they are the only physical representation for traditional heterosexual male-female bonding found on any of the victims. Knowing Tumblety's hatred for "lewd women" who decoy young men from homosexual relationships, if he was the murderer, it is not a surprise that these rings were targeted, especially in light of the fact that no other inanimate objects were taken.

The wedding ring and keeper ring were a set. How curious that years later Tumblety had in his possession at the time of his death his usual assortment of valuable diamonds and

diamond rings plus "two imitation set rings (valued at $3.00),"
as recorded on the inventory by the public administrator
Gerrard Strode. One alternative possibility is that this is
referencing two rings set with fake gems, but there are a
number of problems with this interpretation. While the jewelry
on his person was reported numerous times in his adult life
in the papers, even highlighting his large diamonds and gold,
never were two lesser set rings reported. Also, this statement
was part of an itemized list with estimated values on each
and every piece of jewelry. In view of this, if it was recording
two rings set with imitation gems, it would have listed each
separately, likely valued at $1.50 in each case. Even if they
combined the two, there is still a conflict. The fact that it
states, "valued at $3.00," instead of, "valued at $1.50 each,"
suggests the rings came as a set, as opposed to two separate
rings each set with fake gems. Regardless, how interesting
that the only inanimate trophy taken by Jack the Ripper is the
only physical representation of the very kind of relationship
Tumblety hated, then we see Tumblety had "two imitation set
rings" on his possession at a time he knew he was going to die.

The indoor murder of Mary Kelly also showed signs of both
reassurance-oriented and anger-retaliatory behavior if the
murderer was both gay and a misogynist. Occurring indoors,
the offender had hours with the body, not fearing someone
would happen upon him. The offender had full opportunity to
actualize his reassurance-oriented behavior through display,
which is categorized as offender signature. Kelly's body was
positioned exactly how the offender wanted her and was
displayed *exactly* like the Anatomical Venus wax effigy. The
Anatomical Venus was a very popular nineteenth-century wax
museum model of an attractive female lying prone, nude or
partially nude, on a bed with her internal abdominal organs
exposed. Some Anatomical Venuses even had the breasts
removed and placed to the side, as the killer did with Kelly's
corpse. These controversial, sexually-charged models were
banned in English museums since 1873, but every dime
museum in New York City's seedy Bowery District had them
and promoted them. Tumblety, a man known to walk the
streets at night, lived within a mile of four of these museums.

Although the murder was performed in only minutes, the
body of Catherine Eddowes was also displayed in the likeness

of an Anatomical Venus. When the City of London police surgeon, Dr. Frederick Gordon, arrived at Mitre Square by 2:00 a.m., he stated that the body was on its back with the head turned to the left shoulder, as in the case with Mary Kelly, and the arms by the side of the body and palms facing upward. The right leg was bent. If Jack the Ripper had any intentions of putting the body of Eddowes on display, then the likeness to an Anatomical Venus is uncanny.

Reproducing an Anatomical Venus not only fits reassurance-oriented behavior, but it also fits anger-retaliatory behavior if the offender was both gay and a misogynist. The Anatomical Venus finds its origins in the famous paintings of the erotic reclining Venus. Venus was the Roman goddess of physical love, seduction, and the Uniter of Man and Woman; the embodiment of heterosexual lust. Examples are the *Venus of Urbino* (1538) by Titian, in Florence, Italy, and the *Rokeby Venus* (c. 1650) by Velazquez in the National Gallery in London, England. Being against heterosexuality and being a misogynist, Tumblety would have hated these paintings and their underlying message.

The Anatomical Venus, though, exhibited the goddess of heterosexual love mutilated. That would have fit perfectly into Tumblety's narcissistic fantasy world. Tumblety even claimed to have visited these museums:

> *The Louvre was once a royal palace, but it is now the most extensive museum in the world (with perhaps the exception of the British), adjoining the Palace of the Tuilleries on the east, and of course reached on foot. Among its notable features, apart from the extent and beauty of the building itself, will be found the great picture gallery, filled with rare paintings, sculpture and curiosities, is said to be about ten miles, affording one of the costliest and most celebrated of collections. Chief among these is the Grand Gallery, filled with works by the great painters of antiquity, scarcely a notable name unrepresented, and the whole rivaling the galleries of the Vatican at Rome and Escurial at Madrid.*

How curious that the four Anatomical Venus models in New York City were destroyed by the New York City Police in

January 1888. The police acted in cooperation with Anthony Comstock, a crusader against gambling, prostitution, and obscenity. Tumblety was likely aware that the images of the mutilated goddess of heterosexual love were themselves mutilated, and this occurred in the very same year as the Whitechapel murders.

Jack the Ripper's reasons for collecting the organs may very well have been a combination of anger-retaliatory and reassurance-oriented behaviors, but there is another FBI serial offender motive that may have been involved: personal gain. If true, the killer was harvesting organs for himself. George R. Sims refers in the *Sunday Referee* in 1907 to the harvesting of uterus specimens theory he received from Scotland Yard officials:

> *The other theory in support of which I have some curious information, puts the crime down to a young American medical student who was in London during the whole time of the murders, and who, according to statements of certain highly-respectable people who knew him, made on two occasions an endeavour to obtain a certain internal organ, which for his purpose had to be removed from, as he put it, "the almost living body."*

Note the Tumblety-esque report in the *Chicago Tribune* on October 7, 1888, again written by E. Tracy Greaves, which followed the Philadelphia gynecologist story in the same article:

> *. . . An American who used to live in New York keeps an herb shop now in the Whitechapel district. A detective called at his place this week and asked him if he had sold any unusual compound of herbs to a customer since August. Similar inquiries were made at other shops in the neighborhood. The basis of this investigation has a startling Shakespearean flavor. An eminent engineer in London suggested to the police the theory that the murderer was a medical maniac trying to find the elixir of life and was looking for the essential ingredient in the parts taken from the murdered bodies; that, like the witches in 'Macbeth,' he spent the time over a bubbling caldron of*

the hellbroth made from the gory ingredients looking for the charm.

Greaves' statement of "murdered bodies" does sound like what Sims meant by "almost living bodies." In an Associated Press article in the *Bucks County Gazette*, December 13, 1888, written by their London correspondent, James McClean, and titled "AH THERE! TUMBLETY":

> . . . *His 'herb doctoring' finally became unprofitable in America; so he went to London, located near the Whitechapel road and for a while did a big business. His oddity of manner, dress and speech soon made him notorious as the 'American doctor'; but he enjoyed notoriety and turned it into money, till the Whitechapel horrors caused a general overhauling of suspicious characters.*

The veracity of this article comes from the phrase 'American doctor.' All other newspaper articles in 1888 reporting Tumblety arrested on suspicion only commented about his history as an Indian herb doctor. The London correspondent could not have received this information from any US sources, but only accurate London sources (since it was true). The importance of this is that a credible London source stated Tumblety had an office "located near Whitechapel road."

The *New York Sun* had a Sunday multicolumn article published on November 26, 1888, that was actually written near the time it was discovered that Tumblety was arrested on suspicion on November 17/18. It was then sent across the Atlantic Ocean on ship mail, arriving in New York around November 26:

> *An American doctor named Twomblety is now held because he is an erratic character, and because one theory is that some American medical institution wants specimens of the female uterus, which it happens that Jack the Ripper often takes from the bodies of his victims.*

The only logical scenario for the *Sun's* London correspondent to have a story on Tumblety so quickly is that once the *Sun's* headquarters in New York got word of "Twomblety" being Kumblety, on November 18, they sent an immediate cable to their London correspondent to dig further. This suggests the London correspondent received the information from the source, Scotland Yard, as was the practice of the foreign London correspondents, meaning the story of the police connecting Tumblety to the uterus is true. It also demonstrates that this particular harvesting theory was still on the minds of Scotland Yard even after Tumblety's escape, corroborating Sims' article in 1907 in the *Sunday Referee.*

Tumblety claimed he could cure all disease with his particular herbal/botanical system of medical treatment, and once he realized he himself had a chronic disease, according to his early autobiographies, he seems to have searched for a cure within his medical system. He quoted Dr. A. R. Porter in an address to the *Botanical Medical Reformer*, but this statement became so significant to him that he published it as his own words in his later autobiography versions:

> . . . *In the vegetable kingdom there may be found the elixir of health—there may be found the healing balm. Would to Heaven that the study of this extensive division of natural objects was more generally pursued and appreciated; because, if it were, and the medicinal properties of plants better understood, disease might be more easily and successfully treated . . .*

The uterus is the organ where life begins. If someone was attempting to create an elixir of life by mixing ingredients from a woman's body—something not available in a man's body—with herbs, this is the organ. It is coincidental that Francis Tumblety was reported on numerous occasions to still have an herbal store open, was an herbal expert, and realized in the very same year of the murders that his own skills were not good enough to cure himself.

In his autobiographies, Tumblety did state the primary reason why he went to Europe in the first place beginning in 1869, which was "research" for his profession:

> *Since the publication of the foregoing* [his 1866 autobiography] *I have visited many far off places, including the*

*golden region of California, Great Britain and Ireland, and
the European continent. My tour was not one of mere pleasure, but rather of research in behalf of my profession . . .*

Tumblety's seismic shift in priority in 1880 of focusing
upon his health as opposed to earning money confirms that he
recognized his medical system had no cure for his ailments.
Being in constant dread of sudden death sounds like a man
at his wits end. Tumblety knew that there were three other
popular medical systems in the late-nineteenth century, and
it would be a surprise if desperate Tumblety did not research
possible cures in these other systems. It is also clear he would
not have publicized this research, since the main thrust of his
autobiographies is the dominance of his particular botanical
medical system over all others. Publicizing a search in other
systems would have contradicted his claims. Even so, there is
evidence that Tumblety did research in other areas of medicine
after 1880.

The second popular system of medical treatment Tumblety
would have been aware of was homeopathy, which was
developed in 1796. Even today, homeopathic alternative
medicine is quite popular, albeit considered a pseudoscience by
medical experts. The basis of nineteenth-century homeopathic
medical treatment was, "what makes a person ill also cures
them." "Homeo" means the treatment is "the same as" the
ailment. The goal was to administer a diluted concentration
of a drug that duplicates the disease, such as elevating a
person's temperature if they have a fever. This is different
from Tumblety's botanical cures, where a patient was treated
with an herb that directly attacks the disease. His treatment
was "hetero," or "different," from the ailment. In these terms,
botanical/herbal treatments are "heteropathic." If a desperate
Tumblety did experiment with homeopathic cures, that fact
that he died from his diseases shows he did not find any.

The third system of medical treatment in the nineteenth
century was the method endorsed and used by the
professional medical community. It is called allopathy and is
still the only method fully endorsed by the medical community.
It is a "heteropathic" treatment, but instead of administering
strictly natural botanical/herbal remedies, it focuses upon
synthesizing pharmaceutical drugs through chemistry, which

includes chemical compounds found outside of the botanical world. While we see today that the allopathic approach has produced amazing results, in the late-nineteenth century it was in its infancy. Allopathic remedies included ineffective, painful, and even lethal solutions, such as ingesting mercury, and the practice of bloodletting. Likely finding himself in the hospital because of his medical conditions, Tumblety would have discovered that there was no common allopathic medical cure for his diseases either. Physicians would have confirmed his chronic heart and kidney condition.

The fourth system of medical treatment was part of an esoteric occultist philosophy very popular in the nineteenth century, called theosophy. It begins with a credible and appropriate scientific question, "Why does life decay and die?" The conclusion was that if science discovered the answer, then extending life should be a possibility. If God truly does exist, and we know Tumblety was a devout Catholic, then the mysteries of nature—including cures—can be understood by discovering the relationship between nature and its Creator. Theosophy is an umbrella term for mystical and esoteric western philosophies that deal with the mysteries of life and nature. Theosophy means wisdom of the gods, which is hidden knowledge (Gnosticism) from the ancient past. The release of this hidden knowledge allows for enlightenment and salvation. Christian Theosophy states that the two trees in the Garden of Eden, the Tree of Knowledge of Good and Evil and the Tree of Life, or Kabbalah, are symbolic for all divine knowledge, and the expulsion of man from the Garden due to Original Sin blocked this knowledge from us—albeit still in our minds. Rediscovery and release of this ancient knowledge is the cornerstone of theosophy. If death and decay is the direct result of Original Sin, then hidden knowledge holds the key to cures and even everlasting youth. Man should be able to create an elixir of health and life.

The Theosophical Society was founded in Tumblety's back yard in New York City in 1875, by Helena Blavatsky, William Quan Judge, and Henry Steel Olcott. Interestingly, the foundation of the Theosophical Society was a book written by Blavatsky called *The Secret Doctrine*, which was published in 1888, the same year as the Whitechapel murders. According to French scholar of Western Esotericism Antoine Faivre in *Theosophy, Imagination, Tradition: Studies in Western Esotericism* (2000), theosophy has a connection with alchemy, astrology, Hermetism, Christian Kabbalah, Paracelsism, philosophia occulta, and Rosicrucianism. Note what author Tukaram Tatya, author *of A Guide to Theosophy* (Bombay, 1887), stated in a chapter titled, "The Elixir of Life":

> *In the first place we have the actual visible material body – Man, so called; though, in fact, but his outer shell – to deal with. Let us bear in mind that science teaches us that in about every seven years we change skin as effectually as any serpent; and this so gradually and imperceptibly that, had not science after years of unremitting study and observation assured us of it . . .*

Compare this to what Tumblety stated in his 1893 autobiography, commenting upon the very same physical change by seven years:

> *Our bodies are always undergoing change, constantly wearing and wasting away . . . it is estimated that the soft parts of our bodies become entirely changed in the space of about one year, and our bones in seven years; hence all the flesh of our bodies at the present time will . . . giving us entirely a different body from our present.*

In Tumblety's 1893 autobiography, he connected the human body and the nutritious portion of the blood called chyle:

> *The human body, consisting of bones, muscles, sinews, blood vessels, organs of reproduction, nutrition, respiration and of thought, etc., is constructed, nourished and sustained in accordance with certain laws common to organized beings. It is made up of the elements that surround us, such as animals, vegetables and water. These substances, taken into the stomach, undergo the process of digestion, and the chyle or nutritious portion enters into the composition of the blood, and by this means is brought in contact with all parts of the system.*

Surprisingly, Tatya discusses the principles of the human body and chyle and connects it with immortality, or the elixir of life:

> . . . The 'Dhatu' of the old Hindu physiologist had a dual meaning, the esoteric side of which corresponds with the Tibetan 'Zung' (seven principles of the body – chyle, flesh, blood, fat, bones, marrow, semen). We, Asiatics, have a proverb, probably handed down to us, and by the Hindus repeated ignorantly, as to its esoteric meaning. It has been known ever since the old Rishis mingled familiarly with the simple and noble people they taught and led on. The Devas had whispered into every man's ear —Thou only—if thou wilt—art 'immortal.'

Notice the connection between Tumblety and blood. Recall that he displayed a glass model of the circulatory system showing blood flow in the entrance to his offices. Alchemy itself takes into account chyle and the elixir of life. Julian Scott, coauthor of *The Alchemist* (2000), wrote an article titled, "The Inner Gold of Alchemists" (*India North*, May 12, 2014). In it, Scott comments upon the elixir of life and its connection with chyle:

> Alchemy seems to be an almost universal science. Not only do we find it in Medieval Europe, but also in China and India, amongst other places . . . It was believed, for example, that all the Spirits of the Elements were subject to him [the Alchemist]. There is also a tradition that, owing to his knowledge of the Elixir of Life, he still lives, as an adept who will disclose himself to the profane at the end of a certain cycle . . . What the Alchemist is doing, then, is following the process of natural creation. Thus, Paracelsus speaks of 'Natural Alchemy': 'Natural Alchemy causes the pear to ripen and produces grapes on a vine. Natural alchemy separates the useful elements from the food that is put into the stomach, transforms it into chyle and blood, into muscles and bones, and rejects that which is useless. A physician who knows nothing of alchemy can only be a servant of nature . . . but the alchemist is her lord.'

Paracelsus (1493 – 1541) was a Swiss surgeon-physician and alchemist with a single-minded focus to discover the latent forces of nature, especially in healing. His name was originally Theophrastus Aureolus Bombastus von Hohenheim, and he was a lifelong Catholic. In 1526, he was appointed professor of medicine at the University of Basel, Switzerland, but for much of his life he traveled and studied. In alchemy, he stressed the discovery of medicines based upon the harmony of man—the microcosm—with nature—the macrocosm. His Christian beliefs on nature are categorized as Christian Mysticism. Throughout the philosophy chapter in Tumblety's 1893 autobiography, he connects God with nature and natural cures, demonstrating he also fit into the Christian Mysticism category. As with Tumblety, Paracelsus extracted his chemicals from "natural plants." He discouraged the alchemical practice of attempting to make lead into gold and encouraged the discovery of natural healing. Paracelsus also believed in the ancient hidden mystery called "arcanum." In the arcanum was the knowledge of philosophers' stone, or elixir of life. In Paracelsus' time, it was believed that there were three forms of the philosophers' stone, the *lapis vegetablilis*, the power to preserve man's health and cure sickness with the vegetable world; the *lapis animalis*, the health of the organs and physical senses of man; and third, the *Minerall*, the transformation of metals by fire. Paracelsus created an *elixir vitae*, or life elixir, which eventually became known as a Swedish Bitter. While it never extended life, it was thought to improve life.

The late-nineteenth century public was quite interested in the possibility that medical science might extend life, as evidenced by the following article. A newspaper in Rochester, New York, published an article, "Alchemist Secrets":

And now we are going to let our readers into a few of the secrets in search of which men of old spent their lives and their fortunes. . . . This is how to prepare the elixir of life, which Paracelsus did not—with all respect to Sir Thomas Browne—hold capable of rendering the physical body immortal, but only of prolonging life. Take half a pound of pure carbonate of potash and expose it in the air until dissolved. Filter the fluid and add as many leaves of the plant Melissa as it will hold. Let it stand in a well-closed glass and in a moderately warm place for twenty-four hours. Remove the leaves and throw them away; on the top of the fluid pour "absolute alcohol" to the height of one or two inches, and let it remain until the alcohol becomes intensely green. Take away the alcohol and preserve it, and go on repeating the operation until all the coloring matter is absorbed by which 'man may rejuvenate his constitution by purifying it so that it may be able to receive without any interruption the life-giving influence of the Divine spirit.

—*Brockport Republic,* October 6, 1887

This article on Paracelsus and his elixir of life was published in the New York papers by the time Tumblety returned from England to New York in September 1887. The search for an elixir of life had actually made mainstream medical science and, thus, was for a time recognized as allopathy. There was research in Europe in the late-nineteenth century searching for an elixir of life. The following article on elixir of life ideas from London in the late-nineteenth century, appeared in *Urology Today*:

M. L. Miller discussed the use of 'Injection, Ligation and Transplantation: the Search for the Glandular Fountain of Youth.' She began with the Emerson quote: 'All diseases run into one: old age.' So everyone seeks the fountain of youth. She believes that modern endocrinology began with Brown-Sequard, who self-injected crushed testicles and 'got new vigor.' Physicians soon tried this on their patients. Then, (as noted above), the Steinach rejuvenation procedure of vasectomy also became popular. Voronoff went a step further by transplanting sliced ape/monkey testes into the abdominal wall. This became so popular that the French government eventually had to ban primate hunting in their colonies. . . . C. Nicholson continued the ideas of rejuvenation by filling out the discussion of Brown-Sequard's Elixir of Life: Pioneer Andrology and Genitourinary Endocrinology. The famous physician received his MD degree in 1846 and subsequently held positions in London, Paris and the USA. He is most famous for the description spinal cord hemi-transection and

its resulting neurologic syndrome. But he also pursued
the 'Elixir of Life' and in 1889 reported on his studies of
injection of a mixture of dog blood of the testicular veins,
semen and juices of the testis.
  —*Urology Today*, 2006

On July 31, 1889, Dr. William A. Hammond, the alienist
who was quoted in the papers in October 1888 about Jack
the Ripper being a monomaniac, commented positively about
Brown-Sequard's research and even began research of his own:

Dr. Hammond's views – Washington, July 31. –Dr. Wil-
liam A. Hammond of this city is experimenting with the
elixir of life recently discovered by Brown-Sequard of
Paris, and thus far, he says, the results are fully equal
to the promises given out by the great Paris physician. 'It
is true,' said the doctor, 'that when Dr. Brown-Sequard's
discovery was first reported to the American people I was
rather dubious and inclined more or less to think as oth-
ers hinted, that either the report was a French joke or that
Dr. Brown-Sequard "was another good man gone wrong."
The first report did not give a complete idea of the treat-
ment. It indicated rather that the elixir was a compound
made from various glands from various animals, and on
the showing I was willing to say the thing was impossible,
but when I obtained further and more accurate details I
was willing to believe there might be something in it . . . I
would hardly be safe to inject the fluid into a body twen-
ty-four hours after the liking of the animal, for it is well
known that to inject the essence of decayed beef would
kill. As soon as the lamb is slaughtered by the butcher no
time is wasted in pounding and filtering . . .'

Recall George R. Sims' 1907 *Sunday Referee* harvesting-
of-uterus-specimens theory he received from Scotland Yard
officials. Hammond's comments about injecting only freshly
killed animal fluids into the human body for an elixir of life
makes Sims' "almost living body" comment understandable,
which suggests that the American medical student's hidden
agenda for collection was to create an elixir of life.

While Dr. Brown-Sequard published his research just after
the murders in the June 21, 1889, in *Comptes Rendus* of the

Paris Societe de Biolegie, he stated he began experimenting in 1875. Brown-Sequard also stated that another physician, Dr. M. G. Variot, independently made "experiments of the same kind," injecting fluids into three elderly patients.

Numerous articles were published in Europe and the United States in the early 1880s that attempted to bridge the gap between an allopathic medical approach and a theosophical approach. In the *Scientific American*, October 27, 1883, Dr. J. H. Gladstone, PhD, FRS, VI'CS, president of the British Association, published an article titled "Chemical Science," which connected the early alchemical search for the philosopher's stone, or elixir of life, with advances in chemistry. Gladstone stated, "It was in the salts of gold and silver that he [Geber] looked for the universal medicine [elixir of life]. . . . led to the placing of the conception of simple and compound bodies upon the foundation of scientific fact." John Uri Lloyd published a book in 1883 titled, *Pharmaceutical Preparations. Elixirs: their history, formulae, and methods of preparation . . . with a resume of unofficial elixirs from the days of Paracelsus*, which is another example of the well-respected medical community taking the theosophical approach seriously.

Paracelsus, in addition to being an early practitioner of allopathic medicine, is considered a high authority and master of the Brotherhood of the Rosicrucians, or Rosy Cross, a Masonic-style Order devoted to the attainment and application of medical and spiritual knowledge. The Brotherhood of the Rosy Cross state that they are a branch of the original fraternity of "theosophists, or true Rosicrucians; a brotherhood and sisterhood of Christ and blessed Sophia of holy wisdom and mystical illumination; alchemists and adepts of hermetic knowledge, religious, and spiritual truth." They claim to study the metaphysics, or the hidden forces of nature.

One particular esoteric secret society was called the Order of the Golden Dawn, whose central philosophy was Rosicrucianism. According to Jeff Dannes of Washington and Lee University:

The Hermetic Order of the Golden Dawn (G.D.) was a secret fraternal organization dedicated to the study (with practical focus) of occult and esoteric practices. The organization was founded in the late 1880s by prominent Freemasons, and drew heavily on the tradition of Victorian

*Freemasonry, and from the German Rosicrucian move-
ment. The Order also based much of its ritual practice on
ancient texts, particularly the Egyptian 'Book of the Dead'
and the Hebrew Kabbala, but G.D. never identified itself
as a religion or substitute for religion. Like Rosicrucians
and some Kabbalists, G.D. adherents (called adepts)
sought to 'penetrate the mysteries of nature,' that is, to
reform philosophy and science to reveal divine truths. The
Order used alchemy, astrology and other such practices to
reveal a member's 'true life.' Golden Dawn adepts could
be of any religious persuasion and any gender. The group
recruited members from all sections of European Society,
though many were members of Britain's intellectual elite:
W.B. Yeats, Aleister Crowley, and Bram Stoker all be-
longed to the Order . . .*

As stated, Bram Stoker was the business manager of the
Lyceum Theatre in 1888 and close friend of J. W. Brodie-
Innis, an artist, who was a member of the Golden Dawn.
Brodie-Innis convinced Stoker to hire fellow Golden Dawn
member Pamela Colman Smith at the Lyceum Theatre. Being a
practicing Catholic, a church strongly opposed to all versions
of Freemasonry, Stoker would not have become a direct
member, at least publicly.

There was a connection between the Lyceum Theatre and
the Whitechapel murders. Some believed Jack the Ripper was
a kind of dual-natured killer like Dr. Jekyll and Mr. Hyde, a
prominent physician by day turning into a medical maniac by
night. Note the Tumblety-esque article about the physician-
turned-medical-maniac seeking the elixir of life. Surprisingly,
just three days before—arguably—the first Whitechapel
murder of Martha Tabram, Mansfield's *Dr. Jekyll and Mr. Hyde*
opened at the Lyceum Theatre. It was also only three weeks
before the Polly Nichols murder, the first of the canonical five
murders. On August 5, 1888, the *New York Tribune* published
the following in London:

MANSFIELD AS JEKYLL AND HYDE.
[By Cable to the Tribune.]
Copyright: 1888: By the New York Tribune.
*London, Aug. 4. – Richard Mansfield appeared here to-
night at the Lyceum Theatre as Dr. Jekyll and Mr. Hyde.*

A great audience attended. Many distinguished persons were present, both American and English, and the welcome accorded to Mr. Mansfield was extremely cordial. Upon his first entrance as 'Jekyll' two distinct rounds of applause welcomed him, and in the course of the night he was called back five times. Mr. Mansfield had not intended to appear in London until September 4, but hearing that one of his imitators was making ready to appear here on August 6, at the Opera Comique, in a version of "Jekyll and Hyde" substantially a copy of his own, he changed his plan, and by expeditious movements he has thwarted all attempts to forestall his piece. . . . The two sides of one nature are vividly depicted, but the fatal result is one man, not two. . . . but Mr. Mansfield places strenuous emphasis on Jekyll and portrays a high and fine nature at war with itself and miserably despoiled by the evil which it vainly struggles to extirpate. . . . The scene of the transformation from Hyde to Jekyll greatly excited the spectators, and here, as at home, Mr. Mansfield's passionate outburst and impetuous action, the volume of his ever-increasing vehemence and power capture the house and set upon his effort the seal of unequivocal success. At this climax the theatre resounded with plaudits most energetical and sincere . . .

Among the spectators was H.R.H. the Duke of Teck and the Princess Mary and suite, the Minister of the United States, Miss Mary Anderson and the Countess of Pembroke, Alma Tadema, Clement Scott, Joseph Halton, Sir Morell Mackenzie, Lady Hardy, Mrs. Louise Chandler Moulton, T.P. O'Connor, Percy Fitzgerald, Joseph Knight, Max O'Rell, G.W. Smalley, B.L. Farjeon and wife, Oakey Hall, Beatty Kingston, Edward Ledger and wife, C.J. Parkinson, G.F. Rowe, Charles Dickens, Saville Clarke, Carl Rosa, Miss Agnes Hewitt, Miss Grace Hawthorne, Joseph Arthur, H.C. Jarrett and F.C. Burnand.

It is not Mr. Mansfield's intention to make a long run for the piece, the strain being hurtful to his voice and injurious to his health. "A Parisian Romance" will be presented later, and a production of his new play of 'Nero' is contemplated.

Mr. Henry Irving, who is in Switzerland, telegraphed congratulations, and Mr. Mansfield received a host of friends after the play was ended. –W.W.

The author of the article, William Winter, was an editor and critic for the *New York Tribune*. In attendance was George W. Smalley, the chief London correspondent for the *New York Tribune*.

There are countless eyewitness testimonies of Tumblety's lifelong passion for the theater, so much so that he knew the names and backgrounds of all the actors in the New York theatres. Young Martin McGarry, hired by Tumblety in 1882 as a travel partner, stated:

> *Usually he went up to the Morton House, where he pointed out the actors to me and told me who they were and what they did. Sometimes in the afternoons we would drop in to the matinees.*
> —*New York World*, December 5, 1888

Tumblety likely watched Mansfield's performance in *Dr. Jekyll and Mr. Hyde* in these New York theaters in 1887. When Tumblety returned from England a year before the Whitechapel murders, in September 1887, Mansfield's *Dr. Jekyll and Mr. Hyde* was playing at the Madison Square Theatre until October. In early winter, Mansfield and his acting company performed in Washington DC, but quickly returned to New York performing at the Fifth Avenue Theatre around Christmas. In February 1888, his company performed at the Grand Opera Theatre. Tumblety himself commented upon frequenting the many London theaters in his 1889 autobiography, comments that are not in his earlier versions:

> *London theatres are very numerous and celebrated for the splendor of their entertainments, though scarcely one of them but is dark, dingy and uncomfortable to those familiar with the handsome entrances and fine lights of the American houses.*

It would be out of character if Tumblety did not make the opening of Mansfield's *Dr. Jekyll and Mr. Hyde* at the Lyceum Theatre in London's West End on August 4, 1888, especially since prominent British and American figures were in attendance. He would have reveled in informing anyone seated next to him his vast knowledge of Mansfield and his company of actors. He did state in his January 1889 interview with the

New York World reporter that he frequented the Beefsteak Club, a club that enjoyed a strong relationship with the Lyceum Theatre. Attendance in the club was by sponsorship, so even if he did not get into the club, he certainly knew about it.

Another connection between Tumblety and the Lyceum Theatre was Sir Henry Hall Caine, his intimate young friend between late 1874 and March 1876. Eighteen-year-old Hall Caine claimed to have met famous British Actor Sir Henry Irving and manager of the Lyceum Theatre in 1871 or 1872. At that time, Irving was associated with the Lyceum Theatre and also went on tour. Hall Caine and Irving's friendship was reported to have been "always affectionate and sometimes intimate." Note Hall Caine's comments he made about Irving, who had just passed:

> *I knew Henry Irving through so many years. . . . I was 18 years of age when I met him first* [Since Hall Caine was born on May 14, 1853, it was when Irving performed The Bells in London in 1871 or Liverpool in 1872] . . . *He was then playing his first famous engagement in 'The Bells' and after seeing his performance on two successive nights from the front row of the gallery I exercised the only gift I was conscious of in writing out the entire play from memory. That led to the beginning of our acquaintance, laid the foundations of our friendship and paved the way to lifelong relations that were always affectionate and sometimes intimate. Thirty-four years ago* [1871], *and Irving was then a young man in his thirties . . . –The St. Louis Republic, October 16, 1905*

Hall Caine later contacted Irving in the summer of 1874, when he was preparing his first issue of a monthly Liverpool magazine, *The Rambler*. He asked Irving if he could use his portrait in an article titled, "The Very Modern Stage," and Irving immediately gave his approval. Irving was well aware that Hall Caine also wrote articles and theater reviews for the Liverpool *Town Crier*.

Concurrent to Hall Caine's blossoming friendship with Irving was his whirlwind relationship with Francis Tumblety. Tumblety opened his Liverpool office in September 1874 and began advertising in the Liverpool newspapers. Being an avid fan of theater, or a "play-goer," and frequenter to newspaper offices to pay for his huge advertisements, it is not a surprise that Tumblety would eventually meet Hall Caine. They may also have met, or recognized each other, at the London premiere of *Hamlet* on October 31, 1874. Irving invited Hall Caine to attend the premiere, of which Hall Caine gave an outstanding review, which further cemented their friendship. The performance was advertised for weeks, and tickets sold out early. In the *New York Herald*, November 23, 1874, an article titled "The London Theatres" and dated November 2, 1874, commented upon prominent British and American play-goers crowding the sold-out performance, stating "Mr. Irving is an enormous favorite."

Tumblety began his relationship with Hall Caine in late 1874, employing him as an amanuensis in order to assist him in his legal troubles and write his European version of his autobiography by January 1875. Tumblety abruptly left his flourishing business in Liverpool in January 1875, clearly because of legal cases against him involving slander and an accidental death. He stayed in London for the next six months and left Hall Caine to handle his Liverpool affairs. In view of this, their relationship must have started in late 1874. Hall Caine visited Tumblety in London in February 1875. Irving continued to perform *Hamlet* at the Lyceum Theatre until June 19, 1875. On September 25, 1875, *Macbeth*, also starring Irving, premiered at the Lyceum Theatre. Although extant records of Tumblety's and Hall Caine's correspondence ends in the spring of 1876, the last letter gives no indication that their friendship ended.

In October 1876, Irving was in Liverpool and gave Hall Caine an interview for the *Liverpool Argus*, and Hall Caine helped Irving with some personal issues. Irving then went to Dublin, Ireland, which is where he met Bram Stoker in November 1876. When Irving became the manager and sole lessee of the Lyceum Theatre in September 1878, he quickly hired Stoker as the business manager, a relationship that lasted for the next thirty years. Hall Caine finally met Stoker at the Lyceum Theatre in December 1878 during the yet another performance of *Hamlet*, and they eventually became the best of friends. In the ensuing years, Hall Caine supported Irving's acting career by writing excellent reviews, and in turn, Hall

Caine's fame as a writer blossomed, even into writing for the stage. Stoker eventually acted as Hall Caine's literary agent.

This is when Tumblety spent most of his time in England and Europe. Tumblety arrived in England from New York on May 2, 1878, and is recorded returning to New York in April 1880. It would not be a surprise to see Tumblety attending the 1878 opening of *Hamlet* at the Lyceum Theatre.

If Tumblety was Jack the Ripper, why begin the murders in August 1888? It may not have been a coincidence that the opening of Mansfield's *Dr. Jekyll and Mr. Hyde* in London was just days before the Whitechapel murders began. Mansfield's performance of a physical transformation due to the ingestion of an elixir was a powerful visual representation of one of nature's most closely held secrets being revealed. Reading in the newspaper of possible cures would not have the same effect for a show-goer seeking such a thing. The similarities between Dr. Jekyll's elixir and the elixir of life did not go unnoticed, even by the medical community. In the *Medical Bulletin: A Monthly Journal of Medicine and Surgery*, Volume 11, October 1889, Dr. John V. Shoemaker, AM, MD, states in his article titled, "Science in Fiction":

> *Much discussion was excited during the past summer by Brown-Sequard's statement that he thought it possible to prolong life and recall some portion of departed strength. The ancient idea of the "elixir of life" was that of a wonderful potion which would be able, by one draught, to regenerate the physical system, to recall and preserve indefinitely the vigor of youth. Modern science, if it should harbor the conception at all, would search for some agency able to maintain nutrition and prevent degeneration, not by a sudden influence but by habitual use. The old theory was utilized, or, rather, intended to be utilized by our great romancer, Nathaniel Hawthorne. For 'Septimius Felton,' published after the lamented author's death, was an uncompleted fragment. Hawthorne, however, lays little stress upon the elixir, but makes use of the idea of prolonged life to discuss, in his inimitable style, questions concerning life, manners, and morals. A pseudo-scientific conceit furnishes the motif of Stevenson's 'Dr. Jekyll and Mr. Hyde' . . .*

Hawthorne's *Septimius Felton, Elixir of Life,* was published in 1872 and again in 1883. Note the part of the story where the ingredients of the elixir of life are revealed:

> *The naturalist looked steadfastly at him . . . 'Flower, do you call it?' said he, after a reexamination. 'This is no flower, though it so closely resembles one . . . It is a certain vary rare fungus . . . What sort of manure had been put into that hillock?' 'The hillock where it grew,' answered he, 'was a grave.' 'So it grew out of a grave! Yes, yes; and probably it would have grown out of any other dead flesh, as well as that of a human being; a dog would have answered the purpose as well as a man . . . So superstition say, kill your deadliest enemy, and plant him, and he will come up in a delicious fungus, which I presume to be this; steep him, or distil him, and he will make an elixir of life for you.'*

Tumblety believed his deadliest enemy was the type of woman able to decoy young men. He told young Norris in 1881 just after revealing his collection of surgical knives that all night walkers should be disemboweled. Connecting Tumblety with the Whitechapel crimes in 1888 just after *Dr. Jekyll and Mr. Hyde* opened in London makes sense, especially when Scotland Yard was notified that a medical maniac was indeed attempting to create such an elixir. The engineer from the West End who heard the rumor took the theory seriously enough to contact Scotland Yard.

Tumblety makes a curious omission in his comments about London theaters in his 1889 autobiography, comments that he added only two or three months after his arrest on suspicion for the Whitechapel murders. After his statement about the splendor of the London theaters, he states:

> *The Haymarket, Adelphi or Olympic, and Princess's are the best, at any one of which the time spent is not likely to be thrown away, especially with the opportunities which performances supply for studying the play-going habits and manners of the Londoners.*

How strange that Tumblety ignored the Lyceum Theatre, which was managed at the time by the famous Sir Henry

Irving, an actor so famous he was eventually knighted. Irving was a household name in the United States, visiting the US on numerous occasions. The *Evening World*, October 8, 1887, reports in a large article titled "Henry Irving Here Again" on Henry Irving and Bram Stoker arriving in New York onboard the steamship *Aller* and performing in *Faust* at the Star Theatre. Irving stated, "The production of 'Faust,' which will be seen at the Star Theatre, will be exactly similar to the London Lyceum Theatre production. I have brought my company and my surroundings will be identical. I think the American theatre-going public will enjoy it." Tumblety was known to namedrop in order to demonstrate his higher social status, but he declined to mention the Lyceum Theatre showing *Dr. Jekyll and Mr. Hyde*. Even though he dedicated an entire chapter complaining about his maltreatment by Scotland Yard involving the Whitechapel murders, he did so by omitting any mention of them or London.

If Tumblety was Jack the Ripper harvesting organs for personal gain, he did not continue to kill after he returned, suggesting he admitted to himself that his years in the 1880s searching for an elixir of life cure were a dead end. After the completion of his 1893 autobiography, Tumblety's traveling lifestyle was devoted entirely to dealing with his chronic pains; not curing them. There is evidence of him accepting his fate. Notice what he stated in his 1893 autobiography, a statement *not* written in his 1889 version:

> Since, however, there is no panacea that can give us everlasting youth, let us bow before this inexorable law, but endeavor to prepare for ourselves a green old age by avoiding every other source of organic deterioration.

How curious that Tumblety never commented about this in his earlier versions. In order to maintain his legacy of creating a new medical system and give it credibility, he stated the chronic medical conditions that afflicted him were not diseases, but the product of extreme rheumatic fever.

9

Window into the Mind
of the Doctor

Man is a selfish being, endowed with faculties in harmony
with his animal nature, and with the external objects of the
world.

—Francis Tumblety

Francis Tumblety was plagued with the specific intersex
condition formerly known as Hermaphroditism, possibly
possessing both male genitals (nonfunctioning) and female
genitals. Recall Tumblety reportedly saying to his Baltimore
attorney, Robert Simpson, soon after Tumblety's pants
dropped when he passed out in Simpson's office, "Do not ever
tell that to anybody; that is a misfortune which has followed
me all through my life." His belief that his genitals were a
misfortune plagued him throughout his lifetime. He identified
as a male, and possessing a useless micro-penis was a sexual
dysfunction with the inability to perform as a male. A long-
term psychological study done on intersexed children and
adolescents in 1998 focused upon how their condition affected
them psychologically and socially. It was undertaken at the
Department of Child and Adolescent Psychiatry, Erasmus
University, in Rotterdam, Netherlands, by psychiatrists
Slijper, Drop, Moleaar, Muinck, and Keizer-Schrama. They
determined that 39% of the intersexed children evaluated
exhibited severe general psychopathology, specifically
depression, anxiety, sexual problems, and oppositional defiant
disorder. The general modern definition of psychopathology

is one who possesses a mental disorder, both psychological and behavioral. This was a modern study, and Tumblety was born and raised at a time when society ignored efforts to improve the mental health of individuals, so the percentage of psychopathology was likely much higher.

If Tumblety was the Whitechapel fiend, it was not because he had an intersex condition. The intersex condition, though, may have contributed to his feelings of inadequacy during his formative years. Tumblety would not have felt "normal," especially during adolescence, as his sexuality developed. He was seventeen when he arrived from Ireland, and Captain Streeter recalled young Frank Tumblety as a loner, suggesting he had or began to have antisocial personality disorder. Recall that he experienced the brunt of the Great Famine in Ireland as an adolescent. Not only did he have a sexual dysfunction, but he outwardly identified as a male and was attracted to young men, a sexual orientation labeled illegal under British law. Additionally, Tumblety was a devout Catholic, raised by a Catholic family, and Catholic tradition states that marriage is for the purpose of procreation—something physically impossible for Tumblety to accomplish. This may have caused further feelings of abnormality, which is clearly the reason he kept this a secret all his life.

Feelings of inadequacy in the developmental stage of human beings have the possibility of becoming hardwired into the brain, manifesting as a personality disorder or even psychosis. Peter Vronsky, criminal justice historian and author of *Serial Killers: The Method and Madness of Monsters* (2004), discusses how psychopathology in adults likely began in the formative stages of some serial offenders:

> *An infant that is denied human touch and affection develops a sense of only itself—it becomes completely oblivious to others. This is necessary for the infant to survive. When that infant becomes an adult, that sense of self and disregard of others becomes defined as 'psychopathology.' Thus what starts in the infant's brain as a purely defensive mechanism can become a destructive trait in adulthood.*

There is evidence that teenage Tumblety behaved abnormally and may have been plagued with a psychopathological disorder. Throughout Tumblety's life, countless eyewitnesses considered Tumblety eccentric, or odd, and Tumblety himself even added the term "eccentric" to the title of his 1889 autobiography. Under oath, Eleanor R. Elsheimer stated that her father, John McMullen, a long-time acquaintance of Tumblety, said Tumblety was always "off." She even recalled seeing Tumblety's unusual behavior of hiding motionless in a dark alley in Rochester, New York. Many eyewitnesses who interacted with Tumblety in his later life stated he would walk on the streets dressed like a homeless person, speaking to himself. For the last five years of his life, Tumblety rarely changed his dirty clothes and lived as a homeless person even though he was, by today's standard, a millionaire.

Psychopathology has been identified with serial murder in certain cases. Most experts agree that nearly three-quarters of all serial offenders studied—including those exhibiting psychopathy—have a behavioral personality disorder, either antisocial personality disorder, narcissistic personality disorder, or borderline personality disorder, or a combination of these disorders. Doctors diagnosed serial killer John Wayne Gacy with antisocial personality disorder and he, like many serial killers, kept a secret nefarious life as he lived a public, married life as an upstanding citizen. This is exactly what Tumblety did all his life with his public life as a wealthy and successful doctor and his private life prowling for young men at night in the slums. Tumblety even kept his life hidden from his young male interests. He would constantly travel alone as he had a relationship with Hall Caine in the mid-1870s. The fact that Hall Caine had to write to Thomas Brady asking if he knew where Tumblety was, shows Tumblety kept Hall Caine in the dark. Richard Norris stated Tumblety never told him about his family.

Few would argue against Tumblety being a narcissist, with a lifelong history of self-aggrandized behavior and exaggerated sense of self-worth immortalized in his autobiographies. If he did resort to murder and mutilation in 1888, his intersex condition would not have been the reason for his lack of remorse; it would have been his narcissistic personality disorder, or NPD. Recall the signs of NPD: exaggerated sense of self-importance, expecting to be recognized as superior, an exaggeration in achievements, preoccupied with fantasies about success, having a sense of entitlement, expecting special treatment, taking advantage of others, lack of remorse, and arrogance. An aggressive, or malignant, narcissist, sometimes titled as Narcissistic-Aggressive (NA) is identified with being intensely ambitious, has troublesome relationships, is always on the move, has a proclivity to travel, and is hypersexual. This matches Tumblety perfectly as an extremely successful alternative doctor, constantly traveling, and cruising the city slums at night preying upon older boys and younger men.

According to the Mayo Clinic, narcissism is a "mask of extreme confidence hiding a fragile self-esteem having trouble handling criticism." Someone with NPD comes across as pretentious, often monopolizing conversations, and belittles those they perceive as inferior. Deep-seated feelings of insecurity in a person with NPD cause them to show contempt and even strike out in rage.

Sexual dysfunction has also been a contributing factor to serial murder due to low self-esteem and abnormal socialization.

Sam Vaknin, author of *Malignant Self-Love: Narcissism Revisited* (10th revision, June 2015), discusses the sources a narcissist uses to receive adulation, compliments, admiration, subservience, attention, and being feared, which he calls narcissistic supply. Possessing a certain level of narcissism, or self-love, is healthy, the foundation of self-confidence and high self-esteem. Gregarious humans need positive feedback, approval, affirmation, and admiration from others, yet it is not pinned to our psychological health. Vaknin explains that narcissist's demand for affirmation and admiration from others is constant and insatiable, "the mental equivalent of an alcoholic." A narcissist's entire life is fashioned around receiving a continuous dose of narcissistic supply, and without it they believe their life will fall apart. For a level of security, the narcissist creates what Vaknin calls a False Self, a fictitious perfect and famous version of themselves, demanding, and even extorting special treatment. Narcissistic supply can come from fame, communicated impersonally through written form, or personally through dominant interactions with sex, politics, financial, military, or spiritual power. Economic safety, social acceptability, and upward mobility are also important, as well as being conspicuous in wealth, including running a successful business.

The term Malignant Narcissism is occasionally used to refer to NPD but is also used for a person exhibiting both APD and NPD. In an article titled, "The Malignant Narcissist," April 21, 2008, Pamela Kulbarch, RN, BSW, a psychiatric nurse who is a member of San Diego's Psychiatric Emergency Response Team, states that a narcissist's fundamental problem is the lack of empathy. They are intrinsically grandiose. They are extremely manipulative, complain and criticize, and will do something illegal, immoral, or violent if they believe they can get away with it. They do not feel responsible for their actions, because they believe they are the victims of injustice, discrimination, or prejudice. Malignant narcissists are predators who hunt easy prey, and are serial bullies, serial adulterers, gold-diggers, pedophiliacs, rapists, child molesters, terrorists, and serial killers. Cambridge psychology professor Simon Baron-Cohen also stated in his book, *The Science of Evil: On Empathy and the Origins of Cruelty* (Basic Books, 2012), that those with NPD have no empathy for others, which suggests prefrontal and limbic abnormalities.

Another name for Malignant Narcissism is Aggressive Narcissism. The following is the Hare Psychopathy Checklist for traits of an aggressive narcissist along with comments about Tumblety:

1. Glibness/superficial charm	Effective for Tumblety in building up wealthy patients
2. Grandiose sense of self-worth	Decades of examples in the case of Tumblety
3. Pathological lying	Lying was a tool for Tumblety
4. Cunning/manipulative	Tumblety's attorneys and banker referred to him as cunning. Judge J. Jones called him shrewd.
5. Lack of remorse or guilt	Many cases, such as hiring young Joseph Mitchell for four months, promising pay, and putting in will and never did. Tumblety sneaked out of town.
6. Shallow affect	Expressed in autobiographies

7. Callous/lack of empathy	Exploited patients for money
8. Failure to accept responsibility for own actions	Always blamed others

The following are Hotchkiss' Seven Deadly Sins of Narcissism, along with comments:

1. Shamelessness	
2. Magical thinking	Wrote that he was a highly esteemed medical doctor occupying the highest of social circles.
3. Arrogance	Countless examples
4. Envy	
5. Entitlement-DEFIANCE OF THEIR WILL IS A NARCISSISTIC INJURY THAT CAN TRIGGER NARCISSISTIC RAGE	Tumblety's attorney feared for his physical well-being when Tumblety was in his office in 1902 exhibiting rage
6. Exploitation	Cornerstone of his Indian herb doctor business
7. Bad boundaries (societal norms do not pertain to them).	Continuously arrested for pushing the boundaries of social norms.

In Tumblety's will and testament, he bequeathed thousands of dollars to the Catholic Church for the poor. Did Tumblety honestly do this because he was concerned about the poor; especially in the very country where he personally experienced the Great Famine? Tumblety became a millionaire by 1857, yet never did he contribute to the poor unless he was receiving publicity to further his business. There is no evidence that Tumblety gave to the poor of Ireland except in the very same year of the Whitechapel murders. In "Forest of the Boar," Joe Chetcuti discusses additional Irish research accomplished by himself and Adam Wood. A private meeting was held in Dublin, Ireland, on July 20, 1888, by an Irish charity called the Roomkeepers Society. In the minutes, the secretary detailed an alleged charity of £1,500 left to them from an "American doctor," and explained that "no portion thereof had reached the coffers of this Society—and that the whole thing was a myth—as he believed no such Charity money existed. The Trustees were of this opinion also." Three days later, the *Freeman's Journal* reported on the "American doctor" not honoring the claim of contributing to the poor of Ireland. Throughout the 1870s and the 1880s, Francis Tumblety was known in England as the "American Doctor," or "The Great American Doctor." While promoting "The Great American Doctor" in his ads, he never put his name to them. Interestingly, "Great American Doctor" ads were placed in the Dublin newspapers, and we know Tumblety left for England just a few months prior to this. In all likelihood, Tumblety conducted business in Ireland before making his way to London.

While it is true that Tumblety engaged in immoral behavior all his life, sodomizing young men, he actually had a relatively strong faith in God. In his 1893 autobiography, Tumblety added a chapter on his philosophy of life, which is grounded in Christianity:

> *How sublime are the exhibitions of the Wisdom, the Power and the Benevolence of our Creator . . . In whatever direction we turn our attention we see the impress of Deity. We instinctively turn to that power as our Creator, our life, our hope, our guide, our God. . . . God is our Author; God is everywhere. . . . Man is the noblest work of God.*

Tumblety was a practicing Catholic all his life, with numerous eyewitness accounts of him going to Catholic Mass every Sunday—albeit bringing attention to himself during his money-making days with tithing publicly and excessively:

> *MORE ABOUT TWOMBLETY. Globe Reporter's Recollections of the Whitechapel Suspect.*
> *The writer first met Dr. Twomblety in 1857, in Ottawa, where he opened an office and advertised himself as a specialist . . . His first move on arrival was to make a small deposit in the local branch of the Quebec bank, and on the following Sunday, preceded by his secretary*

carrying a large, gorgeous prayer book, he marched up
the middle aisle of the principal Catholic church of Ottawa
and presented a $100 bill as his offering.
—*Boston Daily Globe*, November 27, 1888

A cigar and tobacco storeowner in Hot Springs, Arkansas, stated in his sworn testimony that he knew Tumblety from around 1888 to 1903 and even had a personal relationship with him for the last four years. He stated that when Tumblety visited Hot Springs, usually during the winter months, he would see him every Sunday just before he attended church:

He came on Sunday morning when he went to church;
he came up to my place and stayed there sometimes ten
minutes, sometimes half an hour, until the church com-
menced. He left his papers there, and when church was
out he came back and got his papers. . . . he was com-
plaining often. He always pointed to his heart when he
came in, and would say that he had heart trouble. He
spoke very often of his heart trouble, and would say that
he knew it would not be long before he had to go.

In the last few years of his life, Tumblety preferred Catholic hospitals, and he even entered St. John's Hospital to die. In his will, he bequeathed $20,000 to two separate dioceses of the Catholic Church: Baltimore, Maryland; and John Ireland, Archbishop of St. Paul, Minnesota. While Tumblety was not known to have visited Minnesota, Archbishop Ireland was a prominent figure in American Catholicism in 1903. The very person who assisted Tumblety in "spiritual matters" and in his will at St. John's was a Catholic priest named Father J. J. Conway. A Father John Conway worked for the diocese of St. Paul in 1885 before leaving, thus, Conway may have been why Tumblety selected the Archbishop Ireland. Testimony from a New Orleans eyewitness stated when Tumblety believed he was going to die, he wanted the local priest to come and administer his will.

Tumblety arrived in the United States at age seventeen, and since the Tumblety clan was Catholic, his religious beliefs began in Ireland. Not only is there evidence that the seeds of his misogyny were sown in Ireland but also possibly due to how his family practiced their faith. The Book of Genesis in the Bible refers to a human-induced curse to mankind: Original Sin. Even today the Catholic Church does not allow ordination of women priests on the basis that Original Sin has changed the relationship between man and woman. In 2004, Pope John Paul II issued a letter to the bishops in the Church on gender relationships. He stated that as a result of Original Sin, the relationship between the sexes has been distorted and damaged. According to the Bible, in a relationship, the woman is subordinate to the man:

> *To the woman he said, 'I will make your pains in child-bearing very severe; with painful labor you will give birth to children. Your desire will be for your husband, and he will rule over you.'*
> —*Genesis 3:16 (NIV)*

Even before the Great Famine occurred, Tumblety and his brothers were treated differently than his sisters when it came to formal education. The 1850 census shows Francis, Lawrence, and Patrick as literate, while all of his sisters are recorded as illiterate. Francis' nephew, Michael Fitzsimons, recalled in his testimony when he was in Ireland at the age of five when Francis, aged ten, walked him to the schoolhouse. In the same pattern, while Michael and his brother Charles are recorded as literate, their only sister, Mary, is recorded as illiterate. School was not compulsory for children in early nineteenth century Ireland, especially for Catholics. They were taught in informal "hedge" schools, yet these schools were open to both Catholic boys and girls. This means the decision to educate only the boys was a family decision, and the head of the family was Francis' father, James Tumilty.

On the surface, a person with strong religious beliefs would seem not to harbor such extreme feelings of hatred toward women, even one from a family favoring the sons over the daughters. Well known in nineteenth-century Europe were teachings of a few early fathers of the Church with even more extreme views on women, blaming them for the downfall of all mankind. Tertullian (155 – 245 AD) stated, "You [woman] are the first deserter of the divine law! You are she who persuaded him (Adam) whom the devil was not valiant enough to attack!

You destroyed so easily God's image, man! On account of what you deserved—that is, death—even the Son of God had to die!" Jerome Gratian (1545 – 1614 AD) stated, "today because of sin, which woman brought into the world, women are admonished by the Apostle . . ." The Franciscan Sicardus of Cremona (1181 AD) stated, "because a double curse lies on the feminine growth. For she carries the curse of Adam and also the (punishment) . . ." Guido de Baysio (1296 AD) stated, "Moreover, woman was the effective cause of damnation since she was the origin of transgression and Adam was deceived through her . . ." Note the similarity of this view in eyewitness accounts of Tumblety's own words. In the *Chicago Daily Inter-Ocean,* December 4, 1888, a Rochester, New York, resident stated Tumblety ". . . constantly spoke of the gentler sex as a curse to the land." Recall that young Martin McGarry stated, "he [Tumblety] often said that all the trouble in this world was caused by women." Indeed, proof was all around Tumblety in Ireland at the age of fifteen when the Great Famine—a clear curse of the land—altered his world forever.

The significance of understanding Catholic doctrine with respect to Tumblety is why someone who lacked remorse would bequeath $27,000 in today's value in his 1901 Baltimore will to the Home for Fallen Women. The Catholic faith is categorized as Pauline Christianity, as in salvation occurs through faith in Jesus Christ. How one enters Heaven is called justification, and a component of justification in the Catholic Church, besides faith in Christ, is accomplished by doing good-works inspired by the Holy Spirit. James 2:24 states, "You can see that man is justified by works and not by faith alone." Many practicing Catholics incorrectly interpret Catholic doctrine, believing one can earn their way to Heaven through good-works. The good-works must be inspired by the Holy Spirit, and attempting to earn one's way to Heaven is at its core selfish, thus, not inspired. Although Tumblety was a lifelong practicing Catholic, he only gave to charity for selfish reasons, noting the last time he did was in the early 1890s when he was finishing his 1893 autobiography. Around the turn of the twentieth century, he believed he was near the end of his life, as evidenced by writing his will and testament numerous times. He believed he was either going to eternal Heaven or going to eternal Hell, so in Catholic Tumblety's mind, bequeathing a large sum of money to the class of people he hated most was accomplishing good-works. Thus, this charity was not out of the goodness of his heart, but for the selfish reason to avoid eternal damnation.

Although we do not know if Francis' brothers were such extreme misogynists, they likely were not, so understanding the origins of his hatred is only part of the story. The fact that he blamed women, especially fallen women, for decoying young men clearly had a profound effect on his treatment of women. In addition, an emotional attribute that all serial killers share is a lack of remorse, and Tumblety's brothers likely had the ability to experience remorse.

Another possible reason for Tumblety's extreme hatred of women who might decoy young men into a life of heterosexuality is that during his adolescence, a young man he desired was lured away by an attractive young lady. We do know that Mark A. Blackburn, the young man out of New York he bequeathed thousands of dollars to, was twice married to women during his employment with Tumblety. Tumblety bequeathed to no other young man of his interest, including Sir Henry Hall Caine. Mark Blackburn was certainly special.

A person may have an extreme hatred for someone or a particular group of people, but if they have compassion or remorse, they are likely not going to murder. If the person has a complete lack of remorse, though, and is unconcerned about the bounds of societal norms, then this may be a recipe for poor, aggressive behavior, including homicide. One of the characteristics of Narcissistic Personality Disorder is a lack of remorse, which is why many serial offenders are diagnosed with this developmental personality disorder. Captain Streeter stated Tumblety had become very aristocratic during his absence. Creating the persona of a high-end physician and upper-class gentleman, dressing extravagantly, living in the best hotels, and spending liberally on advertisements, was an effective business plan. It convinced a wealthier class of people to walk into his office or receive him on a home visit for his services and herbal medicine. This highly successful business plan also became a narcissistic supply, which would have fed perfectly into a narcissist's False Person of a better class of person and omnipotent physician able to cure all. In sworn testimony taken in Rochester, New York, in 1905, a

Nicholas Hadley stated he first met Francis Tumblety around 1855, and recalled the time he came back to Rochester as a doctor. Hadley stated that Tumblety was a tall, aristocratic-looking man, and then added, "He always looked to me like a man that was off." Hadley stated that, "he would have taken for him to be a man in a circus." Because Hadley was staring at him, Tumblety asked if he knew him. Hadley replied that he did not but had seen him before. Tumblety replied, "I am worth a million," and then asked if Hadley knew his brother. The fact that Tumblety had to inform Hadley in their first meeting that he was worth a million, indicates his desire to show his social superiority. Recall that an element in the *Diagnostic and Statistical Manual* used to diagnose narcissistic personality disorder is, "expecting to be recognized as superior."

In his 1866 autobiography, Tumblety discusses his practice in Canada between 1856 and 1860, and in so doing, reveals his narcissistic False Person:

> I had been practicing my profession in Canada with dis-
> tinguished success, and, in the course of a prosperous ca-
> reer, I accumulated an equal amount of profit and of fame.
> So far as the latter went, I trust the reader will not deem
> me an egotist, when I state that in the British Provinces
> I had acquired the respect and consideration of the first
> citizens, in proof of which I was importuned by an influ-
> ential body to represent them in the Colonial Parliament,
> in opposition to the celebrated Thomas Darcy McGee, a
> gentleman whose literary and political reputation is well
> known in this country.
>
> In order to substantiate this position—for I do not wish
> the public to take my word upon credit—I will here intro-
> duce some documentary evidence, which must speak for
> itself.
>
> In the year 1857, after being waited upon by a del-
> egation representing a large body of Canadian citizens,
> urging me to enter the political arena, a course which my
> habits and my inclination strongly repudiated, and which
> I declined, it was rumored that I was nevertheless about
> to become a parliamentary candidate, and paragraphs to
> that effect found their way in the Canadian press. One of

many I have before me. It was in the Union, Ottawa City, and reads as follows:

'It is hinted that Dr. Tumblety will offer himself as a candidate on grittish principles, in case of a vacancy in this constituency, and that he is now feeling the pulse of the people. The Doctor having amassed a fortune in the treatment of all "the ills that flesh is heir to," in which treatment he has ever been successful, now philanthropically proposes to devote his brilliant abilities to the cure of the dangerous diseases affecting the body politic, and is proudly conscious of the success that awaits him in the effort.'

His omnipotent and fanciful claims and successes, supported by testimonies from the elite, were publicized in the paper, but he also promoted them in his advertisements. Vaknin states that the written word is also a source of narcissistic supply further feeding into a narcissist's illusions, and supporting this in Tumblety's case, he published his favorite newspaper clippings and ads in his later autobiographies.

Vaknin commented upon how narcissists feel a need to document their lives,

Prone to magical thinking, the narcissist is deeply convinced of the transcendental meaning of his life. He fervently believes in his own uniqueness and 'mission.' . . . His every move, his every act, his every decision and every scribbling is of momentous consequence. The narcissist often documents his life with vigil, for the benefit of future biographers. His every utterance and shred of correspondence are carefully orchestrated as befitting a historical figure of import.

Throughout Tumblety's life, he published multiple versions of his autobiography, constantly being updated, beginning with version 1866, then 1871, 1872, the 1875 English version, 1889, 1893, then the unpublished but written 1901 version. The constant writing and updating of an autobiography conforms closely to Vaknin's discussion of the written word as a narcissistic source. In Tumblety's New Orleans lawyer's testimony, George Bartley stated that Tumblety asked him to read his autobiography to him over and over:

I noticed a good many peculiarities about him. Of course I saw his negligent appearance; his wearing apparel was not too clean; and I immediately saw that he was a man of rather eccentric habits . . . He would tell you who he was, what was the result of his travels, his business as a doctor, his well-known fame in a medical line. He had a history of his life in printed pamphlet form, and he would hand that to you and ask you to read for him, select certain passages that were particularly complimentary to him, and ask you to read it again, and it seemed that he was very much satisfied with the reading. He produced letters from the royal families of Europe, showing that he was in some close contact with them or had been at one time . . . I remember on one particular occasion that he produced a balance sheet from Henry Clew & Company, bankers, showing a total account to his credit of some one hundred and twenty-five thousand dollars . . . I learned from my brother that he went through the same program with him.

Even the titles show a progressive approach toward internalizing his narcissistic False Person. The title of the 1866 version focused upon responding to his poor treatment by the US government after the Lincoln assassination:

A FEW PASSAGES IN THE LIFE OF DR. FRANCIS TUMBLETY, THE INDIAN HERB DOCTOR, INCLUDING HIS EXPERIENCE IN THE OLD CAPITOL PRISON, TO WHICH HE WAS CONSIGNED, WITH A WANTON DISREGARD TO JUSTICE AND LIBERTY, BY ORDER OF EDWIN STANTON, SECRETARY OF WAR. ALSO JOURNALISTIC AND DOCUMENTARY VINDICATION OF HIS NAME AND FAME, AND PROFESSIONAL TESTIMONIALS

The 1871/1872 versions focused upon eliminating his Indian herb doctor name, a name now synonymous with quack doctors:

NARRATIVE OF DR. TUMBLETY: HOW HE WAS KIDNAPPED, DURING THE AMERICAN WAR, HIS INCARCERATION AND DISCHARGE. A VERITABLE REIGN OF TERROR. AN EXCITING LIFE SKETCH, WITH IMPORTANT

LETTERS AND DOCUMENTS FROM GENERALS LEE AND SHERMAN, EARL DE GREY, LORDS STANLEY, HEADLEY AND TENTERDEN, SIR EDWARD THORNTON, HORACE GREELEY, ABRAHAM LINCOLN, AND OTHER NOTABLE CELEBRITIES, INCLUDING PRIVATE PASSAGES CONCERNING THE EX-EMPEROR NAPOLEON, WHO ENDOWED THE AUTHOR WITH THE CROSS OF THE LEGION OF HONOR; PRESENTATION AND FRIENDLY RELATIONS WITH KAISER WILLIAM, OF PRUSSIA . . .

While his 1889 version was written in response to his treatment due to the Ripper murders, note that the title suggests a full-fledged narcissist:

DR. FRANCIS TUMBLETY, A SKETCH OF THE LIFE OF THE GIFTED, ECCENTRIC AND WORLD-FAMED PHYSICIAN, PRESENTING AN OUTLINE OF HIS WONDERFUL CAREER, Professional Successes and Personal Intimacies with Renowned Personages of Two Hemispheres, INCLUDING LETTERS FROM THE LATE EMPEROR NAPOLEON, PRESIDENT ABRAHAM LINCOLN, RIGHT HON. BENJAMIN DISRAELI (LORD BEACONSFIELD), LORD STANLEY, SIR WILFRID LAWSON, CHARLES DICKENS, PROF. WILLARD PARKER, RIGHT HON. J. WARD HUNT, LORD HEADLEY, P.A. ROEBUCK, M.P.; PROF. S.B. MORSE, INVENTOR OF THE MAGNETIC TELEGRAPH; FRIEND JOHN BEST, W.W. LELAND, ESQ.; REV. FATHERS A.. HOECKEN AND THOMAS B. CHALMERS; AND GENS. SHERMAN AND LEE.

One aspect of narcissism psychologists use as a distinction between NPD and healthy self-confidence is an unusual anger toward criticism. Three of the versions, 1866, his English edition, and 1889, were all prompted by another narcissistic element: responding to criticism. Judge Jones out of Hot Springs, Arkansas, explained that Tumblety often felt wronged by others.

Newspaper reporters in late 1888 were searching for any stories from acquaintances of the elusive American Jack the Ripper suspect Francis Tumblety, and in one account, it stated he periodically battled rheumatism. In the *Evening Star*, November 19, 1888, an article on Tumblety states, "He is said to have not practiced for several years, and has been a familiar figure for several seasons at the White Sulphur Springs, which he visited for some rheumatic affection." Corroborating his rheumatic condition later in life is Tumblety himself. In January 1902, Tumblety was in New Orleans and sent a poorly handwritten letter to his Baltimore lawyer, Frank M. Widner Jr. It stated:

> Dear Sir, In reference to my case now in your hands – [I] would say that owing to an attack of rheumatism I have been unable to give the matter my attention. Just as soon as my condition permits I will leave here for your city— finding my absents [sic] you will of course have to continue the case. Upon my return I shall have all necessary papers. Of course I will request you to give me notice in order that I may protect [illegible] so this statute of limitation shall not operate against me.
> With regard
> Yours Truly Dr F Tumblety

Tumblety then left for Washington DC, but not knowing this, his lawyer sent a return letter to New Orleans. Weeks later, Tumblety eventually received this letter in Washington. His next letter he sent to his lawyer was typed; dated May 19, 1902. It stated:

> Dear Sir: -- Your amiable letter has been forwarded from New Orleans to me. I have been very ill with a bad cold, or I would have been to see you before this. I hope soon to be able to pay you a visit at your office. Respectfully, [signed] Francis Tumblety MD"

In Tumblety's very first advertisement ads out of Canada in 1857, he claimed to have been able to cure rheumatism, and in his 1866 autobiographical pamphlet, he published numerous patient testimonials claiming a complete cure under his care. While the evidence indicates Tumblety believed—or at least publicly announced—his chronic condition was rheumatism, he had also been on record claiming to cure it every time. Interestingly, in his 1893 autobiographical pamphlet, he seems to have resolved this apparent contradiction:

The nature of the cause that has produced the disorder of the heart is a very important item; heart disease originating in an attack of rheumatic fever is usually more serious and brings on more rapidly and more frequently an organic lesion than when it is due to alcoholism . . . A hydro mineral treatment at Neris, Plombeires or Ais-les-Bains will do wonders in checking or lessening attacks of rheumatism, and in order to avoid more certainly their recurrence it is well to follow a perfectly regular life . . . A person afflicted with a lesion of the heart is not necessarily an invalid . . . But although they are not ill, they are, through the fact of their lesion, continually exposed to serious trouble.

In narcissistic fashion, Tumblety created an excuse as to why he had a chronic medical condition. It was not from a disease *per se*, but from a high fever. This also allowed him to continue to boast that he cured all diseases.

This particular explanation of one cause of heart disease was not in his earlier autobiographical pamphlets, from his 1866 version to the 1889 version. As noted, the November 19, 1888, issue of the *Evening Star* commented upon his "rheumatic affection," but it also stated that for several seasons prior to 1888, he was a familiar figure at White Sulphur Springs. This was in reference to White Sulphur Springs, West Virginia, which was an upper-class summer resort in the nineteenth century and claimed its mineral springs had healing powers. It was known as the "Saratoga of the South," referring to a posh nineteenth-century summer resort in Saratoga Springs, just north of Albany, New York. This town also claimed its mineral springs had curative properties. Tumblety was known to visit Saratoga Springs for extended stays in the early 1880s. Martin McGarry, a young man Tumblety recruited in July 1882 as a travel partner, stated in the *New York World*, December 5, 1888:

After we saw everything about Rochester we went to Saratoga. The Doctor took room at No. 151 Congress St. It was the finest suite of rooms at the springs . . . We stayed there two months and enjoyed life . . . We came back to New York, where we spent the winter.

The fact that this explanation in his 1893 autobiography coincides temporally with reports of him having received periodic mineral baths for rheumatism in the 1880s is telling. It suggests Tumblety had a chronic condition that was worsening as he aged. His progressive chronic condition seemed to have degraded to both a state of internal organ damage and an emotional breaking point in January 1888, the year of the Whitechapel murders. Tumblety stated to a *Toronto Mail* reporter that he:

> . . . *was suffering from a kidney and heart disease, and that he was constantly in dread of sudden death.*
> —*Toronto Mail*, November 23, 1888

Hydromineral treatments must have lessened his pain since he continued to visit the spa towns until the year of his death in 1903. After he escaped from England in 1888, his favorite spa resort seems to have been Hot Springs, Arkansas. In 1891, we know he was in Hot Springs because reported being the victim of a series of robberies, losing thousands of dollars of cash and jewelry. It was also reported that before he came to St. Louis in 1903 to die, he had visited Hot Springs. Just as he feared in 1888, heart and kidney failure were his downfall. His death certificate stated the chief cause of death was "Valvular Disease Heart" and the contributing cause was "Nephritis," or kidney disease.

Both the heart and the kidneys can be affected by rheumatoid arthritis (RA), which is acquired by a weakness in the body's immune system, but there is additional evidence that Tumblety suffered from a disease that mimics RA: syphilitic arthritis. Syphilitic arthritis is the result of the contraction of the venereal disease syphilis, an infectious systemic disease caused by the *Treponema pallidum* bacterium that enters the body through mucous membranes or breaks in the skin. Ninety percent of the cases are acquired through sexual contact, including male on male, and has been a public health problem since the sixteenth century. Untreated, syphilis goes through four stages: primary, secondary, latent, and tertiary. The first signs of the primary stage are small, blister-like sores and swollen lymph nodes. After weeks to months the disease goes into the second stage, marked by flu-like symptoms, aching joints, and red skin rashes on the body, including the face. After a period of latency, the tertiary stage begins between three to ten years later and is marked by tumor-like growths. Ten-to-fifteen percent of the patients in the third stage develop cardiovascular syphilis after ten-to-twenty-five years, beginning with inflammation of the arteries, scarring of the heart valves, and possibly followed by heart failure or a heart attack. Eight percent of the patients in the third stage acquire neurosyphilis between five-to-thirty-five years, marked by brain inflammation, aches, irritability, disorientation, loss of memory, irresponsible behavior, delusions of grandeur, and even complete psychosis.

Both diseases share symptoms of joint aches and swelling, and damage to the heart and kidneys. Even so, the end stages of the diseases are different. If RA was the reason for Tumblety's heart and kidneys to be so damaged as to cause his death, then he would have been in stage four. While stage three is characterized by joint deformities and swelling causing decreased mobility, stage four is characterized by lack of function of the joints, i.e., loss of mobility. Francis Tumblety was reported to have gone for walks while checked into St. John's Hospital in St. Louis, Missouri. Additionally, the physician who signed Tumblety's death warrant was asked by the judge assigned to the disposition of Tumblety's will if Tumblety's body had anything unusual about it. The physician stated nothing about stage four rheumatoid arthritis deformities. A unique indication of syphilis, on the other hand, is an unusual red rash on the face in many cases, and Francis Tumblety was known for his florid cheeks. In likely the last newspaper article referring to Francis Tumblety, the *Washington Times* has a comment in the "Heard and Seen" section of its August 8, 1918, issue stating:

> *And speaking of Beau Hickman, does anyone remember Dr. Tumulty, his florid complexion, his riding boots and whip?*

His red cheeks were so apparent that someone sent their recollection to the papers. Incidentally, Colonel Beau Hickman was called Washington DC's "Great Gentleman Loafer" and "the King of Bummers" who came to the capital in 1833 at the age of twenty with family money. He spent it all in two years, then lived off other people's money for the next thirty-eight years by charming them with his "patrician demeanor."

Tumblety's New Orleans attorney, J. M. Goodin, stated under oath about his client's general appearance as to cleanliness at that time he knew him. After an objection was overruled, Goodin stated, "Why, his appearance was very dirty; his clothes were sloven; from his face I judge he had syphilis—I don't know what it was—it was more." This was immediately objected to by the opposing attorney.

Francis Tumblety fit into a particular group considered today to be in the high-risk category for contracting syphilis: prostitutes of either sex *and* their customers. Tumblety never had a monogamous relationship yet was sexually active all of his adult life. Besides luring young men into sex, he was known to cruise for young men in countless cities. Case in point, his gross indecency charge concurrent with the Whitechapel murders investigation was with four young men he was intimately involved with between July and August 1888 and possibly earlier. It was common for him to be hauled into the police station for soliciting young men on the streets for casual sex. For example, in the *New York World*, June 6, 1889, less than a year after he sneaked out of England, he was arrested for an encounter with a young man:

> *The notorious Dr. Francis Tumblety . . . was arraigned in the Jefferson Market Court this morning on charges of assault and battery, preferred by a young man named George Davis, of 168 Allen street. Davis said that Tumblety met him on Fifth avenue, near Clinton place, about 10.30 o'clock last night, and engaged him in conversation which led to his calling Tumblety a vile name. Thereupon the doctor broke his cane across Davis's face . . .*

If the attorney was correct that Tumblety's face was scarred with syphilis, there should be evidence of decreasing health not only physically but mentally until his death on May 28, 1903, in St. Louis. Not only is there evidence of a progressive rheumatic disease, but Tumblety's well-known eccentric behavior changed. While McGarry stated he and Tumblety stayed in Saratoga Springs for two full months allowing Tumblety to take advantage of the medicinal properties of the springs, his behavior seemed to be classic Tumblety. He continued to have a desire to travel and reside in luxurious hotels, enjoy the theater, and even avoid speaking with anyone for weeks. Upon his escape and return from England in late 1888, Tumblety continued to travel, got into scuffles with the law, and completed his last autobiographical pamphlet in 1893.

Specific to the Whitechapel murders and the possibility of Francis Tumblety being Jack the Ripper, might neurosyphilis have played a role in him mutilating women? If Tumblety was the Whitechapel fiend, his motive was likely anger-retaliatory, one of the numerous serial offender motives discussed by Dr. Brent Turvey. Corroborated newspaper reports of Francis Tumblety's bitter hatred and poor treatment of women go back as far as 1860, when Tumblety was thirty years of age and staying in Saint John, New Brunswick. There is even one uncorroborated newspaper report stating his hatred was observed during his teenage years in Rochester, New York, around 1850, when it was stated that women were the source of our man's problems:

> *A few years after reaching manhood, he* [Tumblety] *evinced a great dislike for women, and constantly spoke of the gentler sex as a curse to the land."*
> —*The Inter-Ocean,* December 4, 1888

This is corroborated by the statements of Martin McGarry in the *New York World,* December 5, 1888:

> *When asked about Dr. Tumblety's aversion to women, McGarry said: 'He always disliked women very much. He used to say to me: "Martin, no women for me." He could not bear to have them near him. He thought all women were impostors, and he often said that all the trouble in this world was caused by women.'*

Prior to 1888, there is evidence that Francis Tumblety treated women poorly, but not so much as to murder them. Neurosyphilis, though, attacks the emotional stability and judgement of its victims. Recall Tumblety's mindset in January 1888 and his constant fear of sudden death, clearly suggesting he was at the breaking point. Tumblety already exhibited the traits of a narcissist, living in his own imaginary self-aggrandized world where people were objects for him to use for his benefit. Additionally, at the time of the murders, we have a window into Tumblety's unusual behavior when forced to be next to women:

> *During the past summer and early fall I* [C.A. Bloom] *was in London, England, for three months. One pleasant day in October* [1888], *in company with my wife and another lady, I was going down Regent street. At Oxford street I was greatly surprised to see this same Dr. Tumblety enter the omnibus. . . . But what surprised me was his actions when he found that I was in company with the ladies. When I introduced my wife to him his actions were so strange that she has spoken about it several times since . . . He seemed to be very ill at ease and never raised his eyes from the floor after he had learned that the ladies were with me.*
> —*Buffalo Courier*, December 7, 1888

His trips to Hot Springs, Arkansas, for hydrotherapy began in 1880. The bodily pain was enough to change his obsessive lifelong money-making agenda to a single-minded focus upon his personal health. If his condition was caused by syphilis, eight years would have been ample time for the disease to progress to a more serious neurosyphilic psychological state. Syphilis may not have been the cause for Tumblety's chronic kidney and heart disease, but what is clear is these diseases were progressive, and the Whitechapel murders were a full eight years later.

Tumblety does attempt to justify lack of morality in his writings. While the tenet of most devout Christians, regardless of denomination, is to walk like Christ and avoid immorality, Tumblety's philosophy-of-life chapter in his 1893 autobiography explains the natural loss to the path of righteousness. Note how he begins:

> *Man is a social being, and his relations to his fellow-beings call for the proper exercise of his social nature – the result of which is pleasure. Man is a selfish being, endowed with*

faculties in harmony with his animal nature, and with the external objects of the world. These give force and energy of character, and provide for the wants of man. Their exercise, therefore, is essential to our happiness. So man is endowed with a moral nature, with all the aspirations and emotions which distinguish him from the lower animals; and his relations to his fellow-beings, to his God, and to a future life, call for the active exercise of this part of his nature. Man is also an intellectual being, with powers of observation and reason, adapting him to the acquisition of knowledge, which is the great key to his power, not only over the beasts of the field, but over all the elements that surround him.

Tumblety is explaining that seeking earthly pleasures is a good thing. He then explains that the mind can be adversely affected by disease or poor organ function:

. . . but if the body is diseased, or the functions of any of its organs deranged, the equilibrium of the mind is immediately disturbed, and all the mental operations are affected by it.

Tumblety connects these mentally disturbed operations with morality:

Attention to the laws of health, then, becomes not only a privilege but a duty, as connected with the moral and religious nature of man.

Just five years before writing his 1893 autobiography, he explained to a *Toronto Globe* reporter that he had chronic kidney and heart disease, so he knew he had deranged functions of at least two of his organs. Because of this, Tumblety was explaining, and even justifying, his continuous acts of immorality, the sodomizing of young men, and the extreme hatred and maltreatment of women. Tumblety explains how mental derangement can even end up in madness, violence, and murder, specific to true love:

If disappointed in 'true love,' the pensive sadness and the gloom that shadows the countenance, bespeak the burning embers that are daily consuming the entire being, and will bring the subject to an early grave. In an unbalanced mind, it often results in madness and violence, and the murder of the one so dearly loved is quickly followed by the self-destroying lover.

Numerous eyewitnesses stated Tumblety believed he might die at any moment, or in other words, be brought to an early grave. Tumblety had chronic heart and kidney disease, thus, in his words, the equilibrium of his mind was disturbed, and an unbalanced mind often results in madness, violence, and murder. He was in a permanent state of mental unbalance and accepted it. For Tumblety, true love only came in the form of young men, and while in London in 1888, Tumblety was writing letters to four young men. The contents of these letters convinced the authorities that Tumblety had an intimate relationship with these men. Tumblety was making biannual trips to London throughout the 1880s, and as evidenced by Richard Norris out of New Orleans, his pattern was to reconnect with the same young men each year. If madness did occur in Tumblety, his wrath would have been for those women who best decoyed young men: night walkers.

Francis Tumblety was an eccentric narcissist who dedicated his life to exploitation. He had a bitter hatred of attractive women and prostitutes and was convinced they were the curse of the land. This man, who was known to favor his uterus collection during the Civil War, knew in the same year of the murders that his kidney and heart disease may cause his sudden death—and then we see Jack the Ripper collecting these three organs. No other suspect can be connected to all three organs. How curious that Scotland Yard was aware of a West End rumor that the killer was attempting to create the elixir of life by mixing the ingredients from a freshly murdered female with herbs, and Tumblety was a woman-hating herbal doctor who lived on the West End. Then, in his 1893 autobiography, he admits there is no elixir of life, as if he tried to create one himself but was unsuccessful. Victim Mary Kelly, part of a crime scene that exhibited the offender's signature in full, was displayed exactly like the Anatomical Venus. The Anatomical Venus was a model of the goddess of heterosexual physical love being mutilated; Venus was a goddess Tumblety would have hated. In the very same year of the murders, Anatomical Venuses in four New York City wax museums in the shady Bowery District were destroyed. Tumblety lived near these museums and loved to walk the streets of every city at night. In his 1901 Baltimore will, the devoutly Catholic Tumblety bequeathed $1000 to the Home for Fallen Women, or prostitutes, in a clear attempt to earn his way into Heaven. Not only does this strangely connect him to the Whitechapel murders, but when Tumblety checked himself into the St. John's Hospital to die, he used the alias Frank Townsend. The only other time he used this alias was when he escaped England just after the Whitechapel murders.

While we may never know the true identity of Jack the Ripper, the old arguments rejecting Francis Tumblety's candidacy as a real contender conflict with the evidence. Few suspects fit the bill as well as Francis Tumblety, and no other suspect made such a "Ripper-like" statement about disemboweling night walkers while showing off his collection of surgical knives *before* the murders occurred.

Bibliography

Aeragon, *The US Civil War, the First Modern War,* 2009. available at http://www.aeragon.com/03/.

Allen, J.M., The Elixir of Life, *The Locomotive,* September 1889, 138/9.

Altonen, B., MPH, MS, The First "Indian Doctors", *Public Health, Medicine and History.* https://brianaltonenmph.com/6-history-of-medicine-and-pharmacy/hudson-valley-medical-history/the-post-war-years/the-first-indian-doctors/

Amalux Herbal Products, *Paracelsus Elixir – The Original Swedish Bitters Formula,* http://www.amaluxherbal.com/paracelsus_elixir_swedish_bitters_schwedenbitter.htm

Annie Chapman aka Dark Annie, Annie Siffey, Sievey or Sivvey, Casebook: Jack the Ripper (Stephen Ryder & Johnno), 2009 – 2013, available at http://www.casebook.org/victims/chapman.html.

Arkowitz, H., Lilienfeld, S., Why Science Tells Us Not to Rely on Eyewitness Accounts, *Scientific American,* January 1, 2010. https://www.scientificamerican.com/article/do-the-eyes-have-it/

Austin, E., Early Telephone History of the Fourth, *Southern Telephone News,* Volume 8, Number 8, August 1920.

Bacon, L. et.al., The Brown-Sequard Sensation, *The Independent,* Volume 41, p. 11, August 15, 1889.

Baron-Cohen, S., *The Science of Evil: On Empathy and the Origins of Cruelty,* Basic Books, 2012.

Barnett, R., Lost wax: medicine and spectacle in Enlightenment London. *The Lancet,* Volume 372, Issue 9636, Pages 366-367, August 2, 2008.

Bates, A.W., *"Indecent and Demoralising Representations": Public Anatomy Museums in Mid-Victorian England, Medical History,* V. 52 (1): 1-22, Jan 1, 2008.

———. *Dr Kahn's Museum: Obscene Anatomy in Victorian London, Journal of the Royal Society of Medicine,* V. 99 (12): 618-624, December 2006.

Beatty-Kingston, William, *A Journalist's Jottings,* London: Chapman and Hall, 1890.

Beers, M. H., MD, and Berkow, R., MD., Syphilis, *The Merck Manual of Diagnosis and Therapy,* Whitehouse Station, NJ: Merck Research Laboratories, 2004.

Begg, P., Fido, M., & Skinner, K., *The Jack the Ripper A – Z,* Headline Book Publishing PLC, 1996.

Benis, Anthony, M. M.D., *NPA Theory of Personality* (2017)

Benis, Anthony, *Toward Self & Sanity* (1985, 2nd edition 2008)

Birbaumer N., Veit R., Lotze M., Erb M., Hermann C., Grodd W., et al., Deficient fear conditioning in psychopathy: a functional magnetic resonance imaging study, *Archives of General Psychiatry*, V. 62, pp. 799–805, 2005.

Blanco, J., James Mitchell DeBardeleben II, *Murderpedia*. http:// murderpedia.org/male.D/d/debardeleben-james.htm

Blondheim, M., *News Over the Wires*, Harvard College, 1994.

Bolt, C., *The Women's Movements in the United States and Britain from the 1790s to the 1920s*, University of Massachusetts Press, 1993.

Bourrie, M., *By Reason of Insanity: The David Michael Krueger Story*, Toronto, Hounshow, 1887.

Burn, G., *Somebody's Husband, Somebody's Son*, Faber & Faber, 2004.

Capitalism by Gaslight: The Shadow Economies of 19th-Century America, *Selling Sex* (2012), Library Company of Philadelphia, available at http://www.librarycompany.org/shadoweconomy/section4_10.htm.

Casebook: Jack the Ripper, available at www.casebook.org, Stephen P. Ryder & Johnno, 1996-2013, Thomas Schachner.

Cazeau, T., *A Brief Account of the Thirteenth New York State Volunteer Regiment 1861 – 1863*, Commander, Captain Henry Lomb Camp, S.O.V., Rochester, NY, available at Central Library of Rochester and Monroe County, Historic Monographs Collection.

Central Criminal Court Calendars, London, England, November and December 1888.

Chauncey, G, *The Bowery as Haven and Spectacle* in *The Columbia Reader on Lesbians and Gay Men in Media, Society, and Politics*, 1999.

Chetcuti, J., Knocking on Pall Mall's Door, *Ripperologist 87*, January 2008.

Cook, A., *M:MI5's First Sypmaster*, History Press, 2011.

Coram, J., *Doing 'Write' by Annie – A Closer Look at Annie Chapman's Murder*, *Ripperologist* No. 73, November 2006.

Crawford T.C., *English Life*, Frank F. Lovell & Company (Princeton University), 1889.

Crone, H.D., *Paracelsus: The Man who Defied Medicine*, The Albarello Press, 2004.

Cumming, C., *Devil's Game: The Civil War Intrigues of Charles A. Dunham.* Univ. of Illinois, 2004.

Currie, A.W., Historica Canada Foundation, *Grand Trunk Railway of Canada*, available at http://www.thecanadianencyclopedia.ca/en/article/grand-trunk-railway-of-canada/

Curtis, L Perry, *Jack the Ripper and the London Press*, Yale University Press, 2001.

Dannes, J., *Hermetic Order of the Golden Dawn* (Jan 2009), Washington and Lee University, 'Magic, Science, and Religion', available at http://home.wlu.edu/~lubint/touchstone/GoldenDawn-Dannes.htm

Decety, J., Chenyi, C., Harenski, C., and Kiehl, K., An fMRI Study of Affective Perspective Taking in Individuals with Psychopathy: Imagining Another in Pain Does Not Evoke Empathy, *Frontiers in Human Neuroscience*, September 24, 2013.

DeConick, A., *Holy Misogyny: Why the Sex and Gender Conflicts in the Early Church Still Matter*, Bloomsbury Academic, 2013.

Dynes, Johansson, Percy, and Donaldson, *Encyclopedia of Homosexuality*, Volume II, Garland Pub., 1990.

Eckert, W.C., The Ripper Project: Modern Science Solving Mysteries of History, *American Journal of Forensic Medicine and Pathology*, 10(2), 164-171, 1989.

Edwards, W.C., Steers, E., *The Lincoln Assassination: The Evidence*, University of Illinois, 2009.

Ellis, H., *Sexual Inversion*, F. A. Davis Company, 1897.

Evans, S.M., *Born for Liberty A History of Women in America*, Simon & Schuster Inc., New York, 1997.

Evans, S. and Gainey, P., *Jack the Ripper: First American Serial Killer*, Kodansha International, 1998.

Evans, S. and Rumblelow, D., *Jack the Ripper, Scotland Yard Investigates*, Sutton Publishing, 2006.

Evelyn, D., Dickson, P., *On This Spot: Pinpointing the Past in Washington, D.C.*, 3rd Ed, Capital Books, Inc., 2008.

Faivre, A., *Theosophy, Imagination, Tradition: Studies in Western Esotericism*, 2000.

Federal Bureau of Investigation, U.S. Department of Justice, *Serial Murder Multi-Disciplinary Perspectives for Investigators*, Behavioral Analysis Unit National Center for the Analysis of Violent Crime, 2005.

Ford, P., and Howell, M., *The True History of the Elephant Man: The Definitive Account of the Tragic and Extraordinary Life of Joseph Carey Merrick*, Skyhorse Publishing, Inc, 2010.

Fragoso, J.M., Serial Sexual Femicide in Ciudad Juárez: 1993-2001, *Debate Feminista*, 280, April 25, 2002.

FTL Design, *The Atlantic Cable*, 2014. available at http://atlantic-cable.com/.

Gilbert, R. A., *the masonic career of A. E. Waite*, Grand Lodge of British Columbia and Yukon, available at http://freemasonry.bcy.ca/aqc/waite/waite.html.

Gladstone, J.H., Chemical Science, *Scientific American*, October 27, 1883. https://www.scientificamerican.com/article/chemical-science/

Hawley, M., Charles A. Dunham: for the Better Good, *The New Independent Review* (Issue 2), pp. 10-17, January 2012.

———. Dunham Part II: Tumblety's Anatomical Collection Reconsidered, *The New Independent Review*, Issue 3, April 2012.

Hibbert, Charles, Dictionary of Canadian Biography, University of Toronto, available at http://www.biographi.ca/en/bio/tupper_charles_hibbert_15E.htm.

History Learning Site, *The Great Famine of 1845*, available at http://www.historylearningsite.co.uk/ireland_great_famine_of_1845.htm.

Hobson, F., *Mencken: A Life*, Random House, Inc., 1994.

Hoolihan, *An Annotated Catalogue of the Edward C. Atwater Collection of American Popular Medicine and Health Reform. Volume III, Supplement: A-Z*, 2008.

Irish Wedding Rings, Wedding Bands, 2015, available at http://www.weddingbands.org/irish-wedding-rings/ .

JTRForums, available at www.jtrforums.com, Howard & Nina Brown, 2000 – 2005.

John Sparrow, David, Dictionary of Canadian Biography, University of Toronto, available at http://www.biographi.ca/en/bio/thompson_john_sparrow_david_12E.html.

Johnson, A., *The Blackwell Dictionary of Sociology: A User's Guide to Sociological Language,* Wiley, 2000.

Jones, G., Dictionary of Canadian Biography, University of Toronto, Volume XII (1890 – 1900).

Judge, W.Q., Paracelsus, *The Path,* April 1887, The Theosophical University Press: Online Literature, http://www.theosociety.org/pasadena/path/v02n01p20_paracelsius.htm

KPI Productions, *Jack the Ripper, Mystery Quest,* Season 1, Episode 8, November 11, 2009.

Kulbarch, P., The Malignant Narcissist, April 21, 2008, *Officer.com,* https://www.officer.com/investigations/article/10248968/the-malignant-narcissist

Lander, K.E., A Brief Account of the Use of Wax Models in the Study of Medicine, *Journal of the History of Medicine and Allied Sciences,* Volume XXV, Issue 1, 1970.

Lazo, N., *Sin Clemencia: Los Crimenes Que Conmocionaron, a Mexico.* Mexico City, Mexico: Random House Mondadori, 2007.

Lindgren, C. E., *The Rose Cross in America 1800-1909* (Chapter three of The Rose Cross (1996)), available at http://users.panola.com/lindgren/rosecross-2.html.

———. *Randolph, Paschal Beverly* (Jan 2000), American National Biography, ACLS and Oxford.

Littlechild Letter, dtd September 23, 1913. Sent privately to George R. Sims.

Logan, Guy, *Masters of Crime,* S. Paul, 1928.

Macintyre, B., *The Napoleon of Crime: The Life and Times of Adam Worth, Master Thief,* Crown Publishing Co.,1997.

McBride's Magazine, The Foreign Correspondent. Volume 51. 1893.

McEnnis, John T., *The Clan-Na-Gael and the Murder of Dr. Cronin.* San Francisco: G. P. Woodward, 1889, origin: *Chicago Tribune,* June 30, 1889.

Moore, C. W., Have We Discovered the Elixir of Life?, *Pacific Record of Medicine and Surgery,* Volume 4, August 15, 1889.

National Park Service, U.S. Department of the Interior, The Civil War: Union New York Volunteers, 13th Regiment, New York, Infantry (2016), available at http://www.nps.gov/civilwar/search-battle-units-detail.htm?battleUnitCode=UNY0013RI.

O'Brian, J., *President Lincoln in Civil War Washington* (2014), available at http://www.lincolninwashington.com/.

Palmer, R., Inspector Andrews Revisited, *The Casebook Examiner,* Issues 1, 2, & 4, April, June, & October 2010.

Parker, C., & Sexton, A., "The Great Famine in Cavan", Found at www.irishidentity.com.

Pascoe, C. E., *Our Actors and Actresses: The Dramatic List*, 'Fanny Sterling' (p. 319), Benjamin Blom, Inc., Bronx, NY, and London, 1880, Reissued 1969.

Pemment, J., MA, MS, What Would We Find Wong in the Brain of a Serial Killer?, *Psychology Today*, April 5, 2013, https://www.psychologytoday.com/blog/blame-the-amygdala/201304/what-would-we-find-wrong-in-the-brain-serial-killer.

Pilbeam, P., Madame Tussaud and the Business of Wax: Marketing to the Middle Classes (University of London), *The Emergence of Marketing*, Routledge, 2003.

Pilcher, J.M., *The Sausage Rebellion: Public Health, Private Enterprise, and Meat in Mexico City 1890 – 1917*. Univ. of New Mexico Press, 2006.

Pokel, C., A Critical Analysis of Research Related to the Criminal Mind of Serial Killers, Graduate Research Thesis (Advisor Biggerstaff, E.), University of Wisconsin-Stout, August 2000.

Prescott, A., *Brother Irving: Sir Henry Irving and Freemasonry* (Dec 2003), Director at the Centre for Research into Freemasonry, University of Sheffield, available at http://www.theirvingsociety.org.uk/brother_irving.htm.

Rice, G., "Articles on the History of Navan", *Meath Chronicle*, 1980.

Riordan, T., *Prince of Quacks: The Notorious Life of Dr. Francis Tumblety, Charlatan and Jack the Ripper suspect*. McFarland & Co., 2009.

Rumbelow, Donald, *The Complete Jack the Ripper*, Virgin Books Limited, 1988.

Samuel, D.B., & Widiger, T.A., Clinicians' judgments of clinical utility: A comparison of the DSM-IV and five factor models. *Journal of Abnormal Psychology*, 115, 298-308, 2006.

Sappol, "Morbid curiosity": The Decline and Fall of the Popular Anatomical Museum. Common-Place, *A Cabinet of Curiosities*, Volume 4, Number 2, January 2004.

Scott, J., The Inner Gold of Alchemists, *India North*, May 12, 2014.

Sereno, M., *Types of Crimes: The Relationship Between Narcissistic and Antisocial Personalities*, Department of Psychology, Published by Lavin, M., Ph.D., St. Bonaventure University. http://web.sbu.edu/psychology/lavin/abbey.htm.

Shoemaker, J.V., Science in Fiction, *The Medical Bulletin, A Monthly Journal of Medicine and Surgery*, Volume 11, October 1889.

Skal, D.J., *Something in the Blood: The Untold Story of Bram Stoker*, W.W. Norton & Co., 2016.

Skodo, A., Gunderson, J., McGlashan, T., Dyck, I., Stout, R., Bender, D., Grilo, C., Shea, M., Zanarini, M., Morey, L., Sanislow, C., and Oldham, J., Functional Impairment in Patients with Schizotypal, Borderline, Avoidant, or Obsessive-Compulsive Personality Disorder, *American Journal of Psychiatry*, Volume 159 (2): 276-83, February 2002.

Slijper, F. M., Drop, S. L., Moleaar, J. C., Muinck, Keizer-Schrama, S. M.: Long-term psychological evaluation of intersex children. *Arch*

*Sex Beh.*1998; 28: 103-5. https://www.ncbi.nlm.nih.gov/labs/
articles/9562897/

Smith, P., and Brain, P., Bullying in Schools: Lessons from Two Decades of Research, *Aggressive Behavior*, Volume 26, pp. 109, 2000.

Smith, William, Dictionary of Canadian Biography, University of Toronto, available at http://www.biographi.ca/en/bio/smith_william_1821_97_12E.html.

Stone; an Illustrated Magazine, The Hennessey Monument, Volume 5, The D.H. Ranck Publishing Co., 1892. The New York Public Library.

Storey, N., *The Dracula Secrets: Jack the Ripper and the Darkest Sources of Bram Stoker*, The History Press, 2012.

Strand, Ginger, *Killer on the Road: Violence and the American Interstate*, University of Texas Press, 2012.

Tatya, T., *A Guide to Theosophy*, Bombay, 1887.

Tetens, K., Sir Thomas Henry Hall Caine, Dramatist, with a Special Study of Mahomet (1890) and its contexts, Doctor of Philosophy Thesis, University of Leicester, 2015.

The Fraternitas Rosae Crucis Fraternity, 'General Ethan Allen Hitchcock', available at http://www.soul.org/E%20A%20Hitchcock.html.

The Practice of Banking, Effingham Wilson, Royal Exchange, London, Volume 2, June 1883, page 526, (John Hutchison).

Theosophical Society in America, *The Expulsion From Eden.* www. Theosophical.org, https://www.theosophical. org/component/content/article/23-online-resources/ online-books/1738--sp-123799616

Tumblety, Francis, *A Few Passages in the Life of Dr. Francis Tumblety, The Indian Herb Doctor,* 1866. (Originally self-published in Cincinnati). Casebook: Jack the Ripper, available at www.casebook. org.

———. *A Narrative of Dr. Tumblety: how he was Kidnapped during the American War, His Incarceration and Discharge, A Veritable Reign of Terror,* 1872. (Originally published at Russells' American Steam Printing House, New York, NY.). Casebook: Jack the Ripper, available at www.casebook.org.

———. *A Sketch of the Life of the Gifted, Eccentric and World-Famed Physician, Presenting an Outline of His Wonderful Career,* 1889. (Originally published in Brooklyn, Eagle Book and Job Printing Department). Casebook: Jack the Ripper, available at www.casebook. org.

———. *A Sketch of the Life of Dr. Francis Tumblety, Presenting an Outline of His Wonderful Career as a Physician,* 1893, (Originally published in New York, NY), Harvard College Library, 1918.

Turvey, B., *Criminal Profiling: An Introduction to Behavioral Evidence Analysis*, Academic Press, 2012.

Turvey, B. *Forensic Victimology*, Academic Press, 2009.

Urology Today, 'History of Urology', *AUA*, 2006, available at http://www.urotoday.com/287/conference_reports/ history_of_urology/2024/.

Vaknin, S., *Malignant Self-Love: Narcissism Revisited*, 2015 (10th Revision).

Vronsky, P., *Serial Killers: The Method and Madness of Monsters,* 2004.

Warren, J., Burnette, M., South, S., Chauham, P., Bale, R., and Friend, R., Personality Disorders and Violence Among Female Prison Inmates, *Journal of the American Academy of Psychology and Law,* Volume 30, Number 4, 2002.

Western Union Telegraph Company, Postal Telegraph Pamphlets, 1868.

Wetsch, E., *Yorkshire Ripper,* available at www.crimezzz.net, 2005.

Williams, David Ricardo, *Call in Pinkerton's: American Detectives at Work for Canada,* Canadian Heritage, 1998.

Williams, M., *Round London, Charles Dickens and Evans,* Crystal Palace Press, 1892.

Wijngaards, J., Wijngaards Institute for Catholic Research, *Women Can Be Priests,* 2014, www.womenpriests.org.

Index

About the Author

Michael Hawley was honored to lecture in Liverpool, England, on September 23, 2017, at the Jack the Ripper Conference, and in Baltimore, Maryland, in April 2016, at RipperCon 2016. He was interviewed in Dublin, Ireland, for the Jack the Ripper episode of *Hunting Evidence* (Icon Films) on the Travel Channel in its 2018 season. Hawley is the author of *The Ripper's Haunts* (Nonfiction, 2016) with the top book reviewer and author, Paul Begg, stating, *"Hawley's Magnum Opus"* is *"head and shoulders above the new Ripper offerings in 2016,"* and *"for that matter, 2015."* He was honored to be interviewed in numerous podcasts for *Rippercast.* He has published over a dozen research articles in journals dedicated to the Whitechapel murders/Jack the Ripper mystery, namely *Ripperologist, Whitechapel Society Journal, Casebook Examiner,* and *The Dagger,* and has published online articles for numerous websites. He was awarded *Article of the Year for 2016* for the most popular Jack the Ripper website, which is based out of London, England, and has been asked to write another article for the current year. He is also the author of *The Watchmaker Revelations,* a mystery/thriller fiction trilogy: *The Ripper's Hellbroth* (2017), *Jack's Lantern* (exp. 2018), and *Curse of the Bayou Beast* (exp. 2019). He is also the author of *Searching for Truth with a Broken Flashlight* (Nonfiction, 2010), which was awarded *June 2011 Book of the Month* for the mega-website, *ReligiousTolerance.org,* and was the subject of an article in the *Buffalo Spree,* June 2011. Hawley holds a master's degree in science (invertebrate paleontology) and secondary science education at State University of New York, College of Buffalo, and a bachelor's degree in geology and geophysics at Michigan State University. He is a commander and naval aviator in the US Navy (retired), and is currently enjoying a career as a secondary earth science and chemistry teacher. He resides with his wife and six children in Greater Buffalo, New York.

Printed in Great Britain
by Amazon

37732207R00169